From Kona to Lake Placid
50 Great U.S. Triathlons

From Kona to Lake Placid
50 Great U.S. Triathlons

Edited by
Michaela Gaaserud and Renee Dexter

Rainmaker Publishing LLC
Oakton, Virginia, USA

Acknowledgements

Thank you to all our authors for sharing your fondest triathlon stories and for your assistance throughout the publication process. A special thanks to David Glover of EnduranceWorks LLC for your time and dedication to this project. Your experience and extensive network in the triathlon community was a valuable asset, and we appreciate you going the extra mile to help bring this book to our shelves.

Foreword

If you're reading this book, you are probably part of the cause of the tremendous growth in the sport of triathlon over the past decade. As more and more people try their hand at the sport and more often than not, become addicted to the swim, bike, run trio, new races are born each year to accommodate the growing demand.

Selecting the right triathlon can influence your training as well as vacation plans. It can provide a new challenge, offer an opportunity for a personal growth or represent a professional accomplishment. Whatever your reason for competing, the reward of participating in the right race can leave years of fond memories.

Since every triathlete is different, we turned to literally thousands of athletes across the nation to provide input on the races included in this book. Triathlon club members and independent competitors from coast to coast provided nominations for their favorite races and many of them offered to contribute chapters on those that made the cut. Our featured authors are a solid blend of both amateur and professional athletes of all ages and abilities. Each graciously volunteered their time and talent to share their most memorable triathlon experiences. As such, each chapter represents the opinion of the author and his or her experience at a particular race.

There are four standard triathlon distances as designated by the National Governing Body for Triathlon, USA Triathlon. The formal names for these distances are Short, Intermediate, Long, and Ultra. The standard distances for each are as follows:

Short:	750 Meter Swim, 20K Bike, 5K Run
Intermediate:	1500 Meter Swim, 40K Bike, 10K Run
Long:	1.2 Mile Swim, 56 Mile Bike, 13.1 Mile Run
Ultra:	2.4 Mile Swim, 112 Mile Bike, 26.2 Mile Run

Although other common names are often used to describe each race distance, most are trademarked by private entities and will not appear in this publication except in reference to specific race names owned by those entities.

This book addresses races at the intermediate, long and ultra distances. We agree that there are numerous excellent short distance races in the United States, so many so, that they may at some time warrant a separate book. In order for this book to be a valuable resource, however, the focus needs to be narrow enough to include more than just a handful of races for each featured distance. We selected the longer distance races to begin with because our research shows that more athletes travel greater distances to participate in the longer races.

It is important to note that none of the sponsors or race organizations for the triathlons featured in this book asked to be featured or lobbied for inclusion in any way. Although we are grateful that most provided an outpouring of support, we approached them only after the selection process was finalized, not the other way around. This book is truly a coordinated effort of advocates for the sport of triathlon and the love and dedication to this sport is evident in every chapter.

This book is intended to be a fun "where to" resource and in no way provides training or nutrition advice. Although some of our authors share their personal regiments for race preparation, this information is only provided for interest purposes only and should in no way be construed as training or medical expertise or advice.

We extend a special thank you to our friends at EnduraceWorks for their assistance with this publication. Their dedication, expertise, and extensive network in the triathlon community was a valuable asset to the success of this publication. We sincerely appreciate the endless hours they spent in preparation of this book and their extensive knowledge of the subject matter.

Race courses and logistics are always subject to change from year to year. Although great care was taken to provide accurate, up-to-date information at the time of publication, don't be surprised to find variations in each race from the accounts in this book.

Whether you are racing to finish or racing for the podium, we hope you find this book to be a fun and valuable resource as you select your next triathlon.

Michaela Gaaserud and Renee Dexter, Co-founders
Rainmaker Publishing LLC

Table of Contents

Intermediate Distance

March

April

May

June

July

November

Non-traditional

May

June

August

September

October

November

Lavaman Triathlon

waikoloa, hawaii

Race Distance: Intermediate
1.5K Swim, 40K Bike, 10K Run
Month: March
Race Web Site: www.lavamantriathlon.com

Author: Jeff Recker
Racing Category: Age Group 45-49

In retrospect, the experience bordered on surreal. On my back, massaged, deeply sated, sun on my face admiring palm trees pushed gently in the breeze under a rich blue sky. Pacific Ocean lapping along the shore. Then, Lavaman Red Ale flowing from a tap. White sand between my toes. Live music. BBQ. Who's that? The triathlete and legend, Scott Tinley sitting in with the band strumming a guitar. Awards. None for us but we're happy. Riding bikes back to the hotel. Lavaman buzz. Steering bikes, badly. Horrible behavior. Fun. Kath Laughing. Paradise Found at T3.

We never intended to enter Lavaman. A planned romantic getaway to Hawaii took a tri-twist when a subsequent search for events pulled us in. A course that shares some of the same ground as the Ironman Triathlon World Championship® tortured my idealist-romantic psyche. A frequent loser of the Ironman® lottery, I became slack jawed with the thought of racing on Queen Kaahamanu highway, the hallowed stretch of lore and legend where the world's best triathletes battle each year to remind the rest of us that we're, uh, not them. With 10 triathlons under my belt and less than desirable results, I also understood that I would never be one of them. But I could pretend for a day, right? So I walked around my house for weeks repeating the word "lava" for no other reason than I liked the way the "L" rolled off my tongue, momentarily sticking to the roof of my mouth before it spilled out like, well, lava.

"So much for that romantic getaway," Kath said, upon hearing my discovery. "It's fate," I insisted. To make my point I reminded her that the race was sponsored by our hotel, the Hilton Waikoloa, and better yet, the Kona Brewing Company which brews one of the finest beers I've ever tasted, Lavaman Red Ale.

LAVAMAN TRIATHLON

"So what came first, the tri or the brew?"
She asked.
"Does it matter?"
"No."
"We should enter."
"I've never done a tri!"
"True but you've drank plenty of Lavaman,"
I quickly pointed out. "Besides, there's a
beach party afterward." That sold her.

The Lavaman is an intermediate distance triathlon that takes place the last weekend
of March at the Waikoloa Beach Resort on the Kohola Coast of Hawaii. Celebrating
its 12th year in 2009 it has enjoyed praise from multiple sources and now ranks
as one of the sport's finest. What makes this race great is its organization, location
and a post race barbeque and awards ceremony that is rewarding of one's efforts
and captures the Aloha spirit of the island. It has grown from a humble beginning
to about 750 athletes. It also offers a challenging course that mirrors the island's
harsh, barren nature.

We certainly noticed that upon our arrival. While driving the 25 miles from the
Kailua-Kona Airport to the Waikoloa Beach Resort we had our first look at it along
the Queen Kaahamanu Highway. "Queen K" cuts through large lava fields that
seem incapable of supporting life, though specked with patches of vegetation,
most notable red flowered bougainvilleas. But even they look like they're clinging
to life, windblown and frayed. There too is an occasional cross or simple shrine,
auspicious in nature, bearing the name of a life lost along this highway, a reminder
that as beautiful and spiritual as one might find this island, Queen K has a nasty
side that has taken her share of sacrifices. Unique to her path are notes of greetings
spelled out on the black lava rocks with starkly contrasting white coral stones.
These messages line Queen K for tens of miles and while they would be easy
to label as graffiti they in fact give the island its distinctiveness and much of its
personality. Many of the messages are notes of encouragement directed at past
participants of the Ironman Triathlon. And in this way the Kohola Coast postures
itself as a stage of hope and achievement. Queen K's face hides nothing; scared and
pocked from its natural elements, emblazed by the human element, it commands a
certain truth and respect from race competitors.

We, on the other hand, really hadn't considered this. The drive up Queen K
Highway was sobering. Furthermore, we had blindly thought this was going to
be a small, noncompetitive race where everyone wore a flower in their hair and lei
around their neck. Certainly, that's precisely what we had in mind for ourselves.
Checking in at the host hotel, the Hilton Waikoloa contributed to our thoughts of
a soft race. The Hilton, a sprawling oasis dug out of the lava fields some 20 years

earlier, offers guests the option of a taking a boat anywhere in the resort along a man-made canal. Basically, it felt like an amusement park. And basically we said uncle and hopped on the boat anytime we ventured out of our room, which at one point delivered us to the race expo. Only hours removed from the mainland, but already feeling soft without will or guilt, bubble-gum-blowing, sand-between-the-toes, wanna-be-vacationers, we were now face to face with several hundred very fit looking athletes. Visions of an ill-fated day long ago danced in my head: a 3,000 meter track race I had entered in the running Mecca of Boulder Colorado. A sub five-minute mile pace still placed me next to last out of 27 runners and that was in the Citizen's wave. If Boulder was a Mecca of running, the Big Island of Hawaii was the Mecca of triathlon. While the race caters to special groups like the Leukemia Society's Team In Training® which can make up a third of the entire field, like any race on this island it draws an elite field too that contests the race at a very high level. Ensuring stiff competition lottery slots into the Ironman World Championship® race are also awarded to two lucky age group winners; the prize drawn from a hat. Details overlooked. Oops.

"Not really feeling it," Kath dropped.
"Really, had no idea."
"Let's bail, see a whale."
"Come this far."
So we reluctantly picked up our ill-fitting rental bikes with the cantaloupe-sized saddle bags. The bikes looked pregnant.

"They'll stand out in transition," Kath pointed out. The beautiful thing about being in Hawaii is that it's hard to get worked up about much of anything. After all, it's Hawaii. Isn't that enough to flip your cares and anxieties? So we took it in stride and had a good laugh anticipating our fate. Better make sure you can swim, I said.

Off to the beach to figure that out. Kath took one look at the choppy water which had been roused by boat traffic.

"No way," she said. "I'm pulling out."
"Look, it won't be any worse than the bike. You've never been on a road bike."
"You're filling me with confidence."
Well, damn if she didn't run down the field and miss the podium by one spot in her first, and, four years later, only triathlon, pregnant bike and all. I figured she was hooked. She told me never again. People like you bother me, I said.

The race starts innocently enough with a pleasant two-lap bikini swim (no wetsuits) in the flat, clear waters of Anaehoomalu Bay, or for us multi-syllable challenged athletes, "A-bay." True to the spirit of Hawaii the race director reminded us to swim Aloha, relieving any anxiety and setting the tone for a friendly race. Indeed, there were times I forgot I was racing; caught up in watching the sea turtles and colorful fish beneath me and feeling the cool water wash over my back with each stroke. This was truly swimming Aloha. It was quite a treat coming from Colorado where my swims had mostly been in murky lakes that tasted like gasoline and geese droppings. Kath's goal, in her first open water swim, was to avoid being touched at all costs. If this were a track she swam the entire way in the 8th lane.

Once out of the water the bike quickly transitions to a moderate, rolling section of Queen Kaahamanu Highway, part of the World Championship course. Any dreamers among us, me included, likely broke into fantasy about being in the Big Dance, the white coral messages meant to offer encouragement for the competitors of that championship race keeping my dream alive. There is nothing overly demanding about the bike course. It stays away from the steep climbs up to Hawi and typically this part of Queen K Highway does not experience the brutal cross winds that are found farther north. Though, a defining element during this bike leg is that one becomes wholly aware of the intensity of the sun which builds on every minute, baking asphalt, burning skin, threatening to melt one's will once off the bike. Things heat up fast on this island and without the cooling effect generated on the bike, what's left of a disagreeing athlete isn't much.

The run takes place on the grounds of the Waikoloa Beach Resort along its winding golf cart paths, an out-and-back maintenance road that I referred to afterward as the Easy-Bake Oven section, and finally a mile long dash along the beach pocked with lava rocks and loose sand. Typical of Hawaii the course is hot and humid and offers little shade. It will quickly unravel an under trained or unmotivated athlete. Personally, with all the twists, turns, and undulations, I found the run to be difficult and somewhat annoying. At one point we ran along the edge of the Hilton where weary-eyed vacationers stare at you like an apparition of sorts, scratching their heads like what in the hell is this all about? It's a collision between two worlds.

And I was torn. I sort of wanted to be one of those weary-eyed vacationers with the baggy swim trunks and drink in hand at 9:00 a.m. The promise of Mai Tais, French fries, and boat rides had been made long before we signed up for this race. So this section, where athletes encounter the only spectators, surprised and confused as they might be, was somewhat refreshing and a reminder that after having been through T1 and T2, another transition, often overlooked in most races, would soon take place at T3, that of a vacationer. After all, this was intended to be a romantic getaway.

About the Author

Jeff Recker has been a competitive athlete for nearly 20 years. Starting out as a runner, a series of injuries drove him into triathlon. Jeff lives by the motto "Enjoy Your Evolution" because 10 years ago he never saw himself as a triathlete but has thoroughly enjoyed the journey into the unknown. When Jeff dies he'll likely be remembered by friends and family as the guy who entered the Ironman lottery 60 times and never got in.

St. Anthony's Triathlon

st. petersburg, florida

Race Distance: Intermediate
1.5K Swim, 40K Bike, 10K Run
Month: April
Race Web Site: www.satriathlon.com

Author: Jenn Brown
Racing Category: Age Group 25-29

"Cara, Hilary, and I tried to stay as close to each other as we could as we moved forward with the 100 other women in our age group, farther down the chute toward the starting coral closer to the water's edge. I knew that in a few minutes there would be a flurry of light blue swim caps and black wetsuits as we raced into Tampa Bay, and I would probably not see my friends again until we were all across the finish line. Without warning, the gun went off, and my legs started moving forward on their own. My heart pounded. 'Here we go!' I ran into the water with the group already separated from Cara and Hilary. I waded until the water was to my mid-thigh and then dove in, ready to get the party started. It was barely 8:00 a.m., but the sun already shone brightly off the water's choppy surface. My vision narrowed and I began searching the horizon for the line of orange buoys I had to follow out to sea."

The above excerpt is from my race report from my first triathlon in April 2004. After completing a marathon with Team In Training® (TNT), I was on the hunt for a new challenge and had re-joined with TNT to give the mulit-sport world a shot. The St. Anthony's Triathlon in St. Petersburg, Florida was the event assigned to our group, and had it not been for that particular race, I cannot confidently say that I would have continued to pursue the sport. On December 1, 2007, I signed up for my 5th consecutive St. Anthony's event, as I have done every year since running across the timing mats at Spa Beach for the first time.

Location, location, location. I currently live in Arnold, Maryland and have done the majority of my triathlon training in the Baltimore/ Washington, DC area. Spring temperatures usually sit right around 40–50 degrees on the weekend, but by April, we've seen very few great days to ride outside. What better time than spring to escape to the beach to kick off your triathlon season? Arriving in Florida for race weekend has always felt like a quick break from reality and the weather has never disappointed. On average, the water temps are in the mid-70s (wetsuit legal for Age Groupers) and the sun creates a balmy 75–80 degree race-day temperature. (Don't forget your sun block!)

The downtown St. Petersburg location for both the expo and transition area looks like it was made for an event like the St. Anthony's Triathlon. There are a number of hotels within walking (or riding) distance from Vinoy Park (site of transition) and Straub Park (site of expo/registration), and if you don't mind hailing cabs or renting a car, you can find super cheap deals 5–10 miles away from race headquarters. Two years ago I stayed at a Days Inn for $45/night, rented a car for $40/day and was only 10 minutes from Vinoy Park. Parking on race day was easy (although packing all the bikes in the rented SUV was a little more difficult), but it was a great plan for a weekend on a budget. Not to mention Southwest Airlines flies into Tampa and TriBike Transport now ships bikes to St. Anthony's for about $200 round trip. For the same price you'd pay the airlines to ship your bike in pieces, you can now pass your fully-built (including race wheels) bike to a trustworthy handler who will drive your bike down to the race. You can pick it up with your race packet and hand it off after you finish your race. Absolutely worth the price.

In my opinion, St. Anthony's has the best expo ever. Picture a mini-state fair with all triathlon and bike-related vendors. We all arrive at a race forgetting something, and you can be confident you'll find it and everything else you may have never even realized you needed at the St. Anthony's expo. What stands out for me, however, are the mechanics that are available at the event. Nearly every year, I have had to make a small adjustment on a wheel, rear derailleur, or breaks. The mechanics are quick, professional and friendly. While I work in a bike shop and am accustomed to a certain "techy" level of bike-mechanic lingo, I have always really appreciated the interaction with the Chain Wheel Drive guys. You can tell that they know exactly where our heads are and where they are NOT. We're here to race and need our bikes to work. They will make it happen.

While you're at the expo, don't forget to pick up your race packet. Considering the race draws over 4,000 athletes, you'd think that packet pick-up would be a nightmare. It is quite the opposite. Packet pick-up is well staffed with helpful and cheery volunteers (must be the Florida sun), and it is extremely well organized. Athletes are in and out in 10 minutes (and with a can of beer when Michelob Ultra® is a sponsor!).

People, people, everywhere. As one of the biggest Intermediate distance races in the country, St. Anthony's does a great job of making you feel less like herded cattle and as much like athletes as possible. The transition area is huge, so make sure you remember where you racked your bike! The first wave of professionals hits the water at 6:45 a.m., and transition closes at 7:00 a.m. For the last few years, my age group hasn't hit the water until about 8:30 a.m., so I have had to be set up and out of transition well before I was even close to putting on my wetsuit. The best part of a late wave start is getting to watch the professionals coming out of the water and depending on how late the wave is, coming off the bike as well. Speaking of professionals...

Star struck? St. Anthony's has been the season kick-off for a majority of the most recognizable professionals in our sport. Potts, Alexander, Kemper, Chrabot, Haskins, Lavalle, and McGlone are just some of the names on the backsides of race suits you'll see emerging from the water. Since there is no eligibility requirement for Age Groupers to enter, St. Anthony's is one of the best opportunities to race with the best of the best. Newly introduced in 2007 was the Elite Amateur division, where the best Age Groupers can compete head-to-head instead of in their respective age divisions. It's a great gauge for those athletes considering getting their professional license, as the race draws some of the best talent in the sport.

I'll admit that the thought that my very first triathlon was going to require me to swim in open water scared me a lot. I grew up on Cape Cod, body boarding in the Atlantic Ocean my entire life. Heck, the movie Jaws was even based on my hometown of Martha's Vineyard. But I did not consider myself a "swimmer," and I hadn't done any distance swimming outside of the confines of four pool walls. The excitement of the start line was enough to put my head in a completely different place race morning. Between the loud music, great announcer, and cheers from the crowd, you almost can't wait to get in the water! The race kicks off with a run-in swim start on Spa Beach (about a one mile walk from transition); each wave starts five minutes apart. The course is approximately a 600m swim into the bay, 300m swim parallel to the shore, and a 600m swim back toward Vinoy Park. While the water temperature was consistent the last four years, the water conditions have varied. I have seen mirror flat conditions and considerable chop.

Despite the large number of athletes, the transition to the bike course is both fair and easy to maneuver through. There are many volunteers on the course, leading athletes to the exit and clearly announcing the bike mount line. The first 200 yards of the bike course are on cobblestones, though, so consider your bike mount beforehand.

There is really only one way to describe the St. Anthony's bike course—flat and fast. The course takes you immediately over part of the Formula One race course before a quick out-and-back on 1st Ave. (which is closed to cars). After a short trip on 4th street (with securely controlled car traffic), you are back on closed streets heading toward the golf course. This middle section has a lot of overlapping race traffic; a great chance to see the other athletes on the course. There is one water bottle drop/aid station around mile 13 which is well staffed, but comes up quickly. If you are not planning on using this aid station, take it wide to avoid the dropped bottles and other debris on the road. After another out-and-back on Pinella's Point Drive, you head straight for home on closed back streets. I love the end of the bike course, not only because my legs could use a break, but because of the crowds. Spectators line the end of the bike course for at least the last 1/4 - 1/2 miles. No matter how fast or slow you are going at that point, you can't help but feel like a rock star! Again, you'll find a well-staffed dismount line and transition area, as you head out on the run.

As mentioned previously, my age group waves the last few years have started toward the later side. So while it was a bit warmer during the swim, it has also been incredibly hot during the run. The friend I had traveled with competed in the Elite Amateur division and agreed that the conditions between his wave and mine made it a completely different race. Regardless of the heat, I still love the run course. The course is a flat out-and-back route, crossing the Snell Isle bridge and running through the beautiful waterfront neighborhoods on Brightwaters Blvd. With water stops every mile and locals offering to spray down runners with their hoses, it is easy to stay well-hydrated and motivated.

Because of the out-and-back nature, spectating at this event, especially on the run course, is easy and central. As with the bike course, the crowds on the run course spread out along the first and last 1/4 miles. After taking a left off North Shore Drive you'll be ready for the last 200 yard sprint toward the finish. A lot of signs, cowbells and cheering accompany you in the last moments of the race and your run toward the finish line has never been this exciting. Gatorade, water, a cold towel and a finisher's medal are all handed out before you even reach the end of the finish coral. Post-race, the St. Anthony's spread is BBQ, beer, and a live band.

On a personal note, St. Anthony's Triathlon is also a huge supporter of charity athletic organizations such as Team in Training and Challenged Athletes Foundation. There are always hundreds of charity athletes racing each year. There continues to be discussion regarding the competitiveness of the race and arguments made that those charity athletes who are not racing to be competitive are somehow making it more difficult for those who are competitive by getting in the way on course. Race Director Philip LaHaye has gone to great lengths to try to accommodate both the competitive athletes as well as those participating purely for charity. In the last few years, he has created a wave for those athletes who are not interested in competing within their Age Group, and this wave is the last to leave Spa Beach. As both a Team in Training athlete for two years and a competitive Age Grouper for two years, I applaud Philip LaHaye's efforts. While I enjoy being competitive, I also find it hugely inspiring, as a sibling of a relapsed leukemia survivor, to see the hundreds of selfless charity athletes on the course, as well as hearing the morning announcement of the millions of dollars those athletes have raised for that event alone.

Overall, St. Anthony's is one of the best-run, best-venue'd, best valued, and most fun races out there. The late April timeframe is perfect for a season kick-off and you are almost guaranteed good weather. As a newbie, there was something overwhelming and yet completely inspirational about racing St. Anthony's for the first time. As a seasoned triathlete, I love returning to this course year after year and will continue to do so as long as I am able!

About the Author

In her own words, Jenn Brown is an unlikely candidate for triathlon, spending her high school years as a cheerleader, ballerina, and softball catcher. Determined to prove she was an athlete, she walked onto her college crew team and helped row her boat to the top 10 in 2000. Jenn discovered her love for running while training for crew and post-college, was introduced to multi-sport through Team in Training. She signed up for her first ultra triathlon in 2005.

Since her first race (St. Anthony's) in 2004, Jenn has competed in over 20 triathlons of all distances. She recently found that she was more attracted to mountain biking and specifically, XTERRA racing. Jenn qualified for the XTERRA Nationals in Lake Tahoe in 2007 and plans to continue competing both on and off-road in 2008. Professionally, Jenn is the Executive Director of Girls on the Run of Northern Virginia, an after-school, experiential learning program for girls ages 8–14 that combines training for a 5K running event with life-changing lessons designed to build self-esteem and instill a healthy self-image in its participants. In her free time, Jenn is an associate coach for Principle Fitness, certified by both USAT and USAC. She coaches cyclists and on and off-road triathletes.

Columbia Triathlon

ellicott city, maryland

Race Distance: Intermediate
1.5K Swim, 41K Bike, 10K Run
Month: May
Race Web Site: www.tricolumbia.org

Author: Daniel Frost
Racing Category: Age Group 35-39 (currently races pro)

The Columbia Triathlon is known, and remembered by athletes, for its difficulty. Much of that difficulty comes from its hills. Steep hills. Winding hills. Nothing but hill after hill after hill for many miles.

One hill at Columbia, however, is not feared. It is steep, but athletes don't mind climbing it. It is big, but athletes embrace it rather than feel intimidated by it. It's the grassy hill. The one that rises above the shore of Centennial Lake at the start and finish lines of the Columbia Triathlon. It is the hill that rises above all others as the symbol and signature element of an event with nearly a quarter century of history.

Just like the Columbia Triathlon itself, this hill is where my story begins…and ends.

As the sun rises on the third Sunday in May over the trees of a forest, this unnamed grassy hill takes on a unique, energetic character. This hill, steeply stepped, provides an onlooker with the best vantage of the Columbia Triathlon. From here, you can see the final two thirds of the swim course, sections of the run course from across the water, and the final stretch to the finish line all within a beautiful park setting. The energy comes from the triathlon's 2,100 participants who marshal on this hill adjacent to the swim start, watching friends take off while waiting for their own waves.

The venerable triathlon has been in existence for many years though it always seems to be a little different from year to year. The race has a storied history that includes the hosting of the USA Triathlon age group national and regional championships, course changes and

varying degrees of weather. Its list of champions includes Olympic bronze-medalist Susan Williams and then-reigning Ironman® World Champion Peter Reid. Over time, Columbia has adapted with the growth of the sport, deftly supporting larger numbers of racers along with improvements in race amenities.

At this race, the 2,100 triathletes have nearly 2,100 different sets of goals for participating. For most, it is their first triathlon of the young season. For many, it is their only triathlon of the season, or the first triathlon of their life or the first triathlon at the intermediate distance. Many athletes believe that this is the biggest athletic event that they will ever try. Many other athletes do not even consider Columbia their "A" race with a full season of triathlons to follow.

For myself, I come for the food. It is not gourmet post-race fare, but sometimes it is nice to let someone else do the cooking for you.

Some come just to try to finish the course while others aim for earning valuable cash awards and crystal trophies. This race honors every participant throughout that entire spectrum. Every finisher earns a fine-crafted pewter medallion. Competitive awards are bestowed upon those who are fastest in such categories as an expert division, masters, grand masters, Clydesdales and Athenas, military, married couples and first-time triathletes. There is also a special award for the most improved triathlete from the previous year's race.

Columbia is one of the most convenient triathlons to reach and it is held in an excellent location for further exploration and sightseeing. The race site is located 15 miles from the Baltimore/Washington, DC Beltway. This location makes Columbia a favorite event for both the growing numbers of local triathletes as well as the visiting triathletes who love a variety of lodging, transportation, and sightseeing options. The race site itself is easily accessible by road and large overflow parking areas inside the park eliminate significant pre-race traffic jams.

Registration and exposition are located two miles from the race venue at the headquarters hotel in the Columbia Town Center. The expo is comprehensive, filled with items such as CO_2, energy gels, and all the other necessities for racing. It also is indicative of the new season with the latest models of equipment, clothing and personal gadgetry on display. Only the triathlon expos at the Wildflower Festival and St. Anthony's Triathlon are larger and more comprehensive at this time of the season, but the expo at Columbia is comparable in quality and scope.

The registration process is orderly and efficient, fairly indicative of the organization of the Columbia Triathlon Association and its supportive volunteer force. Within short order you receive your race number, timing chip and a goody bag full of items of fair to excellent quality. Inside, there is an event-commemorative 24-ounce water bottle and additional commemorative premium items such as a race hat or gear bag. The 2004 commemorate race shirt, yellow with additional red and blue colors, remains one of my prized possessions. You get quite a bit of quality goods and services for a very reasonable entry fee.

One special aspect of Columbia's pre-race logistics is the mandatory bicycle safety check. The safety check was a routine item at most triathlons in the past, but there are few today that have it and Columbia is one of the largest triathlons that continues to conduct it. At Columbia, however, the extra time spent waiting for the inspection, and the inspection itself, is time well spent. The nature of this bike course is very demanding on a bicycle's machinery. The frame, the brakes, the shifting system and the power train will be repeatedly stressed on this course. Local triathletes have the option of bringing their bicycle to selected bike shops during the entire week prior to the race to have the inspection performed.

The pre-race experience culminates on the grassy hill. Those fellow triathletes who have been here before know that this hill represents the beginning, the end and everything on the course in between. But if the hills are Columbia's enduring constant, than its weather is its enduring variable.

Mid-May in Maryland can bring a variety of weather. Usually the onset of summer brings about pleasant warmth in the morning, but extreme temperatures, haze, rain and wind are not uncommon. If there is anything that draws your mind away from the impending start and the inevitable hills while you wait on this open grassy space to begin your journey, it is the weather.

The water presents your first challenge, and it is unique. It is a small freshwater reservoir that is covered with ice a mere three months before race day. The temperature varies to where a full-sleeve wetsuit may be perfect in one year and downright intolerable the next. Though cloudy, the quality is remarkably good for what is essentially an oversized pond with some marshy wetlands. The first leg of the swim start adds one more challenge beyond the normally difficult endeavor of the mass swim start—bright sunshine. The rising sun shines right onto the initial direction of the travel for the first 500 meters, making navigation a fearful challenge for leading swimmers.

The transition area is large, grassy, and sloped. A 100-yard uphill run to your bike is followed by a shorter but steeper push to the pavement, taking your heart rate towards new heights. Do not expect to catch your breath until after you leave the park and your first climb on the bike course, behind.

What awaits you on the bicycle course is pleasant to your eyes, and generally kind to your tires, but also strenuous to you and your mechanical parts. If the previous day's running of the Preakness Stakes® in Baltimore, Maryland failed to grab your attention, then this course will remind you of Maryland's historic association with horses. In addition to horse farms, the course takes you by numerous other agricultural farms in a genuine rural setting that you would not expect to see between two of America's largest cities. The roads are clear of debris and are generally smooth, with only a few minor rough or bumpy patches. Nonetheless, this race always seems to have a bunch of DNFs or slow times due to flat tires or other mechanical problems. Even early in the race, where I have started in the third or fourth wave, I have ridden past many people and bikes stopped on the side of the road.

The bike course is advertised to be 41 kilometers. It's probably closer to the truth to say that 40 of those kilometers are travelled horizontally and the "extra" one kilometer is the one you travel straight up. There is no piece of level ground on this bike course. Climbs and descents vary in both length and steepness. None of the climbs are excessively long or excessively steep. Yet, the course unfolds in a way where a consistent rhythm or pace of heart rate is unachievable. Speedy declines can be followed by false flats transitioning to steeper climbs that crest into a shallow descent. In a sport where consistency is prized above most other qualities, this course rewards adaptation instead.

The second transition is all downhill and is a needed opportunity to reclaim control of your breathing, if not your leg strength.

The run course is a precisely measured, certified 10,000 meter path to perdition, unless you prove to be mentally and physically strong. Runners are immediately presented with a short but very steep switch backed hill. After having completed over an hour of irregular surges of leg power on a bike, you are presented with the most objective reality of the race on this hill: You either have the strength to run or you do not. If you walk up this hill, you will be destined to walk many more in a difficult six-mile march.

The course does flatten out in the first two miles as it follows an occasionally shady path around Centennial Lake. The third mile begins a series of long and steep climbs that carry you out of the park and through adjoining neighborhoods, with the first climb being particularly long and steep. After four miles, the course is all downhill as you return to the park, except for climbing that one steep hill. With your energy sapped, the unshaded climb up this hill is the toughest climb on the run course. Columbia saves her toughest test for last.

Columbia also saves her best moment for the end. First the sounds, then the sight of the grassy hill filled with spectators start to draw you faster around the lake to the finish. The spectators on the hillside make Columbia's finish one of the better ones in this sport. It makes you feel that the people and cheers are coming from all around, high and low. Welcoming receptions, I have to say, are pleasantly strong and loud. They will send a chill up your spine on a hot day…and I do not mind taking an extra few seconds in the home stretch to express my thanks to those who loudly brought me to the realization of one thing: That Ms. Columbia found me worthy on this day.

I appreciate the Columbia Triathlon course as much for its fairness as I do its difficulty. Although the run segment is a hilly challenge, Columbia is not known as a "runner's" course. Nor is it a course that particularly favors the elite cyclist or the elite swimmer. Success at Columbia demands an equal balance of speed, power, skill and mental flexibility in every discipline. This is why both an Olympic medalist like Susan Williams and an Ironman Champion like Peter Reid can equally shine here, as they possess those elements in plentiful amounts.

In fact, I believe the fairness of this course magnifies its difficulty; Columbia is like a truth serum. It will expose any and every weakness you have. Do you struggle with the power to climb hills, or the skills to handle your bike on curves and slopes, or the speed to slice through the water? Is your equipment in optimal condition or your body properly trained? Columbia answers these questions better than any course of its length. If the word "challenging" suggests "the full use of one's abilities or resources in a difficult but stimulating effort" according to the American Heritage Dictionary, then I find the Columbia Triathlon to be America's most challenging intermediate distance triathlon.

That's why I love to race at Columbia…and climb that grassy hill afterwards to get to the food tent at the summit.

About the Author

According to Dan Frost, no other triathlete is as minimally qualified to be a professional as he, having been an age-grouper for nine seasons before barely earning a pro license at the age of 37. A native of Sacramento, California, Dan has been a full-time active duty officer in the U.S. Navy for 16 years. He has competed in more than 80 triathlons and hopes to become a multisport coach or race director when he retires from the military.

Memphis in May Triathlon

millington, tennessee

Race Distance: Intermediate
1.5K Swim, 40K Bike, 10K Run
Month: May
Race Web Site: www.mimtri.racesonline.com

Author: Bruce Gennari
Racing Category: Age Group 40-44

On the third Friday in May, I headed down to Millington, Tennessee for the Memphis in May Triathlon. I drove in style as a good friend lent me his 32-foot recreational vehicle. Let me tell you that this recreational vehicle had every bell and whistle that you can imagine. I had all the creature comforts of home and then some. I really liked the idea of being able to park at the race site and not have to leave for the entire weekend. Imagine if you will, not having to wake up at the crack of dawn to pack up your gear and then driving to the race? Sounds good, doesn't it? I highly recommend it if you have the opportunity to do so.

Memphis in May has a two-race weekend set up called the Amateur Challenge. Basically you compete in a mountain bike race on Saturday then follow that up with the intermediate distance triathlon on Sunday. You add your finishing times for both races and then you see where you stand amongst all the other people competing in the Amateur Challenge. There is actually some money to be won, and the year I competed at least 150 people tested their intestinal fortitude by attempting both races.

The weekend was spent with another good friend of mine who accepted my invitation to stay with me. We had both signed up for the Amateur Challenge, and we both would have a great time the entire weekend.

The mountain bike race was held on Saturday with distances of a third of a mile swim, 10 mile mountain bike, and three mile trail run. How did I feel after the race? I felt pretty tired and all I could think about was getting back to the rig and getting some rest. I was a little worried as to how I was going to feel the next day when trying to tackle the intermediate distance triathlon. I didn't feel particularly well when I woke up the morning of the mountain bike race and was hoping that some major rest and recovery would put me in a good position to do well the following day. Time would tell.

After some food and rest, I headed over to the expo which ran all day on Saturday and Sunday. Memphis in May does a very good job with their expo. There were about 50 national distributors selling their products including several triathlon specific vendors that make the trip to Millington each ear. If you left something at home that you needed during the race you'd be able to get it at the expo.

I picked up my race packet at the expo. The people (Start 2 Finish, Inc.) who put on this race really know what they are doing. The packet pickup process is a breeze. You're in and out in about 15–20 minutes. Kudos to the staff handling this particular process.

The weather was perfect on race day. It was a little cool in the morning and it didn't look like it was going to warm up too much during the race. The wind was light and even if it did pick up it wasn't going to be that much of a factor. Things were looking good for having an excellent race.

The race starts at 7:30 a.m. with the professionals hitting the water first. I felt good and was excited to be racing. Any doubts that I had the previous day were gone. I was ready to go. My race number was well into the thousands so I knew that I had some serious time before I raced.

Memphis in May is a little bit different in the way that the race gets started. They use a Time Trial format. One person jumps in the water every three seconds (with the exception of the professionals who have 15 seconds between each other). For those people who don't like the wave start with all of its potential wrestling type antics then this race is for you. Now, this isn't to say that you're not going to run into some traffic out in the swim, because you are. But, you're not going to get crushed at the start of your race. This is very appealing to some people. Do I like it? Not necessarily. The only reason I don't like this type of racing format is because you don't know who you are racing. When everyone in your age group starts together, you can tell where you stand at any given time during the race. In this race, you have to really pay attention to who is in your age group and also be pretty sharp in math.

The swim was in Casper Lake. The temperature of the lake race morning was 76 degrees. Wetsuit legal. Just fine with me. Over near the swim start is where the race officials herd you in a line based on your race number. The line moves fairly fast and before you know it you hear the word "Go!" and you're off.

Before I knew it I was in the water and on somebody's feet. Being a better-than-average swimmer and not wanting to get caught up in the traffic of people hugging the buoy line I made the decision to swim wide around the buoys. I might have been swimming a little bit longer than everybody else but at least I was not being held up by slower swimmers. I actually felt good in the water and got into a solid rhythm. I hit both turn buoys at a most opportune time and was able to avoid the usual traffic jam that occurs around them. Before I knew it the swim finish was in sight. I started to pick up my pace toward the end of the swim as I know this is where a lot of people relax. At the age of 41 I need all the help I can get these days. I swam as close as I could to the finish line (basically waiting until both my hands touched the lake floor), planted my feet solidly on the ground and then started running into T1. I had my wetsuit off of my arms and torso and only needed to vacate my legs before jumping into my bike gear and heading out onto the bike course. Overall my swim time was a fairly swift 16:30 and was the fastest swim time of the day.

T1 was solid. I jumped on my bike after the dismount line and then headed out onto the bike course. I was very pleased to get my feet into my shoes with relative ease before I actually made it out of the park. Now I was ready to hammer.

The bike course can be described as mostly flat with a couple of rolling hills. There is one other word that can describe this 40K bike course — fast! If you're looking for a Personal Record (PR) for a 40K bike then this is your course.

I probably had over 900 people in front of me on the bike. About 10 minutes into the bike ride my legs felt awesome. I could already tell I was going to have a good day. But, I had hit a bump early on and lost my water bottle so my mouth was as dry as the Sahara. I was spitting dust. My mind started to wander, and I was trying to think how this was going to set me up for the remainder of the ride and the run. I finally came to the conclusion that I shouldn't think about things that I have no control over. I'll either adapt and overcome or I could just quit. And there was no way I was going to quit. I waited and waited and waited and then, finally, I came to the aid station. I grabbed a bottle of sport drink and drank it down like a person who had been crawling on their hands and knees in the desert. I had never tasted anything so good. After getting about 2/3 of the bottle down I dropped the bottle, got aero again and started to hammer the rest of the course. Again, my legs were feeling great, and I didn't feel any real repercussions of not having been able to drink as much as I wanted to. I tried to put the hydration gaffe out of my mind, but I knew it was probably going to catch up with me on the run.

Getting ready to pull into T2 I had my feet out of my shoes and was ready to hit the dismount line running. I did just that. Perfect landing and I was on my way to my designated rack. I got my bike into my stall, threw on my running shoes, grabbed my hat and race belt and was off.

The run course can also be described as rolling. There are a couple of hills that you'll run up but they are mostly followed by sharp down hills on the other side. The toughest uphill is at the turn around. Another tough part of the run course is right at the end when you have to run across a levy toward the finish line. This grassy trail is very uneven and it is difficult to see where the best line is. Add in the fact that your legs are shot at this point in the race and that makes for an interesting finish.

Out on the run I first wanted to settle into a good pace and try to let the blood flow from my upper thighs down to my calves. I am not one of those people who can start running fast right from the get-go. Unfortunately, I have to warm up before I can really start putting in a good effort. I hit the turnaround and hit my lap timer on my watch. Then, as I was running the opposite way, I searched for the next person in my age group. When I saw him, I learned I had at least a four minute cushion on him and decided that I could win the age group. I cruised the last 3.1 miles back to the park as best as I could. It was painful and I started feeling the affects of dehydration. The finish line couldn't get here fast enough.

Finally, I saw the levy adjacent to the lake and knew I had about a quarter mile to go. I ran as fast as I could across the levy and broke the tape exhausted. I looked down at my watch and saw 1:52:47 (my time actually turned out to be 1:52:43. Not my fastest time at this race (1:50:51) but certainly not my slowest. Plus, I had raced just the day before. I'll take it. It was a well earned time. I ended up first in my age group and first overall in Masters. In the Amateur Challenge I ended up second (for which I pocketed $350). Not too shabby for a weekend of racing.

After the race I enjoyed what most people feel is the best post race food around. Memphis in May really does it up for its athletes. Barbeque with all of the fixings are had by all. I can't even begin to tell you all the food they have there for one to eat. Let's suffice it to say that nobody goes hungry at the end of the race. Factor in the beer truck (with taps coming out of the side of the truck) and you can imagine a good time was had by all.

The awards ceremony for the race is done fairly quickly once they finally get the race results. But, just like with any other race, there are delays. So, if you have someplace to get to in a hurry I wouldn't wait around for the awards to happen.

All in all I would have to say that Memphis in May is one of the "must do" races that you have to compete in during you triathlon career. I've done Memphis in May for the past 10 years and can honestly say that it is flawlessly executed by a hard working event staff from beginning to end. They've put on this race many, many times and know what they are doing. Pre-race, race, and post-race events are top notch. The volunteers are awesome and cater to your every need. So, if you're looking for a different swim start and possibly a Personal Best (PB) time, then I would certainly look to visit Millington, Tennessee.

About the Author

Bruce Gennari is husband to Tammy Gennari and father to two sons, Ian and Noah. He's been in the sport of triathlon for more than 18 years. He was a swimmer at the University of Alabama in the mid 80s and triathlon took the place of swimming once he graduated. Bruce works for Emdeon Business Services (EBS) and has done so for the past eight years. He is a manager for EBS and loves working with his employees. In his spare time, Bruce likes to watch movies and play with his kids.

Over the Mountain Triathlon

kings mountain, north carolina

Race Distance: Intermediate
1.5K Swim, 40K Bike, 10K Run
Month: May
Race Web Site: www.setupevents.com

Author: Mike Guzek
Racing Category: Age Group 30-35

On paper, the Over The Mountain Triathlon is a 1.5K swim, 40K bike and a 10K run. But on race day, you get much more than your typical triathlon. Kings Mountain, North Carolina is not known as a triathlon community. It is a hardworking small town in the middle of the state, and as a result, your race experience constantly changes, oscillating between a quality triathlon production and the people, places, and attitudes of a small American town. It is this contrast that makes Kings Mountain a unique race venue.

The contrasts are hard to miss. The familiar sounds and smells of triathlon registration are offset by southern accents so thick that while standing in line I felt compelled to check my registration information to make sure I hadn't accidentally shown up for a Bass fishing competition. This was great for me as I was actually looking forward to registration as a chance to rekindle the southerna in me. I grew up in North Carolina, but had been living in Virginia for the past five years and was looking for an excuse to come back to visit. I thought I needed a holiday or a death in the family to make a run for the border, but lucky for everyone, I found triathlon instead.

I originally discovered this race in 2003 while browsing setup-inc.com. I had completed plenty of races through Set Up Inc. previously and knew their races were good, and I was eager to try out another of their offerings.

On race morning, I woke up at 5:00 a.m. and was out the door at 5:30. The logistics for this race are pretty hairy with the swim start, swim finish (T-1) and bike finish (T-2) all in different locations. Moss Lake is totally gorgeous and a wonderful setting for a swim, but with the two transitions, you need to catch a shuttle bus to get there.

I was the only bozo on the shuttle holding a wetsuit. With temperatures reaching the 90s the past several days, the water was very warm and I guess everyone who had brains figured out that no wetsuits would be permitted. I tried to hide the wetsuit under my arm so I wouldn't stick out, but had little success.

As luck would have it, my bus driver got lost and the race start was held up until we finally arrived. Sitting in the shuttle bus (while lost), I took in the scenery. This included a guy in a one piece skintight tri outfit (with back fur so long he actually combed it for the pre-race photos) explaining how he shot an eight point buck the previous weekend at his brother's farm.

When we got off the bus at Moss Lake I quickly stashed the wetsuit under a bench until my family could come and take it away. I hadn't even put sunscreen on yet and I was already rattled.

Contrary to how it sounds so far, there is nothing disorganized or out of place at this race. Over The Mountain is managed under the extremely well respected Set Up Inc. staff, and as a result, its collection of contrasts make this race so memorable.

Over The Mountain is small, but it's a North Carolina Triathlon Series (NCTS) race, so the quality is always high despite a field of only about 300 competitors. While loosening up I enjoyed the beautiful lake views and felt happy to be back in my home state.

Like the previous days, race day temperatures were going to be in the 90s and it was already hot shortly before the 8:00 a.m. start. Swimming without a wetsuit suited me fine, but I did start to wonder about the possible drag that may occur while swimming in my race jersey. My main concern was the rear pockets and in the end I opted to roll the jersey up inward to my body so the pockets would not be exposed (as if triathletes don't look ridiculous enough as it is). So there I was with tight spandex, swim cap, and tri jersey rolled up. Lord, if my frat brothers could see me now.

I seeded myself up front and came out of the gate like Richard Simmons on his way to a televised obesity intervention. And given what I was wearing at the moment, it wasn't just my intensity that resembled Richard. I felt I needed to push hard to get clear of the masses. This however, left me suffering in the water several hundred yards into the race with my fast feet dropping me like freshman calculus while my body drowned in its own lactic acid. I decided to try to hang back on the second row and let others do the work and just follow whoever seemed to be the best man to follow. This worked, and after several hundred yards I settled behind two other swimmers in the front pack of our wave (35 and under males + Clydesdales).

The course resembles a lower case "r" as swimmers swim out and make a right hand turn back to shore (at a different location). The pace seemed very leisurely, but I was content to sit back until we made the right hand turn toward the finish. I planned to scoot around the lead guys and finish first in the wave and steal the glory, but it wasn't meant to be. As they picked up the pace on the homestretch, I swallowed some water and a touch of pride and hung on for dear life. I managed to weather the storm and come out second.

By far, the hardest part of this course is the stretch of pavement from the water exit to T-1. It's the steepest boat ramp I have ever seen. I do have one criticism of the race. It's that they don't recommend you bring crampons and a pick ax with you to climb to T-1. Needless to say, I had a slow transition.

The bike course is absolutely beautiful. It rolls through two state parks and one national park. I felt pretty poor on the bike for about the first 15 minutes, but eventually settled in and started to pass some folks who passed me earlier summiting Mount T-1. I love this course because it's very challenging and has some interesting scenery.

The bike course is undoubtedly the highlight of the race. There is 2,752 feet of climbing over 28 rolling miles. As is emblematic of the race itself, the course takes you through a variety of landscapes. Isolated country roads take you to busy "city" roads. Along the way you meander into local neighborhoods and then disappear into one of three parks on the course. There is no better way to explore an area than on a bike.

While riding, my mind tends to wander. I reflected on how lucky we all are to be able to come to these races and challenge ourselves in such a healthy and positive atmosphere and how such an event can bring families together in different ways. Competing in triathlon creates a unique and dynamic connection with those around you and I felt that when I saw my family cheering for me on the course.

I had been in triathlon for five years and had done probably 40 races, some fast, some slow, but most in that gray area in between where you are only a couple of key workouts from greatness (or so your mind tells you). Tipping the scales at a healthy 215 pounds, I often race as a Clydesdale. But don't let the pieces of hay stuck in my tri jersey or the half eaten sugar cube sitting on my top tube fool you, I'm out there for more than just the post race pizza—sometimes there is beer too.

I had difficulty getting water and calories down as a result of the continuing undulations on the course. My heart rate was pegged. No time ever felt like the right time to eat. I ended up taking in about 300 calories less than my goal, but it was the best I could do. About the time I hit the bike aid station the temperature really started to rise and I was noticeably sweating which concerned me. The sun was out on the hunt and he was preying on triathletes.

With about 10 miles to go I began catching the elite females and some of the master male elites from the previous waves. Okay, okay, these guys were 60, and I was 29, but I had heard enough annoying "walking to school" stories and the "virtues of oatmeal and a high fiber diet." It was time to show the old-timers who was boss. It was around that time that I finally remembered to roll my jersey back down.

I rode right up to T-2 and avoided the mistake others made of dismounting without realizing there was still a half mile to go to circle around some train tracks to the T-2 entrance. I got off the bike feeling good and my bike time made it in the top 10 overall. Was I headed for greatness?

T-2 was a bit of a debacle as my shoe somehow came off my bike after I dismounted. By the time I realized it, I was 50 feet into T-2, and I told the volunteer holding it to just toss it to me. Apparently this guy never played baseball or anything requiring a throwing motion because my shoe rolled out of his hand and dribbled to a stop about 10 feet in front of him. Even the spectators lining T-2 seemed disappointed with the effort, flashing the same look of sadness and disappointment you'd flash someone who had just said a swear word in front of kids. I ran back and got it for fear of an abandonment penalty (and out of fear that this guy might try to throw it again) and tried to run to my bike rack.

The layout of the racks was a little confusing, and I couldn't for the life of me figure out where I was. A hot panic-driven flash shot through my body. Was I about to live out many of the disastrous triathlon nightmares I have had over the years? Wait, I still had all my clothes on, no penguins were in sight, and as far as I could tell I was not required to have an umbrella to continue the race. Whew, I was in good shape! Eventually I figured it all out and tossed on my hat and grabbed my race number and headed out. I saw my family cheering madly for me as I exited T-2, and I tried to look as good as I could for the photos they were taking. I swear I even heard my two month old niece call my name.

T-2 is in a park in downtown Kings Mountain. The transition spits you right into the heart of the town. Neighborhoods that have probably been there since before this was ever considered a town serve as the backdrop for the run. Some runners run the street, others choose the sidewalk. I noticed a group of kids sitting on one of the street corners watching the race with their dirt bikes behind them. I wondered if this race might encourage them to give triathlon a try one day. An interaction like this would never have happened unless you mixed triathlon with a town like this. Maybe it's my destiny to inspire a town the same way Dave Scott and Mark Allen inspired the world in the 80s? Hmm, lumbering Clydesdale on the run, maybe not.

The run starts off flat for almost a mile and then has a long descent followed by a long climb. At the top of the climb you make a U-turn around a lone orange cone and return the way you came. You do that twice to get the 6.2 miles for the run.

I started to get a little light headed on the way out, and I regretted not being more diligent about taking in calories on the bike. I had a gel flask, but because it was loaded up by the same chucklehead that brought the wetsuit to the race, it contained caffeinated gel. I have no idea why I would need five caffeinated gels for a 10K run, but there I was holding five of 'em. I didn't want any caffeine because I was concerned that it might create more problems than it would solve. I soldiered on, but nearing the conclusion of my first loop I realized that my speculations were true, I was feeling the onset of a bonk. I knew I had to get something in me so I sucked back on the gel at the turn around and mentioned to my girlfriend that "I think I might be starting to bonk." She responded with intensity shouting "Don't bonk! NO bonk!" while pointing at me and jumping. I felt scolded! But she was right. NO BONK! While my pace slowed on the second loop because of general fatigue, I never completely crashed and burned.

On the second loop, a super fast runner in my age group passed me, putting me in second. By the time I made the climb to the final turn around I was beat. I took just a second to look back on all the runners heading up and down the hill below. What drives all these people to come out and sweat, and hurt and push themselves like this? It's always an inspiring sight to see. I generally find that it's at my worst moments that I see the best in this sport because I am in a place I would never be otherwise.

Several hundred yards from the finish line, a fellow that I swam and biked with went around me. I'm not a runner, but I convinced myself to take the challenge and stay with him. I managed to stay right on his shoulder as we approached the right hand turn to the finishing chute. I would later find out that he had no idea the run finish was around the corner (which would explain why the "move" worked), but nevertheless, when I cocked my head back and ran something that likely resembled a cow milling to some fresh grass in the pasture, I was a god. Run moments like that don't happen to me so it salvaged what was otherwise a fairly dismal run.

As I barreled past the finish line I went straight to a tent where they had cold towels and water. But before I stopped running, I nailed my head on a metal bar at the top of the tent and then collapsed on top of a cooler. I was super hot and now my head hurt, but at least I was done.

I ran 5:45 below my goal which was disappointing. I did, however, end up winning the Clydesdale division by 20 minutes and finished second in my age group. In the end I was very happy with my swim and bike, but disappointed in my run.

The course is spectator friendly and it was great to see my mom, girlfriend, sister and two month old niece cheering me on. After the race I got to hold my niece and show her some triathlon gear. This was her first triathlon so I wanted to make sure she got the full experience, sweat and all. She started crying (going anaerobic) so I quickly handed her back to her mom to get her heart rate down and get her back into Zone 1 intensity. She is pretty young so I wanted her to focus on building a good aerobic base before getting too serious.

As I reflect back on this race I remember so many things I don't typically remember about races and it's very refreshing. I love the run course because I see the faces of the people on their porches who look at me the same way my cat does when I bring in the newspaper each morning—with curiosity, excitement and fear. I also love the train tracks that slice off T-2 from downtown. Kings Mountain has train tracks?? Heck, why hide 'em, let's celebrate them by putting T-2 right on them! Much of what makes this great has nothing to do with the race and everything to do with the slices of life we may not often get to see.

I particularly remember hanging around for several hours after the race talking with other competitors and volunteers, catching some rays and even spending some time discussing race strategy with the race director. Of all my races, this one will always rank near the top for the variety of experiences it offers. My usual race format is to get completely amped the morning of the race, tune everything out while I race, stew after the race about things I could have done better and then go home. At this race, I seem to realize that there is a lot more to see, and that is what makes it unique and one of America's great.

So, having realized all the goodness this race had to offer during my first trip there, I was back the next year to do it all over again. In addition to Gatorade and a handful of gels, I armed myself with a fishing license and a friend's turkey hunting story, just in case I sat on the bus next to the back fur deer hunting guy.

About the Author

Built of twisted steel, Michael Guzek stands a towering 6′ 5″ and weighs 215 pounds. He lives in Boulder, Colorado with his wife Melanie and has completed over 50 triathlons including 11 ultra distance races. An athlete all his life, Michael played five different sports in high school and continued to play basketball through college at the University of North Carolina. His passion for endurance sports was born in 2000 after a friend convinced him to run the Army 10 Miler in Washington, DC. Shortly afterward, he completed his first triathlon and then his first ultra distance race the following year at the Great Floridian.

When not training, Michael enjoys hiking, snowboarding, mountain biking, and bullying the little triathletes out of their Power Gels. He hopes to be the first superhero to complete an ultra distance race in less than seven hours.

Loveland Lake to Lake Triathlon

loveland, colorado

Race Distance: Intermediate
1.5K Swim, 30 Mile Bike, 10K Run
Month: June
Race Web Site: www.lovelandlaketolake.com

Author: Neal J. McLaughlin
Racing Category: Age Group 45-49

The Loveland Lake to Lake Triathlon burst on the triathlon scene in Colorado in 2001 and quickly became a favorite race of many local triathletes. Race Director, Peggy Shockley, schedules this race in late June each year. Staged at Lake Loveland in the middle of the town of Loveland, Colorado, this intermediate distance race features one of the prettiest venues and the most challenging bike course of any race in the region. For those who don't like to run or whose running days are behind them due to injury, there is an Aquabike category (swim/bike), and there is also a relay category. The field is a mix of first-timers, enthusiasts, and elite age group triathletes. As further evidence of the quality of the Loveland Lake to Lake Triathlon, this race has been a USAT Rocky Mountain Regional Championship in past years, as well as being a current qualifier for the Best of the USA Championship.

Registration is located at Loveland High School, which borders Lake Loveland. Race registration is available the afternoon and evening before race day and the morning of the race in the school cafeteria. This process is very easy and quick, thanks to an abundance of helpful volunteers. Event parking at the high school is plentiful and convenient.

To get to Loveland, take I-25 to Highway 34 and go west into the town of Loveland. You will pass Lake Loveland. Take a right turn on Taft, another right on 29th, and you are at Loveland High School. There are several hotels adjacent to Interstate 25, and several in town, closer to the race venue. The first wave is usually in the water by 6:30–6:45 a.m.. Since Loveland is 60 to 90 minutes north of the Denver area (depending on where you live), many competitors choose to stay overnight in Loveland. Summer is a busy time in Loveland and the surrounding communities, so it is strongly recommended that you make your hotel reservations early.

The pre-race meeting is also strongly recommended for all competitors and a must for those doing this race for the first time. The briefing is held at the amphitheater adjacent to the swim start.

The race begins with a swim in Lake Loveland, which is fed by the Big Thompson River. Water temperatures are typically in the low 70s, and the water in Lake Loveland is very clean and clear. The 1,500 meter swim course is a single loop, counterclockwise swim. The start is a beach start at water's edge, and the course is laid out in such a way as to minimize having to sight directly into the glare of the rising sun. Usually, there are six or seven waves with fewer than 100 participants per wave, keeping the swim leg spread out fairly well. The swim exits the lake on a grassy shoreline and you have about a 300 meter run through the park from the swim exit to the transition area.

From the grassy transition area, the bike leg starts in the west parking lot of the high school and begins by winding through the adjacent neighborhoods. Volunteers are plentiful along the course and well-placed, so that competitors are pointed in the right direction. The bike course heads west toward Big Thompson Canyon, before taking a right turn and heading north toward Fort Collins. This section of the bike course is a steady, gradual uphill on a less traveled road. Farms and ranches line the right-hand side of this portion of the course, and foothills line the left. A brief descent is followed by a rather long, hard climb. Again, you descend, and then begin a more gradual climb adjacent to beautiful Horsetooth Reservoir, at the southwest edge of nearby Fort Collins. Once at the top of this hill, you begin a rapid and steep descent with a couple of sweeping turns. A bit of caution is urged on this descent, as you will be moving at speeds in excess of 40 mph. The course turns east, winding through a residential area. Then it's an extended stretch of rolling terrain, through farmland and new subdivisions, south on Taft Hill Road, back to Loveland. Conveniently, there are two aid stations on the bike course, where you can exchange water bottles.

You may want your road bike for this race, as you will find the climbs challenging and the winding descents fast, and a bit tricky. In addition to being hilly, the bike course is long—approximately 30 miles, a pleasing feature to those whose cycling abilities are their strength. Competitors are rewarded for their efforts with pretty scenery and applause from the spectators that gather in the neighborhood sections of the course.

After a fast transition, you are out on a flat and fast 10K run course, which begins by winding through the athletic fields and neighborhood streets adjacent to Loveland High School. From there, you run on a concrete path halfway around Lake Loveland. The run course was originally a trip around the lake, but logistical concerns about the flow of the race caused event organizers to alter the run course to an out-and-back. You are treated to a shady, tree-lined course, and the encouragement of neighbors who come out to cheer on the participants. Aid stations are conveniently located at every mile along the run course. Once you are back on the grounds adjacent to the high school and amphitheater, you are almost home… but not quite. The last quarter mile of the run course passes tantalizingly close to the finish line, but you must first run around the duck pond adjacent to the West parking lot, and finish next to the amphitheater. Every finisher's name is announced, as they cross the line, and the award ceremonies don't begin until the last competitor has finished. The grassy, shaded park adjacent to the finish is the perfect place to recover, grab a cold bottle of water, and cheer your friends as they finish.

The clean water of Lake Loveland, the scenic and challenging bike course, and the tree-lined run course around Lake Loveland are hallmarks of this race. But there are some other important ingredients which set this race apart – volunteers and food. The volunteers who support this race are among the friendliest, most enthusiastic, and most supportive you will find anywhere. As evidence of this, I can remember being asked how my race experience was by no fewer than six of these fine volunteers, after my first Loveland Lake to Lake. They really do care! The local police department has also been very supportive in managing the course to keep it safe for the athletes. Secondly, this race has a truly excellent post-race feed (read: real food!), featuring pasta, fruit, baked goods, etc. No one goes home hungry.

Loveland Lake to Lake has given me some fond memories, including a couple of breakthrough races, my first race on Zipp wheels (yes, they do make a difference), and my first sub 40 minute 10K in a triathlon. Every year, I make it a point to enter a few key races the day registration opens, and Loveland Lake to Lake is one of them. This is one I don't want to miss.

So, if an intermediate distance triathlon in late June fits into your summer racing schedule, I highly recommend Loveland Lake to Lake.

About the Author

Neal McLaughlin is an Account Executive for Group Life and Disability with The Hartford. He graduated with a Bachelor of Arts degree from Williams College in 1981. Neal is married to Kathy, and they have two children.

Neal has been competing in triathlons since 1998, and is a five time USA Triathlon All American and a five time member of Team USA. He represented the United States at the 2008 ITU World Age Group Triathlon Championships in Vancouver, BC.

Neal is a Director of COMPA Food Bank Ministry in Denver, Colorado, having served as Board President from 2002 -2006, and currently serving as Board Vice President.

Neal coaches a U-14 Girls Soccer team for Real Colorado and a Boys JV Inline Hockey team for Mountain Vista High School in Highlands Ranch, Colorado. He has been a spinning instructor since 1996.

Neal is also a past member of the Winter Park Ski Patrol from 1981-2002.

Pacific Crest Triathlon

sunriver, oregon

Race Distance: Intermediate
1.5K Swim, 28 Mile Bike, 10K Run
Month: June
Race Web Site: www.racecenter.com/pacificcrest

Author: Linnea Alvord
Racing Category: Age Group 35-39

I stood at the boat ramp at Wickiup Reservoir in Sunriver, Oregon amongst hundreds, but feeling completely alone and panicked. The lake looked so big and the buoys impossibly far away. Tears were in my eyes but the goggles hid that. Quick, back to the porta-potty, the one way off on the right where nobody seems to be in line. How am I ever going to make it through this swim, those buoys are so far apart...

This would be my first intermediate distance race and while I'd been successful racing the short course distance, the new distance was daunting. Moreover, the Pacific Crest Triathlon has a very competitive field; not a race you have to qualify for, but one you have to be brave enough to undertake. It occurs early in the Pacific Northwest racing season, when the ice has barely melted off the roads. And so, of course, I signed right up to challenge myself and to start off what would be a season of racing local intermediate distance triathlons in order to gain a Pacific Northwest ranking.

My fourth triathlon didn't start with any less fear at the swim start than the prior ones. Not because I'm scared of the water, but because it just seems so long and it's worse when you're at the edge of the lake and you can see the whole course. Double UGH! With the cold, I'd been extra careful to bring wool socks and old sneakers to stand in because it was cold in the mountains, and my extremities are always the first to go numb. Wickiup, the largest of all the Cascade Lakes along the Deschutes River, stands at an elevation of 4,350 feet. The water was supposedly 62 degrees, but so was the air! Oh man, my teeth were chattering, thank god it was wetsuit legal! I just wanted to get started. My stomach was acid, and I was shaking from fear more than from the chill. The announcer was chatty and chipper and tried to calm and psych us up at the same

time with gossip on the previous wave leaders, the weather forecast, anything he could think of.

Finally the ladies started—a huge group of more than 200. The water didn't feel cold at all with adrenaline surging through me and I tried to focus. The day prior I had executed a "race day preparation" 20 minute swim that turned out to be one of the best confidence boosters. Several 90 second bursts followed by 60 second recoveries gave me the courage to push myself in that huge lake of freezing water and know that I wasn't going to die out there. Now on race day if I could realize I was backing off, I knew I could summon up the memory of the intervals and push forward.

The swim was a thrasher right at the start, but by the first buoy I was already coming upon guys from the prior wave. The course is executed clockwise and the second buoy is nearly to the opposite shore. I stopped a few times to ensure I was really going the right way and then promptly veered off course on the way back into shore, but wonders never cease, I was finishing!

The swim course is highly spectator friendly, and people line up on the exit chute to cheer. My fans yelled for me as I exited, "You actually passed some people… you're in the first half of your wave." Later I would recall how I had chuckled as I swam off course, I was merely preparing myself for that eventual need to swim a whole bunch farther one day! Even though I was just doing my first intermediate distance, I had the sneaking suspicion that longer distance racing would be an interesting challenge.

Transitioning onto the bike was hard! My hands were incredibly cold so I immediately pulled on gloves and then dizzy still, couldn't get anything else accomplished smoothly. Funny how preservation instincts can take over a well-planned mental checklist. But once I got my act together, I was able to perform my latest learning, to run down a very long transition chute with one hand easily steering the saddle, the other pumping along in normal running style. That felt great; taking my mind off of how difficult it was to run in bike shoes with frozen feet. Just add one little triathlon trick per race and maybe one day I'll get to be really fast, I smiled to myself.

The Pacific Crest intermediate distance bike course starts off pretty flat and tame while your heart is still heaving and you're shaking the water out of your ears. But quickly you come to a mild grade that starts to separate the novices from the pack.

It was as beautiful as it could be, there was early morning sun as you passed the next lake and snow lingering on the sides of the roads.

Central Oregon is known for its infamous "chip seal" roads that are definitely not smooth. But, the scenery makes up for it. There are plenty of things to take your eye off of the bike computer and the road. WHOOMP!! One huge pothole! Oh how freaking scary. Of course it was on a descent, too. Struggling to refocus, I finally got to the last long flat stretch, about eight miles from Sunriver Village. I knew from my pre-ride of the course that it was not too far to the end.

My average speed was 21 mph and I was spinning easy, keeping my heart rate right in the (correct) zone. There are no spectators along the bike course since it's closed to traffic, except for right at the last stretch, where people who live along the road set up chairs and cheer the athletes on. So just when you are feeling a bit like "it's time to get on to the run," a little extra energy is nice.

At last I heard music. YEAH! I thought, I'm almost there and I am really doing this! Now just get through transition. Pacific Crest is a "split transition" race, and it was the first time I'd done that. We had to place our running gear at T2 before we started the swim and bike up at Wickiup, 26 miles away. My hotel room, the local Red Lion Inn, had been the scene of much debate and consternation as I created two separate piles of gear to check at each transition spot. I had checked and re-checked to make sure I had left what I needed. But now as I approached, the doubt entered my head. Did I get it right? Would it all be there, intact? Shoes, hat, drink. In that order. Right? Special yellow towel, middle of rack, about five racks in. I tried to focus on the plan for the minutes ahead.

Coming into the run transition area, I rode up upon a gal who was expertly unclipping and slipping her feet onto the tops of her shoes (oh, the envy of that tri skill!). Still new to the rules, I wasn't sure if I was allowed to pass within the coned area, but I carried on and moved in front of her. Unclipped, hopped off, and we ran up into T2 together. She didn't save that much time being so expert after all. I executed my second transition quickly, except for another small brain fade. Did I leave a little vial of Vaseline in my shoe? I paused, shaking out my shoe for several seconds before I remembered that I had not done that. All the while, the precious seconds were ticking. I knew from my short course racing that seconds actually count in these races.

My fans had driven way around the bike course, and I spotted them dashing across the field to get to the run course. They told me I was doing very well, "Top Ten" and that was super helpful. And right there, I passed about three women as we left the field. To think I might be in the top ten females was an unbelievable thought! I kept trucking! My legs felt the normal lead for the first mile and definitely didn't come back as strong as I'd have liked. The run course is winding, little ups and downs on narrow walking paths, and now in Sunriver Village it was 79 degrees. I gratefully grabbed water at every aid station and stayed in any shade available (not much). Many of the homes we ran by had been rented by triathletes, and those who had raced on Saturday were now out in easy chairs, clapping and cheering us on. What a super energy boost they gave me. And oh, the envy of being done! Boy, it sure wasn't like doing a short course triathlon. I would have liked to have had more energy left in my legs. Maybe taking in some additional fuel would have helped but I was too nervous to try and add food into the plan.

As I neared the finish line, the music blared, and the crowd was cheering. I was able to glance over my shoulder as the road bent and didn't see anyone in sight. Go, go, go I thought, push it! I picked up my legs and ran harder. As I came to the finish chute, my two Weimaraners recognized me (smelled me is more like it!) and rushed the fencing. Woof!

And then, whoosh, it was all over…I finished in 3rd place in my age group and 7th overall for females. The volunteers quickly shoved cold drinks into my hands and pulled off my timing chip, threw a medal around my neck, and pushed me on to the shade and food tent!

I moved right in and snacked quickly on the variety of fruit, cookies, and sandwiches, then went to hug my husband, friend Susan and my two dogs. There was even more food for sale, and even non-cola beverages which went straight to my head. The post-race festivities and expo were just as good as the pre-race ones. Product samples, shopping opportunities, and local coaches and teams all had booths there. When my time finally came to get my medal, I reflected how the training and race preparation had paid off. I had made a special trip to Wickiup to ride the bike course. I'd wandered around on the running paths some and gotten a feel for that too. More importantly, I proved to myself that I can take on a new challenge and succeed despite having very little background in the sport. It was a sense of achievement that would carry me on a high note for several days while I focused on how to get better at swimming!

About the Author

Linnea Alvord was inspired to train for triathlons while living briefly in San Diego. Now living in the Pacific Northwest, she has learned how to successfully train through the eight months of rain while also working as a marketing consultant. The year after her Pacific Crest intermediate distance debut, she followed up with a season of long course triathlons, ending up 7th in her age group at the Ironman World Championship 70.3®. Her two Weimaraners remain her loyal training partners and race day fans.

Philadelphia Triathlon

philadelphia, pennsylvania

Race Distance: Intermediate
1.5K Swim, 40K Bike, 10K Run
Month: June
Race Web Site: www.phillytri.com

Author: Rhonda Cohen
Racing Category: Age Group 50-54

The Sure Kill River—that is how Philadelphians refer to their beloved local body of water, the Schuylkill, hugging the shores of the expressway of the same name. When I first told my friends I would be entering the first annual Philadelphia Triathlon (now called the Philadelphia Insurance Triathlon), everyone questioned me as if I had been abducted by aliens. "You're swimming in THAT?"

The river is the stuff of legends, such as people turning green for life if they touch the water and sickness like the plague afflicting you if you immerse yourself in it.

To put it mildly, this made me a bit skeptical. "What kind of antibiotics would I have to take before and after the race? Can you get a shot?" But, despite the fears, these untried waters appealed to the adventurous amongst local athletes. Even more compelling was a race held in downtown Philadelphia that would keep us from schlepping to the Jersey shore on a summer weekend.

So began the first year of the Philadelphia Triathlon. In its inaugural year, 2005, only the intermediate distance was offered. A short course race was added in year two. Both distance races are presented with the assurance that the race director and staff would be in constant contact with the Schuylkill Navy Police, and would test for water quality in the five weeks prior to the race to make sure the river was safe to swim in.

This June event has become extremely popular and now sells out quickly each year. The short course race and two kids' races are held on Saturday while the next day offers the intermediate distance race. Packet pick-up begins on the Friday of race weekend.

A word of caution: the race start is down a very long, steep hill in Fairmount Park by the river (which means a very long, steep uphill on the return after the race).

My friends expected to see dead fish and body parts of some ex-Mafia target floating beneath them. As it turned out, the water was actually pleasant and swimming downstream was a nice addition to a race.

This is a USAT sanctioned race so wetsuit-legal rules apply. However; the second year of the race, Philadelphia had heavy rains the week prior to the race. They did hold the swim for the short course race but cancelled the swim portion for the intermediate and made it a duathlon. For me, the change posed a problem as I had been diagnosed with severe tendonitis in my foot several months prior. I was planning on swimming, biking, and using an AirCast and walking the run course. It was challenging to say the least. People still talk about me to this day as "the girl who did a duathlon in a cast." I'm tough, but it wasn't a barrel of laughs.

One of the nice advantages of this race is support provided by Cadence Cycling & Multisport Centers of Philadelphia. They have been a sponsor of the race since its inception and they offer triathlon classes to get ready for this race. Since I was fairly new to the sport when I signed up and had never raced this distance, it was invaluable to train with world class coaches and extremely helpful to specifically train for the race on the course (we also trained indoors). Cadence also provides bike mechanics at the race and they really take time with each bike to make any necessary adjustments. You can tell I'm crazy about them!

The intermediate distance bike course is not an easy one. There are four technical hills (the literature says short, but not in my vocabulary) that are quite steep. In fact, the first time I tried one of the earliest hills, I could barely get up. Lemon Hill, one of the steepest hills on the USPRO Cycling Championship, is part of this course but goes in a slightly different direction.

There are two loops on the bike course. Some people are better on hills than others, and with the spacing of the swim waves some of the fastest riders will be on their second loop where those "Back of the Packers" and those who started in a late swim wave, are likely to be on the course at the same time. All I can say is to be patient and be courteous, no matter what your pace is.

Kelly Drive and Martin Luther King Drive are two roads on the course that are normally very busy. This course is completely closed so it is very exciting to race on these roads with no cars.

There is some nice shade during the first part of the run, although for most of the course you run in the hot blazing sun without a tree in sight. It is a flat course but can be brutal since Philadelphia, like much of the east coast, is known for its humidity.

There are no qualifications to get into the race and the course stays open fairly long. Some people say this is their favorite race of the year. I have some reservations about recommending the intermediate distance race as someone's very first triathlon. As I mentioned, the course is technical and with the challenging hills on the bike course, it might dissuade someone from trying another. The race is also large. You need to decide whether or not you like the hoopla and energy from large crowds or if a smaller, more intimate setting is more to your liking. Having said this, they do have a first-timers' wave that many other races don't offer. They even have an award for fastest first-timers so in that respect, it's great.

For those of us in the local triathlon community, this is a fun race socially. We know a lot of people and many do this race. It is a very competitive race but accommodates the slow ones like myself. The first year I did the race, I even won 2nd in my division, Athena 40 Plus. It was by default, but I'll take it, and I adore that they have this category!

About the Author

In Rhonda Cohen's own words, "I started exercising at 50 (midlife crisis, what can I say) and being a big-boned gal (I call myself Athena Plus), I am not breaking any records. I'm slow as a slug and despite working with coaches, taking workshops, classes, lessons-you name it, I'm still slow. It's okay though because when people see me during a triathlon, it motivates others out there to try it."

Rhonda has recruited hundreds of people to the sport or any one of the three because it's really terrific for friendship, support, health, and camaraderie. She has done many triathlons of varied distances including long course races and has also done a marathon and several half-marathons, and metric and century bike rides. She is also training for an ultra distance triathlon and considers herself "in it for the long haul!"

Boulder Peak Triathlon

boulder, colorado

Race Distance: Intermediate
1.5K Swim, 42K Bike, 10K Run
Month: July
Race Web Site: http://www.5430sports.com/peak.htm

Author: Neal McLaughlin
Racing Category: Age Group 45-49

It is 5:30 a.m.. The sky in the east begins to glow in advance of sunrise. In the cool of the early morning, the smell of freshly mowed weeds and grass permeates the air. Three miles northeast of Boulder, Colorado, in the makeshift parking lot at the Boulder Reservoir (known to locals as "The Rez"), athletes begin to pump tires, assemble their gear, and prepare for the short walk to the transition area. There is an air of excitement, nervousness, and anticipation of the start of the Boulder Peak Triathlon.

For pro triathletes and age-groupers (both novice and experienced), the long-awaited start of the first wave of one of the premier intermediate distance triathlons is only an hour away. The announcer begins to welcome the athletes and gives them directions regarding the order of events.

What makes the Boulder Peak Triathlon one of the great triathlons in the U.S. is a combination of a challenging course and a world class field. This is typically an "A" priority race on most of the athletes' schedules, and it attracts not only the largest and strongest field of age group triathletes in the Rocky Mountain Region, but also a significant complement of the world's top pro triathletes.

Boulder has long been either a seasonal or permanent residence of some of the top professional endurance athletes in the world. The list of elite triathletes who call Boulder "home" reads like a Who's Who of the best in the sport. This event usually falls on the third Sunday in July each year and is part two of a series promoted and produced by 5430 Sports.

The 10 wave, 1,500 meter wetsuit-legal swim starts east of the transition area in the approximately 75 degree water adjacent to the Boulder Reservoir swim beach. It continues along a single triangular loop and exits north of the transition area just below "Pro Hill." The transition area in the parking lot to the south of Pro Hill is organized by wave/bib number, and it is fairly easy to find your spot in the transition area.

Once on the bike, the 42 kilometer course exits Boulder Reservoir and begins with rolling hills and false flats. It then winds through north Boulder County. About seven miles into the course, athletes begin to climb Old Stage Road, a 2/3 mile climb that approaches a 15 percent grade. Old Stage Road is the signature feature of this course and this triathlon. The mere mention of this hill strikes fear in the hearts of some and earns the respect of others. A favored method for local athletes in preparing for this climb is to include Old Stage Road in training rides in the weeks leading up to the race. Missing from their training, however, are the numerous spectators that line the climb during the race, shouting words of encouragement to the athletes as they ride by. Some athletes climb seated, some standing, and some walk their bikes as they struggle up the hill.

With encouraging messages written in chalk covering the roadway and the cheering crowd, there is an atmosphere that belies a featured climb in a grand tour. Once the athletes reach the top of the climb the road winds along for several hundred meters on undulating terrain before a fast descent. There is a strictly enforced 35 mph speed limit on the downhill portion of Old Stage Road. A right turn onto Left Hand Canyon Road, a left turn onto US 36, and a right hand turn onto Nelson Road leads the riders into gently rolling hills, which with four more right turns, takes you back to the Rez. There are a total of two aid stations along the bike course.

Once the second transition is complete, the athletes head out on the run course which crosses two dams located on the east side of the Rez. It then winds along the Certain Death Canal, before reversing and returning to the finish line. With the exception of the first and last half mile of the course, the run is on dirt trails — flat and fast. Similar to Old Stage Road, spectators line the last quarter mile of the run course, shouting encouragement and willing the athletes to a strong finish. Once across the finish line, the athletes are handed a bottle of cold water and a cold, wet towel.

What I like about this race is that every aspect of the event is consistent with its reputation as one of the top triathlons in the U.S. Race Director Barry Siff truly sweats the details to make certain that the high levels of expectations among the athletes are met. Former Race Director and Founder, Paul Karlsson made this a world class event, and Barry has continued the tradition. Registration and mandatory pre-race meetings are held the day before the race, along with an expo featuring dozens of vendors. One comment on the expo is that if the vendors don't have it, you probably don't need it.

Competitors need to take care not to linger too long at the expo, so they do not get overheated on the eve of this important race. Barry and his team of volunteers are available to assist with issues in the registration process, and do an excellent job of accommodating the athletes with problems that arise. The course is world-class, the volunteers are helpful, and the spectators provide a boost of energy and encouragement to the participants. For the pro race, the run course is altered into four 2.5K loops, to make the race even more spectator friendly. One of the rewards at the finish of the age group race is to grab a cold drink and some food and watch some of the best pros in the world duel on the run course.

The pre-race meetings are always helpful and even more so with the number of questions regarding the speed limit imposed on the descent of Old Stage Road for the age groupers. Much anxiety was originally created by the announcement of the speed trap, yet on race day it proves not to be an issue. These meetings are also instructional for the novice/first-timer, and those not familiar with the course. With a field of approximately 2,100 athletes, logistics are important to maintain flow throughout the race, and Siff and his staff do a good job making the course fast and fair. The rewards for the top three finishers in each age group are merchandise and awards that are handmade by Jodee Siff (and she does a great job!).

Accommodations are available at a number of hotels in the Boulder/Louisville area, and information is available on the race web site.

About the Author

Neal McLaughlin is a four time USAT All-American Triathlete and a three time member of Team USA. His best finishes at Boulder Peak include 3rd place finishes in 2002 (M40-44) and 2006 (M45-49), and a 1st place finish (M45-49) in 2005. The 2006 Boulder Peak Triathlon was Neal's 7th time doing this race. Neal lives in Highlands Ranch, Colorado with his wife, Kathy, and two children, Chris and Megan.

Donner Lake Triathlon

truckee, california

Race Distance: Intermediate
1.5K Swim, 40K Bike, 6.5 Mile Run
Month: July
Race Web Site: www.changeofpace.com/Donner_lake_tri.html

Author: Marissa Axell
Racing Category: Age Group 30-34

In 2003, I joined the Embarcadero Women's Triathlon Club where women of varying levels of abilities come together to train and socialize. I made many friends in my first year and decided to enter the Donner Lake Triathlon, which has been held in Truckee, California for nearly 30 years. I decided on this particular race partly to get my first intermediate distance race under my belt and partly to enjoy a weekend in the Sierras with my new triathlon friends.

I had heard how gorgeous the race setting is and about the beautiful lake swim, tough bike course, and stimulating run course. When I announced my intentions to do the race, my coach made sure that I knew what I was in for. She said, "When I decided that this race was going to be MY first intermediate distance race, I had no idea what I was in for. I burst into tears after the bike ride, it was so overwhelming. I think you can do it, but you do realize it's a long climb at altitude, right?" Of course I nodded, thinking "Hey, I live in the Bay Area, we have HILLS too."

My background as a collegiate swimmer assured me I could finish the swim, so I turned my dedication to training on the bike by climbing our local hills and running with teammates (either long runs in Golden Gate Park or speed workouts around the track). I was very excited about the race.

Planning for the weekend was easy. For accommodations, there are hotels, bed and breakfasts, campgrounds, and vacation rental units nearby in Truckee and Donner Lake. The real deals happen when you bring a group of six or more to the race. The team found a vacation home in the Tahoe/Donner forest through Vacation Rentals By Owner. This made the housing ultra affordable, and we could cook our own food.

By the way, Truckee is a year round sports playground destination with legendary snow in the winter and recreational water sports in the summer so there's a little of everything in the way of restaurants in the area.

The weather at Donner Lake in July is generally gorgeous and in the high 80s. Because it's at altitude, the mornings are cold and the afternoons are warm. It can get pretty windy, but the swim is early enough that the athletes exit the water before any whitecaps appear. Don't forget your sunscreen.

The race is typically on Sunday, and I picked up my registration packet the day before the race. Donner Lake is known as one of the gems nestled into the Sierras, so I planned on spending the entire afternoon at the lake. I packed some snacks, sunscreen, and my swim suit and floated, swam and jogged around the park area as my last tune up workout. There is also ample room for sunning, meeting, and grilling at the West End Beach.

I checked out the triathlon expo set up on the grass area, looking for great deals. Because most everyone must pre-register online, the packet pick up is fast and very organized. The goody bag is well stocked, and the t-shirts are standard and colorful. Only a handful of locals are allowed to register the day of the race.

The swim start is at the West End Beach on Donner Lake. Donner Lake is usually somewhere around the low to mid 60s in July, a bit warmer than nearby Lake Tahoe and a lot warmer than where I practice in the San Francisco Bay. Wetsuits are legal, but many people complete this swim without one.

The swim starts "in the water" with the course following a counter clockwise rectangle for 1,500 meters. With the swim at 6,500 feet, the altitude takes your breath away, so the locals have the advantage and usually dominate this race. The water is crystal clear, clean and cold, three reasons why I love swimming in it. When the sun is out, it's a killer, not just on the bike and run course, but also during the swim since you head directly into it or have it at your side until the final westward leg.

Transition is set up in the West End Beach parking lot. It is all first come first served when it comes to racking. This is a race that many pro's avoid (presumably because of the altitude), and its chock full of local athletes. I'm always conscious and courteous when racking my bike and setting up my transition area, we all have to share the limited space.

Porta-potties and some flush toilets are available and the lines are on the short side. The earlier you get to transition, the easier your race will be. Parking is available only in designated areas on the side of the road, so the earlier you are, the better parking you have, and the easier it is to start your pre-race rituals. Keep in mind, the entire lake is a huge recreation area during the day with a mix of Bay-area families and locals out for weekend play.

The bike course starts with an immediate left out of the transition area and you're on your way up, up, and up Donner Pass Road. The road is closed to car traffic and has ample volunteer support. The terrain is a winding, sometimes steep three mile climb up to the summit at 7,700 feet. I usually race with my road bike. Sure the tri bike is faster in general, but with all the steep, twisty descents, the road bike was a better choice for me.

As I began gasping for air at 6,700 feet, I found I was passing a few folks that were gasping harder than I was. I made sure to smile and say "Hi" as I moved ahead because everyone is friendly at this small race. My advice is to relax and soak up the amazing breathtaking (bad pun intended) views around you. It helps numb the pain of the three mile ascent. Relax your shoulders, even out your breathing and find your rhythm.

I spun up the three mile hill, enjoying every second of it. You can't beat a beautiful, sunny, crystal-blue morning on your bike. The entire ascent offers gorgeous vistas. Every major view point summons your desires to stop and snap photos capturing the bridges and the stunning backdrop of the lake and the Sierras. Spectators have ample viewing areas but beware you have to hike or drive up the road and the road closes for the entire race so if you're driving you might get stuck out there until all cyclists have passed.

Suddenly we crest the summit and are happy to have a little downhill. For approximately nine miles you cycle past some higher alpine ponds and a few of the tiny ski slopes like Donner Lake ski ranch. The course winds up Donner Pass Road and crosses over Interstate 80. At the turn around is the only aid station on the bike course. Here you find many volunteers who offer food, gel, and sports drink. Throw your used bottles and pick up new bottles, and don't forget to thank your volunteers!

After the turn around, the nine mile gradual uphill keeps you honest under the hot sun. There is some shade, but definitely not much. Just after the turn around your fellow athletes begin chatting, commenting on everything from the weather to your bike. I've met several fun characters along this part of the race over the years, from grandpas to very fit teenagers. Once you reach the summit, prepare for a fast, twisty descent down the steep three mile Donner Pass Road toward to the transition area. Please don't cross the yellow line, and if you're a slow descender, please let others pass with care by staying to the left. Major point of interest: you MUST come to a complete stop and place a foot down at the stop sign once you reach the bottom of the hill. This is for safety. Do not ignore those volunteers working hard to keep us safe out there! They will waive you across the street and head back to the transition.

The run is a lovely course around the entire lake because you never have a bad view! It's relatively flat and on pavement, except for a half mile or so on a wide trail through the state park. Many locals are on their porches by this time, barbecuing and watching the athletes. Once through Donner Lake State Park, you'll encounter a hill approximately 200 yard long, the only hill on the run course. After that hill, you only have a few miles left, so I start picking up the pace. Most of the course winds through residential housing.

At about the 10K mark, you realize that the finish is closer to seven full miles, instead of 6.2. But the crowds are large, and I start getting energized when the crowd starts roaring and I hear the announcer as you round the corner heading back to the West End Beach. The announcer manages to shout every competitor's name as they cross the finish line, a spectacular touch to wind up a grueling competition.

The race also boasts a short course triathlon on the same day. The swim is quarter mile with a six mile bike and two mile run..

The after party includes awards that go six deep in each age group, including a Clydesdale and Athena division. Many athletes stick around to enjoy the after party of socializing, free food, drinks, and generally enjoying the lake. It leaves you with the feeling of a community sponsored summer barbeque, a one of a kind in today's day and age of large scale, large budget triathlons. Definitely a gem in the Sierras, not to be missed by any triathlete seeking out their next challenge.

About the Author

Marissa Axell lives and works in San Francisco, California. After a competitive swimming career she turned to a new challenge of triathlons. Her first years of triathlons included the Donner Lake Triathlon and Wildflower Triathlon to name a few. After two years of triathlon experience, she trained for and completed Ironman Coeur D'Alene with her close group of "Iron-chick" friends. After her first ultra distance experience, she was hooked, and went back for more with Ironman Wisconsin a year later. She then spent a year rediscovering open-water swimming, and competing in the Trans-Tahoe Relay, Lake Berryessa two and one mile open water competitions and various other races in Northern California.

Recently, Marissa joined the road cycling and cyclo-cross scene in NorCal, and currently she's training for Hawaii 70.3 and her first trip to Hawaii in addition to preparing for her first year of road racing with her new team. Ultimately, Marissa enjoys the oodles of close friends that the sports of swimming, triathlon, and cycling have brought to her.

Life Time Fitness Triathlon®

Race Distance: Intermediate
1.5K Swim, 40K Bike, 10K Run
Month: July
Race Web Site: www.ltftriathlon.com

Author: Margie Shapiro
Racing Category: Professional

The Life Time Fitness Triathlon, held in Minneapolis, Minnesota each year in mid-July, gained immediate national recognition from its 2002 debut because of its unique race format for professionals. One of very few televised triathlons, it boasted the greatest prize purse in the sport's history (and still ranks among the best). Additionally, its "Battle of the Sexes" format pitted male and female professionals against each other with a pre-determined "equalizer" time, so that the women started ahead of the men, and the first person to cross the line won the grand prize. Since then, the race has changed its format for professionals to a typical non-drafting Intermediate (a.k.a. Olympic®) distance triathlon and continues to thrive as an excellent race opportunity for amateurs and pros alike.

Offering Short and Intermediate distance race options for amateurs and relays, two elite-amateur categories (below 40 and above 40), and a small invitation-only race for professionals (now one of five in the Life Time Fitness Triathlon series), the Life Time Fitness Triathlon allows over 2,500 entrants yearly. Registration opens in the fall/winter of the preceding season and fills quickly. While there are no requirements for amateur entry, those interested in competing in the elite amateur category must provide a race resume for consideration.

Getting your registration in early, traveling to Minneapolis, and taking part in this event are well worth the effort. Good accommodations are available downtown, and it is an easy trip from there to the event site at Lake Nokomis. If you've never been to downtown Minneapolis, there are plenty of sites to see in the city (museums and other attractions), and there is a very nice downtown shopping area with great restaurants and cafes.

Lake Nokomis is an inviting, family-friendly spot to spend the day before the race. You'll find open parkland with trails to walk along the lake and nice Midwest-style neighborhoods to tour nearby, either on foot or by bike. The bike course is safe enough to preview without road closures, and you may even be able to swim the course a day or two preceding the race.

Participants enjoy a large pre-race and race-day expo chock full of vendors offering top-of-the-line wares for us gear and gadget-loving triathletes. There is also a bounteous post-race food tent, a plentiful goodie bag including a high quality t-shirt, and free massages for those willing to stand in line.

My experience with the race came in 2007. It began with a phone call from one of the race organizers inviting me to participate in the small professional field. Despite having raced too much already that year by June and knowing that I would not be at the top of my game in mid-July, I was still very excited for the opportunity to race at the Life Time Fitness Triathlon, one of the most renowned professional races in the country. I remembered seeing television coverage of the race as an amateur and dreaming of one day being among those battling it out for the grand prize. Though I'd been quite intrigued by the battle of the sexes format and regretted not having been a pro when it was contested that way, I was thrilled to be involved.

One perk of racing as a professional is that the race organizers tend to take very good care of you. This race was no exception, in fact, it was my first big professional race, and I felt that they treated us like royalty. Clearly, Life Time Fitness founder and CEO Bahram Akradi shares our passion for the sport of triathlon and the lifestyle it embraces, investing so much into the race beyond the already mind-boggling prize purse.

Aside from airfare and a few meals, the race took care of my expenses and arrangements including hotel, bus transportation to and from the event, and two classy dinner/cocktail parties during the weekend. While it was a humbling experience to hobnob with some of the biggest names in the sport, at the same time it put me at ease to be around them outside of the race itself. At that time in my career I was still a relatively new "pro" on the scene, I hadn't socialized much with anyone outside of the U.S. team, so it was a nice chance to meet other athletes and hear intriguing accents, my favorite was that of the Australians! Also, the race organizers made sure we were comfortable on the course, providing us a bike course preview led by a local elite amateur and a chance to train in the lake prior to race day.

Race morning, you will enjoy the enthusiasm of the announcers (likely including Minnesota's greatest triathlon advocate, Jerry McNeil) as you prepare for a calm one-lap clockwise swim in the lake. Our race was the first wave of the day, and I remember my typical pre-race nerves getting out of hand when in last-minute T1 checks I found that my disc wheel tire (a tubular, not quick or easy to change) had flatted. Although my husband tried to calm me, the most soothing voice was that of the mechanic on hand who promised me that my bike would be ready on its rack by the time I came out of the water.

Oftentimes when a race offers both a professional and amateur field, the pros race on a criterium-style course with multiple bike laps, however, at the Life Time Fitness Triathlon, the pros and age groupers share the same course for the swim, bike, and run. Because of high heat in previous years, our start time was earlier than usual, but the weather happened to be mild anyway.

I hurried down to the race start still a bit flustered, but was calmed even further when I heard the familiar voices of Jerry McNeil and Barb Lindquist (who won the race a few years prior when it was still women vs. men). They had gathered information on each racer and gave short but detailed introductions to each of us as we jogged down to our positions at the beach start. My husband relayed to me later that when the announcers mentioned my name and the fact that I have two kids, several of the other women looked shocked. Maybe if I'd seen their expressions, it would've given me a boost.

The water was clean and fresh, with water temperatures in the mid 70s (wetsuit-legal for amateurs). I enjoyed the clockwise one-loop swim, as I breathe and sight more comfortably to my right, and it was easy to sight off buoys placed along the course. It was an uneventful swim for me (smaller fields tend to be a bit easier to navigate, and we didn't have that many in the group). I exited with Sam McGlone and Mirinda Carfrae, so I felt like I was in great company despite being among the last out of the water.

The roar of the crowd was exhilarating in T1 as I ran to my freshly-racked bike (with two fully-inflated tires). I was ready to attack once I got out of T1 (you ride out down a little park access road a few hundred meters before getting on the main road, and then make a quick turn shortly thereafter). Once I was on the first main stretch of the course, I found a good rhythm. The bike course meanders from Lake Nokomis onto some neighborhood and semi-highway roads. It goes to the Mississippi River, and then back toward the race site and out in the other direction to go around Lake Harriet. While there are no real "climbs" in the course, you'll enjoy some small rolling hills on various parkways with picturesque views of neighborhoods and lakes.

It was a great scenic course for my taste since I love to look out at the water. I suggest practicing your cornering before hitting this course because, although there are only about 10 or 15 turns, a couple of them are quite sharp, including a ramp from one parkway to another.

Perhaps I got overexcited in the early part of the bike course while catching up to the faster swimmers. When I rode past my husband after the first main loop (which comprised about two thirds of the 40K), he had calculated how much time I'd made up on the leaders and how much more I needed to push. I was pleased with my ride so far and got a little distracted on the last third of the course, finding time to take in the scenery, especially as I circled Lake Harriet. I remember seeing boaters and fitness enthusiasts around that area and marveling at what a great life this was.

The run, which goes around Lake Nokomis on a paved path, is flat and very spectator-friendly. By the time I hit the run, my legs didn't respond well to the excitement of the crowds in my two laps around the lake, but I did my best to appreciate the great weather and to savor the experience. I was probably thinking too much about the other racers around me, losing my own concentration, as I noted the running styles and breathing patterns of both male and female pros as they came running by.

I have several very vivid memories of my run at the Life Time Fitness Triathlon. At one point, there is a sharp left turn on the course, followed by a short straightaway, then a U-turn to return on the straightaway before making another sharp turn. I remember seeing the leaders (Vanessa Fernandes was out ahead with Emma Snowsill, Pip Taylor, Julie Dibens, and Becky Lavelle not far behind) turning the second corner as I rounded the first. Another memory was hearing the labored breathing of Greg Bennett, who was on his way to a win, as he ran around me to finish his second lap (while I was still on my first). I noticed how hard he was working (and also how far ahead he was from the next man), and I wished I could push myself to that level of effort. Greg eventually went on to win the grand prize by taking all five races in the 2007 Life Time Fitness Triathlon series. These memories are all part of the learning process, as I aspire to compete at that level someday. On that day, for me, it was all about getting through the run. It was one of those "it's not my day but I'm going to enjoy it anyway" races. I wanted to make sure to hold myself together enough that they'd invite me back!

After the race, I spent the afternoon accelerating my recovery by taking full advantage of all of the great food available as well as a lengthy and free massage. One of my favorite memories of the day was listening to the announcers as they welcomed in each finisher individually, inserting commentary and highlights along the way. Good announcers have the opportunity to leave lasting impressions on race participants, and I always enjoy hearing them celebrate each racer individually and watching the expressions (from pride to disappointment, exhilaration to exasperation) as each one crosses the line.

One great aspect of triathlon (and something racing on the international circuit doesn't always convey) is the camaraderie. Because the awards were presented to pros and amateurs in succession, the Life Time Fitness Triathlon provided a nice opportunity to socialize with triathletes from all over the country (not to mention the pros who'd traveled from abroad) and of all levels (including newbies and multiple world champions). While each athlete's perspective and experience is different, we all share a common bond, and post-race picnics and awards ceremonies highlight that bond.

The Life Time Fitness Triathlon is an event you'll want to add to your list of "must-do's." Race day weather can vary, but you can expect typical Midwest weather for July. I found conditions ideal. The day I raced was sunny and warm without much wind, and I thoroughly enjoyed my experience there. Even without benefiting from some mathematically-derived equalizer, you will leave this race a winner and I'm sure you'll agree that it is one of the United State's 50 great triathlons.

About the Author

Currently in her 3rd year of professional racing, with over 20 U.S. Intermediate distance triathlons and multiple international races under her belt, Margaret ("Margie") Shapiro is a member of the U.S. National Elite Team. She is also a 2008/2012 Olympic hopeful, and was the 2005 overall World Amateur Champion at the Olympic distance. Margie resides in Northern Virginia with her husband Brendan and her two children, William and Molly. In addition to training and racing on the International Triathlon Union circuit and in U.S. non-drafting triathlons, she coaches runners and triathletes and co-owns a chain of successful athletic stores, called Potomac River Running, in the Washington, DC area.

Chicago Triathlon

chicago, illinois

Race Distance: Intermediate
1.5K Swim, 40K Bike, 10K Run
Month: August
Race Web Site: www.chicagotriathlon.com

Author: Austan Goolsbee
Racing Category: Age Group 35-39

The Chicago Triathlon is one of the largest triathlons in the world. That's the first thing that anyone signing up for it should know. It is very different from a typical local intermediate distance triathlon and it is probably very different from even the largest race you have done.

You don't do Chicago for the family atmosphere. You do it because it is an incredible event—a spectacle and a legend. This is the kind of race that you really ought to try at least once in your life and if you are like thousands of others, you might just keep coming back.

Most triathlons don't have enough participants to convince major cities to give them the permits they need to close down roads. In Chicago, the sheer magnitude of participants enables the race to be held right downtown. That can be a little nerve-racking but it's also very special.

Because of its popularity, you need to register early in the season. The event always sells out months before race day. The race typically takes place around the last weekend in August. There is a kids' race and a Supersprint on Saturday and then the big ones—the Intermediate and Short course races on Sunday.

The race organizers have designed the Chicago Triple Triathlon Challenge for those they describe as "multisport zealots." In the triple challenge, triathletes register for all three of the major triathlons and compete in them consecutively—the Supersprint on Saturday, the short course first thing Sunday morning immediately followed by a trip to the starting line for the Intermediate course triathlon.

There is no better organized major race than Chicago. They have to be given the massive size. In recent years the swim has started right in Monroe Harbor across from Grant Park and the famous Buckingham Fountain (the fountain that used to open the TV show "Married, With Children"). It continues next to the harbor wall and then back along an outside lane of buoys.

One of the reasons for the popularity of the Chicago Triathlon is that the course is very beginner friendly. For the swim, there are many, many starting waves—more than 50—so that each one is not overly chaotic. They are grouped by age and gender. I would say the event is overwhelmingly likely to be wetsuit legal, though a lot of people choose not to wear one because the water by late August is very comfortable.

In my opinion, there is no better spectator course for a swim. My wife walked along the wall for more than half the swim waving to me and taking pictures (not an easy assignment given that most swimmers spend the majority of the time with their faces in the water). During other years at Chicago, I have seen whole crews of people with big signs walking along the swim course encouraging their friends and family members so it's very nice for those who are nervous about their swim.

Athletes exit the water onto steel stairs where volunteers are on hand to provide help to those who want it. You then face a third of a mile run on an asphalt path to the massive grassy area of the bike transition. If you don't like running barefoot on a hard surface, you can join one of two types of people—those who try to walk quickly without hurting themselves and the prepared folks who have stashed an extra pair of running shoes or even flip flops along the fence at the swim exit.

Once in the transition area, the number of bikes racked is overwhelming. Make sure you worked out a path to your spot or you could spend a long time circling the grassy hill lost. You enter the transition on the south side and exit on the north side. Once you cross the transition mat you're free to hop on the bike and head on your way.

There's a short uphill on the ramp to Lake Shore Drive. This is the only "hill" you are going to face all day. Chicago is legendarily flat. The bike course follows what is normally a main commuter drag in the city. City authorities close down the inner two lanes of The Drive, as Chicagoans call it, going both ways.

The bike course showcases some amazing urban scenery—the stately Gold Coast mansions, Lincoln Park, the improbable beaches right in the heart of the city at North Avenue—as well as great views of the lake. The short course triathletes make one loop. The intermediate folks do a second one. For a lot of the locals, this is their daily commute so it's actually pretty cool to be riding it on a bike.

More so than in smaller races, you need to be alert on the bike course. This is especially true if you are in one of the later starting waves. With so many bikes on the road, it is crowded and by the end of the day, the road is littered with dropped water bottles and nutrition debris. If you get a flat on the road, I recommend hopping up into the safety of the big plant boxes in the median to change your tire instead of trying to pull over on the side of the course.

The other unusual thing about the bike course at the Chicago Triathlon is that you are supposed to ride on the left and pass on the right. That is because the outer two lanes still have traffic — the inner two lanes are for the triathlon. There are plenty of cones separating you from the cars and it has not felt dangerous to me when I have ridden it, but you don't want to end up causing an accident with other bikers by accidentally cruising slowly in the passing lane.

The bike course is not especially spectator friendly since you ride right down the highway. There are some spots on the northern section of the course where people can go to the park and walk over to the railing and see the competitors easily and there are a couple of overpass pedestrian bridges that are good spots for watching as well (but tell your cheering section not to spend too much effort trying to get your attention from up there because you'll need to keep your eyes on the road!).

When you finish the bike course, you head out of the transition area through a different exit onto Chicago's famous lake front path. The run course parallels the harbor with the park and the historic skyscrapers in the foreground and the Sears Tower and large modern buildings behind them. Then it's down around the back of the aquarium and the Museum Campus, past the weird toilet bowl inside a stadium that is the renovated Soldier Field, and then to the McCormick center. Turn around points vary depending on which distance you are running so pay attention.

There are aid stations every mile with water and sports drinks and there are also a lot of gel stations. It is, again, extremely pleasant lakefront and urban scenery. Keep an eye out for the McCormick Geese. They sometimes stand along the path watching the triathletes go by, apparently confused as to what in the world happened to their normally tranquil pathway.

The weather in Chicago can be anything. The first time I did this race, it was sunny and hot with terrible humidity. The next time I did the race it was overcast and cool but very windy, which made the bike course difficult. Generally you should plan for it to be hot. That's the most likely. But old timers will tell you about the time it was pouring rain and cold. You know the deal.

If you have any interest in seeing the pros race, Chicago frequently runs the pro start waves at times when the age-groupers can conveniently see them — either before or just after the age group race. I always enjoy seeing how fast they cover the course that I just raced on or am about to race on.

In all, the Chicago Triathlon is an amazing event and an incredible spectacle. I didn't want to make it my first triathlon because it seemed so massive, though the thousands of newbies each year suggest others have a different view. For me, my first go at Chicago was actually my third triathlon. I was comfortable with the idea of starting a swim with other people in the open water and going through a transition area, that sort of thing. With that, I could really appreciate what an experience it was to be part of such a mega-event.

Chicago is my home town race so I didn't have to find accommodations. It's a huge convention city, though, so it's easy to find a place to stay reasonably close to the starting line.

The expo, which typically takes place in the big Hilton downtown, is enormous. There must be 100+ booths there. With so many participants in the event, there are 20 or 30 different pick-up lines organized by last name, other lines for check-in points on the computer, more lines to pick up goodie bags, and so on. It feels much more like the packet pick-up of a large marathon than a triathlon. Some people like the energy from the expo. Others find it overwhelming. Whatever your view, try to get a good night's sleep because you will need to get up early to set up your transition area.

In terms of logistics, you can understand why an 8,000 person race's transition area can be daunting. It is just massive. Really though, it's no different than other races - you get assigned to a rack and you put your stuff there. The most important thing to do in the transition area is to orient yourself with the swim entrance on one side and the bike entrance on the other side so you know where to find your stuff. You will often see people come into the transition during the race and just run back and forth trying to figure out where they are. Count the number of racks up or down from the entrance and use that to get to your bike. Some people use balloons to mark their spot, but when you come in all you see are tons of balloons, so I'm guessing this is counter productive. My own method to the madness is to put a bright orange towel under my gear so when I come down the row, it's easy to see where my bike is.

The other unique thing about such a big event with so many start waves, is that you will probably have to do a lot of waiting in the morning. Typically you need to get in and rack your bike very early (around 5:30 a.m.). But the intermediate course waves might not start until around 10:30 a.m. There is a fun vibe among people just sitting and talking on the grassy knoll between the transition and the start which I love but others find a quiet corner and try to take a quick nap. It can be helpful to bring a throw away pair of flip-flops for walking around during this time.

The Chicago Triathlon is a thing unto itself. It's really very different from most events you will ever enter. If you seek a quiet race without crowds where it's easy to find your bike in the transition area, this triathlon is definitely not for you. If you are into the adrenaline rush of huge crowds — spectators, racers, and a massive post-race party, then there really is nothing quite like Chicago. In that case, you may find yourself like most of the other people I know who decided to try the race — they can hardly wait to do it again the next year.

About the Author

Austan Goolsbee is an economics professor at the University of Chicago. He describes himself as a not-particularly-fast middle-of-the-pack triathlete (2:45 for the Intermediate distance) who is okay at swimming and running and lousy on the bike. He mainly does triathlons around the Midwest (including four intermediate course and two long course triathlons).

Given that Chicago is the birthplace of the skyscraper (and is also his home), Austan enjoys stair races and has run to the top of three of America's four tallest buildings including the Sears Tower, the Hancock Center, and the Aon Center. Austan lives in Chicago with his wife and three children.

Luray International Triathlon

luray, virginia

Race Distance: Intermediate
1.5K Swim, 23 Mile Bike, 10K Run
Month: August
Race Web Site: www.luraytriathlon.com

Author: Shawn Clark
Racing Category: Age Group 30-35

There are a lot of things to consider when choosing which races to do in any given season. Among the questions we ask ourselves are, "Where does each race fit into my overall training plan?" and "Will this hinder or help my performance at my "A" race for the year?" If I'm deciding on my "A" race for the year, I ask myself, "Do I want hills or flats?" and "Do I want the race to be technical?" Then there are the convenience concerns: "How far away is this race? Will I need a hotel" How expensive is it?" So we read every race report we can find searching for races that may meet our criteria, hoping to glean from the author/athlete something that grabs our attention, something that leaps off the pages at us, making us want to not just enter the race, but to experience it. In the end we take everything we've gained from these fact-and-fancy-finding missions, and finally we commit. After considering all of these questions, choosing the Luray International Triathlon to be my first intermediate distance race was a no brainer.

It may help to give you a little background to my delving into the land of triathlon. In early 2006, I was sitting at work after coming in from a smoke break and one of my co-workers asked me when I was going to quit smoking. I told her May. I wasn't sure after 15 years of smoking that I could just put down the cigarettes and never start up again (in fact, it will probably always be a battle) but I had set a date so I was going to try. Previous attempts to quit had left me irritable, antsy and ten pounds heavier; okay maybe 20. Knowing those things, I needed a way to fight all three; exercise of course came to mind as something that should combat my dilemmas. So, I shared this with my co-worker, who, knowing I had just bought a bicycle, told me that I should give triathlon a whirl. It seemed like she had reached into my head, looked through

my childhood memories, found the DNA marker for my competiveness and planted a seed that immediately sprouted.

"That's a great idea," I heard myself saying. "Any suggestions for which one I should do?" I surprised myself by asking.

She told me about local triathlete David Glover and how he was directing his first race out in Luray, Virginia.

"Where those caverns are?" I asked (Luray is famous for an underground cavern network called Luray Caverns).

"Yup," she answered.

It wasn't much longer before I signed up for my first short course triathlon in Luray. I should have cut up the credit cards that day because I've been hooked ever since. So, choosing Luray to be my first intermediate distance race as well seemed like a perfect fit. The Luray International course meets all my criteria. It appeals to my sense of outdoors as well as my competitive drive. It is not enough to enter a race just because you hear that the scenery along the course is beautiful, if only to find out that the competition that shows up doesn't push you to race better. That's what training rides are for, not races. Even if you're not vying for first place, you want a deep enough field to challenge you at your place in the pack. Of course, it doesn't hurt to also have that beautiful scenery rolling by when you are riding and running down the country roads. Luckily, for me, Luray has both.

When first driving into Luray, one thing you notice is obvious cycling potential. Luray is located in the heart of the Shenandoah Valley in Virginia. Rolling, beautiful hills are all around, and sparsely populated roads make for perfect conditions for some great rides. The town itself is a mix of Appalachia and coffee houses, a combination that means this small little gem of a town has something to offer nearly anyone.

The lodging is adequate but can get full if you don't get a room early enough, especially since it is a popular tourist town. If you plan a little bit ahead though, you can find a reasonably priced place to stay without a problem. It really helps races when the host town appreciates, accepts and encourages the event; nobody wants to show up for an event and feel local hostility. Luray's residents fit the bill; they are extremely accepting, generous and a little bit curious about the race.

The race's start and finish, along with its single transition area, is set up in Lake Arrowhead Park, which has a small man-made lake just outside of Luray. The day before the event the local population is treated to the sight of eager participants donning wetsuits, tri-suits, bike shorts and running gear while they get in a little training and course familiarity. This garners some strange looks and more than a couple of good natured chuckles from the locals. I've been places where you can meet some serious irrational hostility, but not here.

Race morning the town is abuzz with local organizations providing the much needed coffee to appreciative volunteers and racers alike. Since the race is in August, the temperatures in Lake Arrowhead can vary greatly. Racers should always have their wetsuits with them just in case the cool evening convinces this small lake to drop a degree or two. Illustrating this point was the 2007 race weekend where the first day had the Saturday intermediate course race competitors leaving their wetsuits in the car but the following morning, after a particularly cool evening, they were able to pull them back out again for the Sunday short course race.

The race director, David Glover, collaborated with Setup Events, Luray Parks and Recreation, and a team of fantastic volunteers to have everything on hand to keep the morning events moving along nicely. The professional race announcer, Brad Rex, an apparent mainstay at a Glover race, adds a big race feel, his deep voice rolling over top of the thumping race music giving directions to the frantic racers, wittily entertaining the local crowd and taking the edge off the early morning race nerves. Greg Hawkins with Setup Events helps Mr. Glover put on a first-class event, which is just one of the many great events in their Virginia Triathlon Series (www.setupevents.com). The organization and coordination between these directors helps everything go off without a hitch, at least from a participant's perspective.

The wave start has the racers swimming a two loop, clockwise rectangle in Lake Arrowhead, ending on a sandy beach where triathletes head toward the transition up a set of wooden stairs. This is the only part of the event that could be construed as a short coming, by no fault of the race organizers, but rather the lack of an alternative method in this small park. Really, it's a minor inconvenience, and one that is quickly forgotten as you roll your bike out of transition, heart pounding, and prepare to head out on arguably the best bike course in the local triathlon scene.

For me, the bike course is what makes or breaks a race: the scenery, road surface, and variety of challenges all are taken into consideration. For some people, a flat course with nothing to think about is all they want, just a way to PR their bike split. Don't get me wrong, I love PRs and bike splits are my favorite kind, but I'd trade them in for a challenging course and scenery any day of the week. I joined this sport to improve my health and enjoy the outdoors, something that is much easier to do when I have variety. Luray's intermediate course delivers this and so much more.

The bike course is a lollipop with a double loop through the countryside of Luray and Page County with relatively smooth roads. The course really does offer some of the most varied bike conditions I've seen in my short career. If you want flat fast sections, you got it, if you want short steep climbs, you got it, if you want long slow climbs, you got it, if you want fast descents — yup, that's right, you got it. This course forces the cyclist to be able to tackle several types of riding. It allows you to get into a rhythm, and right before you are lulled into a sense of calm and start thinking, this is pretty easy, she reaches out and slaps you back to reality with something new and challenging.

After the second loop, you head back into the park via the same road that you began your bike leg on to the cheering of friends, family and locals alike. This is really my favorite part of the race; spinning my legs out trying to get them ready to run in just a few short minutes, seeing who is already out on the run, my mind quickly computing what I need to do to catch that calf with my number on it directly in front of me. Then you dismount and struggle to execute your transition while suffering from "exercise brain." There really is nothing like it.

The run course is a double out-and-back that takes you up a rather tough climb after leaving the park but it flattens out into more gentle rolls and leaves you with the promise of a fast descent on the way back, which is always a motivator. And, you get to do it twice! The downside of a double out-and-back is that you have to run by the finish line, which if you are spent, can be really tough mentally. Throughout the run there are volunteers and spectators cheering you along and the course layout allows you to see your competition multiple times so you can figure out what you need to do to catch them. However, the opposite side of this coin is that seeing your competition can be very demoralizing if you realize just how far ahead they are, but then you dig deep. The run is primarily on the road leading out of the park and depending on the temperatures that day, can be very challenging due to its lack of shade. The section near the start/finish is pretty shady, so on a hot day you should relish the time you spend near it, but after that it's open road and hot sun so you need to make sure to stay hydrated.

The finish line at every race is great and Luray International does not disappoint in the least. With the personalized finishing commentary by the announcer you can't beat this finish line.

The awards this past year were stemless wineglasses which were a fantastic gift, something you can use to enjoy a glass of Virginia wine, or as I prefer, a nice glass of top shelf Tequila. We all love a trophy here and there that can sit out at the house and we can say with feigned modesty when someone inquires, "Oh that? Just some triathlon I did." With these wineglasses you get that little bit of boasting plus a functional gift.

About the Author

Shawn Clark was a Clydesdale racer through his second year of triathlon. After winning the Virginia Triathlon Series overall Clydesdale award in 2007 he has set his sights on the 30-35 age group, as well as his first ultra distance race. When not racing, training or writing, Shawn enjoys spending time with his wife and dog as well as the numerous friends he has made through the Reston Area Triathletes Club.

Wilkes-Barre Triathlon

wilkes barre, pennsylvania

Race Distance: Intermediate
1.5K Swim, 40K Bike, 11K Run
Month: August
Race Web Site: www.wilkesbarretriathlon.com

Author: Bob Mina
Racing Category: Age Group 35-39

The Wilkes-Barre Triathlon typifies the definition of a classic in the Northeast U.S. In 2008 the Wilkes-Barre triathlon celebrated its 27th anniversary and it shows no signs of slowing down. As one of the longest running triathlons in the country, the race director, Jim Harris, and his staff know what they're doing from top to bottom and it shines through.

I first raced Wilkes-Barre in 1996, and I was able to sign up for it (via paper application) two weeks before race day. I raced it through 1998, the year they attempted to hold a long course race in addition to the intermediate distance race. This second race never took hold, but the intermediate distance continues to thrive year after year.

After a six year hiatus from the race, I was completely surprised to find out in July of 2005 that registration was still open for the year's Wilkes-Barre Triathlon and for only $65! I was hoping to find a tune-up race in early August and couldn't believe my luck. Could this be true? It was and more. When I walked into registration on a sunny August afternoon, it was like I'd gone back in time. The volunteers were super friendly, and knew exactly what to do, what to say and how to get things done. It was just like I'd remembered in 1996 as a wide-eyed newbie, when the volunteers guided me through check-in with all the care I could ask for. Clearly, the race staff knows they've got it good, and if it ain't broke, don't fix it!

Wilkes-Barre is an intermediate distance race with an extra kilometer added to the run course at no additional charge. It doesn't sound like much, but you will definitely notice the extra distance when you get to the run. The race also has two transition areas. The night before you'll rack your bike at Harvey's Lake, and then on race day you'll set up T-2 near the finish line before taking a bus to the swim start and T-1. Sound confusing? Don't worry, it works.

Race morning you'll want to show up at the Lake Lehman campus of Penn State nice and early (about 6:00 a.m.) so you have plenty of time to set up your T-2 at a reserved space (of course). There will be a long line of yellow school buses waiting and once you're ready to go, hop on the bus, Gus! It's about a 15-minute ride to the lake. You'll carry your stuff in a small plastic bag that was given to you at check-in for your wetsuit and pre-race clothes. I've always thought that a bus ride with nervous triathletes would be too stressful, but every year I've managed to chat with whomever I've sat next to the entire way to the lake.

The swim is a simple out-and-back 1,500 meters on Harvey's Lake in one of the coves. There are no currents, no waves and no problem sighting. When you make the turn back for home, you'll be able to sight off a tall, white flagpole for the Beach Club the entire way back. How's that for a buoy of choice?

The water temperature is always on the borderline of being wetsuit legal. I wore one in 1996, but haven't since. If it's been a hot summer, Harvey's Lake can warm up very quickly. One year the water temperature was 84 degrees Fahrenheit! Even so, people were given the option to wear wetsuits and race in a "non-awards" eligible wave.

So if you've worn a wetsuit at T-1 you'll do the usual dance of joy with your wetsuit and then stuff it. Stuff it? Remember that bag I mentioned? You'll just put everything in that bag for the volunteers to truck back to the finish. Make sure you pick up all your toys and take a second or two to make sure it's in there well and leave it. Note, your wetsuit and cap will be wet (duh) and the warm-ups you wore to the race will share the bag with them, so it's a good idea to have another change of clothes back in your car. Just a tip from someone who hates to drive home damp!

If you are a strong cyclist, you will absolutely love this bike course. Even if you aren't a strong cyclist, you will love this bike course. It's hilly, but fair. Call it rolling with several false-flats. Unlike most rides out of transition where you usually climb away from a lake, you actually descend from Harvey's Lake within the first mile. Those first few miles are downhill and fast, and really let you settle into a good rhythm pretty easily. After about five miles of flats or descending, you'll come to a sharp hairpin turn, then up a considerable climb. It looks worse than it really is when you first make the turn at the bottom because you nearly come to a stop.

Then there's a false flat that seems to go on for days (I think it took me two days in 1997, truthfully). The wind usually blows there, even if it isn't too windy of a day. Despite all this, it's not bad once you're in the middle of it. You just need to sit in a little gear, and spin, spin, spin. As you're riding you'll think, "It doesn't look bad…" but you'll be in your 39x23 wondering just why the heck you can't go any faster. That's normal, everyone feels that way. Stay with it! This is the only long climb on the ride.

Once you get over the faux plane, the rest of the course is rolling. You're either going to be riding up or down, but you can use your momentum to the very end. Work the down hills hard, and then spin the up hills and focus on keeping your power output steady. As you close in on T-2 there are two intersections that make really fun chicanes. Both come at the bottom of descents in quick up/down flicks that can be taken by the daring in the aero bars – whee! It's like skiing. Totally fantastic when you get it right.

You'll know you're nearing the end of the ride as you climb behind Huntsville Lake (great view) and then approach the Lake Lehman campus and T-2. On the approach you'll be on old Route 115, and there are two nasty grades near the end that are short and steep, so don't let them get you down. Just ride them strong and steady, it's not long now! You'll approach T-2 from a totally different direction then when you rode the bus in the morning, so you might be surprised that you're finished when you get there.

Following a quick T-2, you'll take off down the road into the fields of the Penn State Lake Lehman campus (a farming college of Penn State). The course is shaped like a big lollipop with the first and last mile sharing the same road.

The road surface constantly changes, which makes this run a unique challenge. You'll be on a paved road to start as you pass through horse farms, but then it changes to dirt just after mile one. You'll descend steeply past the first mile and then cruise along the dirt road to mile two. The surface changes back to pavement for miles three and four as you run through the quiet neighborhood around the campus, but then you're back to dirt as you pass Lake Lehman High School at mile five. By mile six you're back to pavement for the last stretch to the finish.

The course terrain is spectacular so you'll be busy the entire way. My favorite stretch comes along Mountain View Road, so you can imagine since it's called "Mountain View" that it's not exactly flat. There are some ups, downs, ups, downs, ups, and downs. It's a tough run course, but compared to others it's not bad.

The opening two miles are flat to slightly downhill. Just after the two-mile mark you'll make a right turn onto Ceasetown-Huntsville Road, and this turn brings a sharp climb for about a half mile, followed by a rapid plunge to another sharp turn just after mile three. This is the turn onto Mountain View Road. You'll spend the next two miles on this stretch, be ready.

Mile three to mile four is pretty much uphill the entire way, so as you near the top be sure to look to your left over the valley, you worked for it, so enjoy the view! Once you pass mile four the steep grades drop away, and you'll roll a bit as you approach Lake Lehman High School.

Just after mile five you make what I've always thought of as the "turn for home." You'll have just less than two miles to go and after all the rollers you get a nice, long, sustained descent. The pavement changes to dirt, so you can really let it fly if you've got the legs. Don't be afraid to push it, this is a great chance to open a gap, or close one (depending on what's happening in your race).

When you come up on mile six, just when you think you should be finishing your 10K…that's when you remember that this is an 11K run. Never fails. So just think about how much longer you'll get to celebrate your approach to the finish while you work that extra kilometer, right? You'll cross back onto the out/back section of the course just past mile six, so now you're on familiar turf.

It's paved from there to the finish, and does trend slightly uphill. You'll be able to see and hear the finish line from a half mile away so kick it in, and bring it home! You'll leave the road and jump onto the grass for the last 100 meters; look good for the spectators, and listen for the race announcer to call you out as you smile for the finish. Make sure they can see your number!

When you finish, the volunteers will be at your side immediately. In the past two years, I've had a cold towel draped over my neck and been given a bottle of water before I had totally stopped running (they're THAT good). You'll make your way out of the finish line and probably pick up your finishing schwag along the way. Wilkes-Barre has always had great and unique finishing gifts: In 2006, for example, all finishers received a great gear bag with the race logo.

One of my favorite things (and it's so simple, what can I say?): The Penn State Fitness Center is open for all athletes, so you can take a shower! Nothing like leaving a race clean; it's the best way I know of to go home happy.

Traditionally, August in Pennsylvania means hot and humid. The water temperature for the swim is usually close to 78 degrees Fahrenheit so as I mentioned, wetsuit legality is always a toss up. The air temperature (even with the 8:00 a.m. start) can be in the 80s and will usually climb from there. However, you are racing in the mountains, so you never know what you'll get until race day. Before the 2006 race, I was shivering before the swim start as the air temperature hovered in the 50s.

There are few races out there with the staff as well rooted and professional as this crew. They all live in Wilkes-Barre, and the fact that this is their race shines through at every opportunity. From packet pick up to the pre-race meeting, to the morning logistics of a two transition area setup to transporting all the athlete gear back to the finish line, every aspect of the day at Wilkes-Barre is truly first class. When you race Wilkes-Barre, it will remind you of how triathlon was in the late 80s and early 90s – simple, fun, pure and athlete-centered.

The unique set up of two transitions provides a bit of a challenge for spectators. Taking in the swim and then somehow getting in a car and making it back to the Penn State campus in time to see your athlete is very unlikely. There is limited parking at the lake, so all spectators are advised to stay at the Wilkes-Barre campus all day, where they can see their athletes come in from the bike to T-2 and again at the run finish.

Spectators are allowed to ride the buses to the lake in the morning to watch the swim, but the first bus doesn't head back to Penn State until the last cyclist starts the bike course, so depending on the wave your athlete is in, it's a close call.

There are plenty of hotels in and around Wilkes-Barre and Scranton, Pennsylvania. Most are within a 15-20 minute drive of the Penn State campus on race morning, making any of them perfectly suitable. There is a home stay program available for elite athletes as well, so if you wish to partake, just get faster.

About the Author

After a short USCF Road Racing career (1990-1995), Bob Mina has been racing triathlon. Wilkes-Barre was his fifth ever triathlon back in 1996 (third intermediate distance race). He has been an age-grouper throughout his entire career, and has completed more than 48 triathlons, from the short course through ultra distance, as well as 27 marathons. In Bob's own words, "It doesn't mean I'm any good, mind you – I just like eating, so the longer distances work well for me."

Bob has finished the Wilkes-Barre Triathlon six times. He had the good fortune to win the Clydesdale Division in 2005, but didn't weigh enough to defend his title in 2006 (which wasn't necessarily a bad thing). His personal best on the course is a 2:34:32 (27:35, 1:06:35 and 57:26).

If you read www.xtri.com, Bob is "Hurricane Bob," and has been writing race reports from an age-grouper perspective since 1998. If you don't read Xtri.com, you should check it out, especially if you found this chapter helpful.

Big Lick Triathlon

huddleston, virginia

Race Distance: Intermediate
1,500 Meter Swim, 40K Bike, 10K Run
Month: September
Race Web Site: www.setupevents.com
http://www.setupevents.com/index.cfm?fuseaction=event_
detail&eventID=940

Author: Julie Tanja Gibbons
Race Category: Age Group 40-45

The telltale sign of a great triathlon venue is that once you arrive in town, you find that you would rather just be on vacation there. And though you won't admit it out loud (because you are a tough, dedicated athlete), you secretly wish you didn't have to race. The Big Lick Triathlon, held in Huddleston, Virginia at Smith Mountain Lake State Park, is one of those wonderful races.

After picking up my packet and checking into the Mariner's Landing Hotel, I sat outside on the patio of the hotel restaurant and surveyed the scene. On this beautiful pre-race September evening, looking out at the calm water on Smith Mountain Lake and the clouds rolling past the mountains, I had the uncontrollable urge to order really-bad-for-you appetizers and an apple martini—a bottomless apple martini—and decide in the morning if I still felt like racing.

But no, this was serious business here, I told myself. Even if you're not hung up on carbs and calories, I'm fairly certain that wings and appletinis will make a triathlete hate themselves in the morning. Plus there were important things still left to do that night like race packets to go through, numbers to attach everywhere, liquid breakfasts to prepare, planning, packing, panicking... So, determined to stay healthy and sober, I diligently drank my water, scanned the menu for the perfect pre-race meal, and vowed to come back after the race and do this right. The irony is that, had I been there on vacation, relaxing outside with my cocktail, I would be thinking "What a fabulous place for a triathlon. Someone should really set a race up here. I would totally do it. "

So race morning came and I showed up. The weather was beautiful. I tend to be a complainer, and I wasn't whining about being too hot or too cold that morning, so that actually speaks volumes about how nice it was. The start was also a bit later in the morning than many races; 9:00 a.m., which for me may as well have been dinnertime. Most days I have dragged myself out of bed, worked out, showered and eaten a huge egg sandwich by this point in the morning, so it presents an interesting logistic to the early bird. Also, if you do the math, at 8:55 a.m. you might realize that you would be close to finishing most other races. Try not to think about that. On the flip side, it presents a delightful opportunity to actually sleep later in the morning. (Hmmm, strangely appealing you may think.)

The transition area was well organized, which was no surprise considering the event was put on by Set Up. I chose this race because in my mind, it's a given that everything—packet pick-up, pre-race information, race support, post-race organization—will go well at a race run by Set Up. I don't know how much scurrying around goes on behind the scenes, I'm sure it's a lot, but they make it look easy. I take it for granted. They are truly the underappreciated super mom of the triathlon world. The volunteers and athletes were all great. I love the atmosphere at this late season race as most people have done what they're going to do for the year and are just taking one last go at it.

The race is relaxed and social, and many of the faces are familiar. I saw one woman, who routinely kicks my butt, with her husband and new baby. They are both ridiculously fast and were doing a relay with one other person who I had no doubt was also a ringer. The baby, of course, stayed in the transition area and got passed off to the non-competing athlete. How cool is that? Also, there was a girl there that I see fairly often training at the pool, who does many of the same races I do. I don't really know much of her story, but I know she recently had brain cancer, and is usually advised not to race. But there she was. I think she's so tough. It's humbling. Then I chatted with an older man who is retired and lives on Smith Mountain Lake. He does this triathlon every year because it is in his own backyard. I was so envious, and was secretly hoping he'd adopt me and let me live at his house. It was a refreshing contrast to the tension of the early and mid-season races, where the conversation centers on training regiments, nutritional strategies, and anything else someone is willing to share in the porta-potty line.

Speaking of that, it's worth a mention that there are indoor bathroom facilities at this race. That alone makes it the premier race of the season.

So, like any competitive athlete, I start an event poised, focused, and confident... not. As a runner who came to triathlon, I have one distinct goal in the swim—don't suck. So basically anything about the swim that makes it suck less is a good thing. Unfortunately, this becomes the yardstick by which the success of my swim is measured. That being said, I may go so far as to say that this was an enjoyable swim! The water temperature was great, cool but not cold, probably in the 70s. I didn't freeze at the start, nor did I get overheated in my wetsuit (which was legal). The course was well marked and the water was so clear. (This makes it easier to see the foot in front of you about to knock your goggles off!) The last leg of the swim is a long straightaway and you can see the buoys marking the exit point from far away. For the non-swimmer, this is the proverbial light at the end of the tunnel. Be aware though, that this will highlight any inability to swim a straight line — over and over and over. I speak from experience. More often than not, I think I'm swimming a straight course, but upon sighting realize that I have executed a perfect 45 degree turn. The other day a swim coach asked me when I was going to stop swimming like a runner. I thought that was funny.

Regardless, the swim is lovely and that's saying something coming from me.

Upon exiting the swim, you will do what seems like a 5K run barefoot. No, actually it's not that bad, but it's not short. It's well protected and well marked, and it adds more spectator square footage which is nice. Although I must admit, the exit of the swim is not my best look. Goggle eyes, swim cap hair, stumbling around. Yeah, you know what I'm talking about. Still the cheering is nice. So you zip into T1, and the exit to the bike start is a real slice of life. You mount your bike at the base of a small but steep hill. Let me repeat that last part...at the base of a small but steep hill. Now, maybe you're one of these people who can elegantly swoop their leg over the bike and cleanly strap into their shoes without missing a beat. If so, good for you. I envy you. For everyone else, take note. I'm generally not one to give advice on racing other than "do what works for you." That being said, I STRONGLY recommend that taking the time to jog up to the top of the hill and mount, be something that works for you. Believe me, chances are the few seconds you lose running your bike up the hill will more than make up for the time you spend zig-zagging up the hill on your third try clipping in. It'll also earn you a lot more goodwill among your fellow racers who won't have to try to avoid you on their way up the hill. And who, at the end of the race, will remember you. Again, the voice of experience talking.

The bike course is challenging. To be honest, I have a terrible memory for bike courses, because frankly, I come from the put-you-head-down-and-go-like-hell school of thought. They are all sufferfests to me. I can't tell you which hills are at which point at the race, because I have no cycle computer. I don't want to know. I realize sharing such facts puts me at risk of being shunned by the triathlon community. However, what I can tell you are portions that are burned into my brain. One memory is of long grinds on false flats, the kind where you literally grit your teeth. You grind and you grind, pondering if it is possible to be pedaling and going backwards simultaneously, but take solace in the fact that people are not pulling away from you. I also remember more than once looking up and seeing a LINE of people slooooowly mashing gears up a hill ahead of me. A long hill. When you're approaching a hill like that, spinning at a decent cadence, it's daunting to see how anemically people's cranks are turning up ahead. Surely, you think, surely I won't slow down that much. Ha. Ha. Ha. But though it doesn't always feel like it, what goes up does come down. As a result of the grinding climbs, there are a handful of spots where you feel like Lance Armstrong. It's sweet. Overall, it's a good, tough course that you can really sink your teeth into. And all under beautiful weather, on open, lightly traveled roads with good pavement.

On to T2. Remember that problematic uphill at the start of the bike? Yup, it's still there, only this time you have to stop at the bottom. This is a good time to remember that you're not driving a high performance vehicle that can stop on a dime. Believe me, I forget that sometimes too. Thankfully there are plenty of very nice, very persuasive volunteers who truly care about your safety to remind you to slow down. These people are wise. Listen to them. Lose a little time, keep your skull intact. Call me conservative, but I think it's a good trade-off.

Now on to the run. A word of advice, don't judge the run based on my experience alone. Oh, things were fine leaving T2—a good strong ride under my race belt, people cheering, a quick transition, and only 6.2 to run. It all seemed so great. The first mile or so out of the park is very spectator friendly. The road is lined with people telling you that you can do it, and they are fairly convincing at the time. These people make you feel like a stud. And really, based on what you are in the midst of doing, you are a stud. However, I have found there are different levels of studliness, and in my 15 years of doing triathlons, I think I have spanned the continuum. On this particular day, I was flirting with the ugly end. I'm always amused by how your level of suffering on a run is directly reflected in the cheers you hear. A good, strong run usually elicits an enthusiastic "Way to go!" or "Looking awesome!" or a "You go girl!" Conversely, on a bad day, you get a very sympathetic "Almost there!" or "Not too much longer!" or "Hang in there!" If they throw a "sweetie" in there, you know you're sunk. It's hilarious. You can puff your chest out and try to look good, but these people KNOW. They've seen what good looks like and then YOU came by. Regardless, this was how my day went and good or bad it was the best I could do, which makes it a success in my mind. And anyway, it's nice to be called "sweetie" sometimes.

The run course is a rolling out-and-back with one short dog leg down a steep hill and straight back up just to make sure you're paying attention. And when I say the course is rolling, seriously, I'm not kidding. Once you leave the parking lot and go down a small hill, you climb your way out of the park for about a mile or so. You then turn on a road on which you will constantly be going either up or down. Enjoy the downhills, because if you're having a bad day (like somebody I know), the uphills are the type that make your brain talk to your calves on a random basis to say CRAMP NOW!!!!!! But if you're having a good day and can work the hills, you will eat this thing up. And you might actually enjoy the scenic wooded surroundings, which include rental cabins. I've been in one and they are very cozy little places worth considering as your race accommodations. Just be sure you are not the type that's easily tempted to drop out of a race, as you may very well end up running right past your blankie at a pivotal, low-blood sugar moment.

The reward for all the hills is the one mile down hill before the finish. You have to pop up a moderate hill before finishing but at this point, with only a 1/4 mile remaining in the whole season, even on a bad day you can schlep it over the hump. And a slight downhill to the finishing chute ensures that you can pick up the pace and fool even the veteran spectator into thinking you were strong the whole time. Every race should end that way. Heck, every racing season should end that way.

Fast forward to that night, back at the hotel restaurant. The sun is setting, and I'm almost done with my apple martini. The bartender asks if I want another one, and I look at him and think, duh. Thankfully "Yes, please" comes out. Some nice folks nearby ask if I did "that bike race" today. I think about all that I did that day, and have an overwhelming urge to explain the sport of triathlon to them. But I know their heart is in the right place, so I smile and say yes. They are impressed. I thought back on how I felt sitting there just one day before, all of my anxieties that night, and what has happened from then to now. And I think, everyone should be lucky enough to have my problems.

Simply put, this race rocks.

About the Author

Julie Tanja Gibbons is a part-time accountant and business owner, a full time mom to an active seven year old, and a two-time All American triathlete (2006 and 2007). She has competed in triathlons for 15 years, and at age 38, had her best season in 2007, winning overall female in four of her seven races. When she is not training, working or assembling Legos, she enjoys sleeping.

Kaiser Permanente Los Angeles Triathlon

los angeles, california

Race Distance: Intermediate
1.5K Swim, 40K Bike, 10K Run
Month: September
Race Web Site: www.latriathlon.com

Author: 2nd Lt. Justine Whipple
Racing Category: Professional

If you are looking for a race with the glitz and glamour of Hollywood Boulevard, lovely Southern California weather, and some of the biggest names in triathlon, then the Kaiser Permanente Los Angeles Triathlon is the one to enter. Although the day might start off a bit chilly as you plunge into the water at Venice Beach, the temperate climate of Los Angeles in September typically provides perfect racing conditions.

The Los Angeles Triathlon is a renowned Intermediate distance triathlon and one of the premier races of the Lifetime Fitness Triathlon Series®. The first year I was able to make it out to Los Angeles for the race was in 2007, and despite not being at the top of my game I still had a fantastic weekend. With an early race start, there is plenty of time to pour your heart into a tough race and still hit the beach by mid afternoon.

Thanks to a liberal race purse and race series point accumulation, top triathletes from around the world participate each year. This non-draft legal race provides a challenging course and its unique point-to-point format offers a constant change of scenery as it tours the majority of the city. In addition, the race venue is easily accessible and there are plenty of surrounding attractions. The Los Angeles Triathlon truly provides something for everyone from professional triathletes to first timers.

As in any other race, the only prerequisite for professional athlete registration is to hold an elite license from USAT. There is, however, an incentive for pros to sign up early for this race, because the first professional athletes to make their deposit or those entered in the entire Lifetime Fitness Triathlon Series have the opportunity to stay at the Los Angeles Athletic Club. Although as a fairly new pro and a first timer to a Lifetime Fitness Triathlon Series race, I did not manage to get a room, however I was set up with a homestay where a woman, who happened to be around my age, graciously offered up her spare room. This fortunate circumstance has developed into a good friendship. As for age group athletes, this race is extremely popular and sells out very quickly, so keep an eye on the first day of registration to make sure you can reserve your spot.

The Los Angeles International Airport (LAX) is by far the most accessible airport to the event, but Burbank Airport, Orange County Airport, and Ontario International Airport are also within driving distance. Be prepared to fight Los Angeles area traffic for the majority of your weekend, because whether you want to drive the course or get to the pre-race meeting, you will sit in long lines of traffic resulting from the sheer volume of cars and traffic lights downtown.

The main race sponsor, Kaiser Permanente, treated the professional athletes to a catered dinner on the two evenings before the race at a maritime club near the water. This is an optional event that I encourage athletes to attend. The event provides the race sponsors and various race directors a chance to mingle with the athletes. When I attended we also had the opportunity to hear Sarah Reinstein speak about her experiences as a disabled athlete.

The packet pick-up and pre-race meeting take place at the Marina del Rey Marriot. Athletes are provided two bags at the race meeting. One bag is for items you would like taken from the bike transition area to the finish line (including your goggles and swim cap after the swim). The other bag is for gear you will need when you arrive at the second transition area to transition from your bike to the run (T2 bag). This will typically contain your running shoes, run nutrition, race belt, etc. Athletes drop off their T2 bags at the race expo the day before the race so be sure to bring any items you need for the run to the expo. The race staff will place your run gear at the second transition area in downtown Los Angeles. This is the only way to ensure that your run gear will be waiting for you when you arrive at T2 on your bike.

The race expo is very extensive. Vendors include multiple bike shops, companies selling nutritional supplements, free sample booths, and an efficient bike mechanic. Race apparel is for sale, and you'll be sure to see well-known faces in the triathlon community strolling around.

The race start is on Venice Beach where transition is set up in a parking lot immediately off the beach on Venice Boulevard. Since this is a point-to-point race, a shuttle from the Los Angeles Athletic Club (located around the block from the finish line) to Venice Beach is provided for professional athletes on the morning of the race.

In 2007, the day started off cooler than normal and the surf was a bit rough. From what I heard, however, this was nothing compared to the size of the surf the previous year. Trying to keep warm before the race, I jogged around with full sweats on and brought a long sleeve shirt down to the beach that I could throw away so I wouldn't freeze. Due to the chilly breeze and cool water temperature, I opted to warm up with arm swings and stretch cords rather than hop in the water.

The first two waves sent off were the professional men and women. The first professional wave went off at 6:45 a.m. with 21 men and then the women's wave went off with 13. The age group waves followed.

The race start was a bit tough with the rough surf, but once I made it through the initial breakers it was smooth sailing. The bright sun made sighting difficult, but it was a very straightforward one lap course. On a personal note, I tend to struggle when it comes to keeping up with the women's pro field in the swim and this day was no different. I was less experienced than many of the Australians in the field, and the large waves slowed me down considerably as we headed out into the surf. Luckily I was not alone toward the back of the pack, as another American and I remained within close proximity throughout the swim. Due to unfortunate sighting we somehow missed the final buoy and swam too far. This set us back and caused a slight run-in with the age group men as they entered the water, but this was simply an unfortunate chain of events that could happen in any race. Without loosing ambition, me and my fellow American navigated the huge transition parking lot and hopped onto our bikes.

Although my closest competitor, Lara Brown, got through transition before me, I was quickly able to overtake her on the initial stretch down Venice Boulevard, and we both grinded gears to make up for lost time. Although the bike course does not have any notably tough sections, the point-to-point route from the beach into town makes for an unexpectedly challenging course since it is a constant gradual climb. There are no real technical sections, however, and aside from a few rough sections on the road the course is wide open, and I was able to push hard in aero position.

Normally I would have loved the bike course, but my legs felt the effects of two previous weeks of traveling and racing. Just having competed in the under-23 world championships in Hamburg, Germany the past weekend and in a continental cup race in British Columbia the weekend before, my legs were pretty toasted, and I struggled to keep a fast tempo. As we neared transition number two the hills got steeper. I was happy to see, however, that I had made up some good time on the bike and had a more feasible gap to close on the run course.

With a flow through transition area for the bike, T2 went very smoothly and the race directors had efficiently positioned our shoes and gels in our perspective places. The race map provided to athletes during the meeting laid out a detailed description of where our bikes were to be racked. After exiting the long transition chutes, the ominous run was upon me.

This is a very spectator friendly race and enthusiastic fans line the majority of the two loop run course. There is one major climb on the run, which hits you hard and fast as you ascend toward the Staples Center. Fortunately, you quickly get to turn around afterward and head back downhill. Normally I would be ecstatic that a large hill lay ahead, but my legs were in no condition to hammer out a personal record. At this point, it was all I could do to focus my mind on the runners ahead and put out a steady effort.

Aid stations are available right in the transition area and are appropriately staged at the top of the steep climb and at the turn around point. Although there are no gels provided, Gatorade and water are plentiful.

Using the downhill is essential to keeping up a good tempo on this course, so my advice is to let your arms relax and to keep a nice high cadence moving down the steep hill. Although the sun was out during the race, the temperature was comfortable and the downtown buildings provided partial shade to the early morning sunlight. By the second run loop I was mentally in race mode and pushed into the finish with everything I had left. I was a little disappointed with my 10th place finish, but overall I was very pleased with the experience and look forward to doing the race again.

As a professional, I had full access to the VIP tent were we could pick up some tasty post-race treats and refuel. Another nice perk was the free post-race massage tent in the finish area. With ample massage therapists ready to work on sore bodies, it was a perfect way to start my recovery.

Awards are given after all age groupers cross the finish line. A very simple ceremony was held during which the top eight male and female professional racers were called up. Prize money is quite good in the professional category; however, it only runs eight deep with 8th place receiving $1000. This makes the push to the finish extremely competitive and keeps the top athletes returning year after year.

As a professional athlete, I would say the Los Angeles Triathlon was one of the most efficiently organized races I have attended, and I was very pleased with my first experience there. Many thanks must be given to the countless volunteers who devote multiple days to helping out all of the athletes. There was always someone around to direct athletes to the right location of the race meeting, body marking, bike placement, aid stations etc.

I would advise racers to be willing to deal with a significant amount of logistics at this race, simply because it is a point-to-point event and movement of equipment and staging of pre- and post-race activities requires great coordination. It might be noted that I had to wait over an hour and a half after the race to get back my T1 bag that was transported from Venice Beach over to the finish line; however, once it was brought over, professionals' race bags were separated from the rest of the field so it was easy to identify and retrieve.

After the race, Venice Beach is a relaxing place to spend the remainder of the afternoon or if you are more star struck you can take advantage of the many tourist attractions Los Angeles has to offer.

About the Author

2nd Lt. Justine Whipple is a professional athlete and Marine Corps officer. She began her formal triathlon career in 2004 during her freshman year in college. With over 20 Intermediate distance triathlons (both draft legal and non-draft legal) and one Long course distance race under her belt, Justine has competed as a professional athlete for approximately one year. Her notable accomplishments include:

• 2005 Age Group world champion (21 and under age group - 2nd overall)
• 2x Collegiate National Champion (2006-2007)
• 14th at Under 23 worlds in 2007
• 2nd at 2007 Military World Championships

Make-A-Wish® Triathlon at Sea Colony

bethany beach, delaware

Race Distance: Intermediate
1.5K Swim, 40K Bike, 10K Run
Month: September
Race Web Site: www.tricolumbia.org/Make-A-Wish

Author: Jason Goyanko
Racing Category: Age Group 30-34

Autumn on the eastern shore of Delaware is a beautiful time of year. The hot, humid summer air gives way to dry, comfortable Northern California-like weather. As a lifeguard during college summers, I fell in love with the shores of Delaware and Maryland. It was during those summers that I first learned of the Make-A-Wish Triathlon. This September classic attracts over 600 athletes per year to raise money for the Make-A-Wish Foundation.

The Make-A-Wish Foundation fulfills the wishes of children suffering from life-threatening diseases. To compete in the event, participants used to have to pledge to raise $300 or more for the Foundation. As of 2008 (the 25th year of this race), there was a $125 registration fee, but no pledge requirement. Athletes are, however, encouraged to raise funds to help the foundation fulfill its mission. The incentive for me to raise funds became easy after listening to a child suffering from a life threatening illness talk about his or her wish—to go to Walt Disney World®, see snow, or be in the next Spiderman movie. It is not uncommon to hear of fundraising efforts that generate $10,000 or more.

The Make-A-Wish Triathlon takes place at The Sea Colony Private Beach Resort on Bethany Beach. The looming condominium towers provide a city-like backdrop to the sand dunes and three level vacation homes surrounding the community. The race is run by one of the best race directors in the business, Robert Vigorito, of the Columbia Triathlon Association.

Participants start their day with a pre-race warm-up "stroll" down the beach, 1,500 meters from T1, to the north or south end of the beach.

This is the starting point of the swim. The direction is determined race morning by the littoral current of the ocean. The early fall air should be comfortably warm and dry. Expect ocean temperatures to be around 66 to 70 degrees and perfect for a full or sleeveless wetsuit. Line up according to your swim cap color and be sure to cross the timing mat before the start of the race.

The 1.5K ocean swim begins with an on beach start. Swimmers start out with a short sprint into the ocean. As you enter the ocean, keep your eyes peeled for breaking waves. Also be prepared to duck-dive a line of oncoming waves to get past the breakers. Round the first buoy and get into your rhythm as you swim parallel to shore. As you reach the last buoy make the turn in for shore. Keep swimming until your hand touches bottom otherwise you'll be trying to walk through waist deep water. As you exit the water, volunteers greet you and funnel you over the dunes and up the wood ramps that twist and turn through the Sea Colony buildings on your way to T1. Be prepared to be cheered on by spectators, family, friends, and beach-goers as you grab your bike and head out on the main strip through Bethany Beach.

Expect a mostly flat and fast bike ride as you head north on the Coastal Highway toward Dewey Beach for the out-and-back 22 mile leg. Your bike split will benefit from a tailwind in one direction and a headwind in the other. You won't know which direction it will be coming from until race day. As you ride past the small resort town of Bethany Beach, you'll be greeted by wide, smooth, bike friendly shoulders that are clean and relatively free of debris.

There is only one, short moderately challenging hill on this course and you'll hit it from both directions. The hill comes in the form of a bridge over The Indian Inlet River. You'll be rewarded twice for your climbing effort; first, with a brief but beautiful view of the Atlantic Ocean, then the fast downhill boost as you begin your short descent. You'll continue on toward the outskirts of Dewey Beach where you'll make the turnaround and head back south through Bethany Beach and into T2.

As you exit T2, you'll feel your energy soar as you run through the chute and out onto the run course. The run course resembles the terrain of the bike course; flat and fast minus the hill. You'll head south toward Fenwick Island for the 6.2 mile out-and-back past lines of sand dunes and beach houses. The crowds thin out on the run course, but as you make the turnaround, you'll get a good look at your competition, be able to cheer a buddy on, or yell encouragement to another racer.

After making the turnaround, you'll see the Sea Colony condominium towers in sight. I've always found this as good motivation during this race. As you get closer to the towers, you'll know you're nearing the finish. As you approach the last 200 meters, you'll see the race director who will greet you and announce your name. Make the right turn into the parking lot and sprint down the finishing chute to the cheers of hundreds of spectators. Grab an energy drink and some fruit as you talk it up with fellow racers and cheer on those coming into the chute.

One of the best parts about this race is the post race party. It's held on a nicely manicured park inside the Sea Colony community. Bring a blanket, chairs, and a comfortable change of clothing to lounge around and enjoy the activities. No stale bagels, cold pasta salad, or peanut butter and jelly sandwiches here. You'll be treated to a buffet of barbeque, soft-serve ice cream, and a beer truck to toast your effort. For a few extra dollars, you can bring family and friends to enjoy it with you.

Don't skip the awards ceremony. You'll get to hear some of the Make-A-Wish kids tell their stories and understand why this race is a must-do annual event. Arguably, the coolest wish I have heard had to be that of a young boy from my hometown, Vienna, Virginia. It was his wish to be in the Spiderman 2 movie. As a result of the Make-A-Wish efforts, not only did he have a speaking line in the movie, but he was also invited to the red carpet premiere. The kids are great and make all your efforts to raise money and train well worth it. You'll hear the excitement in their voices, the thrill in their hearts, and hope these wishes have given them. You'll think you're a tough cookie for being able to swim, bike, and run in triathlons until you listen to a ten year old fighting cancer. A fellow triathlete, age-group competitor, and friend, Brady Dehoust, said it best when I asked him about his experience with The Make-A-Wish Triathlon: "I did this race five years ago as my first triathlon. I finished 173rd that year. I had no PRs to break or AG wins to defend. I simply showed up to support a young boy named Joe. Joe was fighting a brain tumor, and his community came together to use donations from the triathlon to help grant Joe his wish. Each year, I show up with my Joe's Team t-shirt to race in his memory. He is, to this day, a big part of the reason I'm in this sport. I'll show up next year. I'll show up for Joe and the rest of the kids. "

This race also makes for a great weekend getaway or family vacation. Just south of Bethany Beach is Fenwick Island, Ocean City, Maryland, and Assateague Island National Seashore. To the north is Dewey Beach, Rehoboth Beach, and Cape Henlopen. Whether it's family fun, beautiful scenery, sunning on the beach, nightlife, or fine dining, this area has something for everyone. With so many reasons to do this race, it's easy to see why it's one of the great U.S. triathlons.

About the Author

Jason Goyanko is a personal trainer and triathlon coach residing in Fairfax, Virginia. He has competed in triathlons and endurance events for the last 13 years and coached triathletes of all levels for 10 years. He is a four-time ultra distance veteran with a 10:40 personal record. Jason recently started his own coaching business called Torque Training Systems and in his spare time enjoys surfing and snowboarding.

Nation's Triathlon

washington, dc

Race Distance: Intermediate
1.5k Swim, 40k Bike, 10k Run
Month: September
Race Web Site: www.thenationstriathlon.com

Author: James P. Toner Jr. (J.P.)
Racing Category: Age Group 41-45

With the election of new Mayor Adrian Fenty (an avid runner and triathlete) and the passage of the Inaugural DC Triathlon Emergency Amendment Act by the DC City Council, the 2007 Nation's Triathlon overcame permit challenges it faced in its preceding inaugural year and saw its first full event become a huge success.

The Nation's Triathlon created quite a buzz all along the Mid Atlantic since its inception in 2006. When official word came in late summer that this race would be a true triathlon for 2007 (instead of the duathlon it was in 2006) slots went quickly. Even though the race is one of the more expensive intermediate course events, it is truly worth every dollar as the race was well organized and provides an overall unique experience.

Having the race in late September makes for perfect weather in the nation's capital. While there is still a touch of warmth in the air, the city doesn't have its usually summer qualities of high heat and high humidity. There was a chill in the air for the start of the 2007 event I entered, and as racers assembled in the transition area a stiff breeze kept it cool. The transition area itself was well laid out and well supported and was located on a small grassy spot a short jog from the entry and exit to the swim.

As racers moved to the swim start the sun began to rise and provided a wonderful view of the Potomac River. To start the day off right, as the national anthem was played two fire boats floated in the river just across from the start and turned on all their hoses. A beautiful sight as the sun glistened off the arcs of spraying water and the Potomac.

As waves of swimmers jumped into the water, discussions began on why people haven't previously been allowed to swim in this great river! Although wetsuit legal, the water was comfortable and could have been done without one. There was no gasoline smell or taste, no debris in the water, and no noticeable current.

Swimmers swam up the river just short of the Francis Scott Key Bridge that connects Arlington, Virginia to Georgetown in DC then turned and headed south past the start of the swim. The swim back down river was a bit difficult as the rising sun was directly in the swimmers' faces. This caused some confusion as some swimmers coming down the river ran into swim waves coming up the river. (Race organizers addressed this issue for the 2008 race and a new swim route was established to prevent this.)

Heading out of the swim and up some steep stairs, swimmers were welcomed by a huge crowd of spectators as well as a misting tent as they headed to transition. A tricky run over sidewalk, road, dirt and grass from the swim finish to the transition area ensued. However, it was clearly marked, well-supported, and kept clear of non-racers. Athletes entered in one end of the transition area and headed out the other for the start of the two loop bike course.

This is truly one of the more spectacular bike rides in triathlon today. It is hard to stay focused on the task at hand while trying to admire the great scenery and history as it flies past you. The Washington Monument, the Smithsonian, the National Mall, the Lincoln, and Jefferson Memorials are all in clear view as you ride the fairly flat two loop course. It is also one of the few races were the streets are entirely closed to traffic which makes for a smooth and less congested ride.

At the start of the first bike loop, riders headed south along the Potomac and past the Kennedy Center, the Lincoln Memorial, and onto Haines Point. Riding south along Haines Point, athletes had a great view of Ronald Reagan National Airport and even enjoy a bit of a tailwind. That all changed when riders made the turn north at the end of the peninsula as a nasty headwind made gear selection a challenge but the view was still something to enjoy.

Once off of Haines Point, the course moved into the heart of DC with a brief pass of the Tidal Basin and the Jefferson Memorial, the U.S. Mint, and the National Holocaust Museum. As athletes passed over the National Mall they encountered a nice straight shot along Constitution Avenue lined with cheering spectators before heading back toward the transition area for a second lap.

The second time around was mostly similar to the first lap, but there was a much stronger headwind along the far side of Haines Point which seemed a lot worse as fatigue began to set in for many riders. Well-placed volunteers directed riders either toward transition or the second lap of the bike.

Once back to the transition area athletes began the run as the day started to heat up. Heading north on the Whitehurst Freeway, it was a bizarre sight as nothing but runners occupied the usually traffic laden road. Being someone who has been caught more than a few times in traffic on the freeway, the stillness and quiet was almost eerie. Just before the Key Bridge runners went up and over the lane divider and headed south on the freeway and into the city. Water stops every mile became vital as the temperature rose quickly as the day went on.

Once off the parkway, runners made their way past the Tidal Basin. Being a back-of-the-pack triathlete, it was here that I was approached by an elderly couple strolling along the water. They asked me, "How long is the race?" I replied and they stood there with a look of amazement on their faces. They wished me good luck, and I thanked them as I moved along. It was this type of atmosphere and support that was prevalent throughout the day from participants, volunteers, and spectators.

There was something unique about the spectators along the route and it wasn't until after the race that I realized just what that something was. Being someone who sees a triathlon as more of a challenge than a race, by the time individuals like myself near the finish line most of the crowds have long dispersed and called it a day. But not in Washington, DC, here the crowds seemed to grow as the day went on. Whether it was for the race or because people were just coming out to enjoy a day in the city, they made themselves seen and heard all along the race route.

It was along the final stretch of the run that went past the White House and down Constitution Avenue that I was pleasantly surprised by not only the amount of people watching and cheering but the intensity of that cheering. Several times folks came out and ran with individuals to keep them motivated and to help them finish strong. As most triathletes know, it is almost impossible not to be urged on by people cheering and screaming for you as you make your way to the finish. For nearly the entire final two miles of the run it seemed like there was rarely a time when a racer was alone. The yelling, cheering, horns blowing, bells ringing were just as loud, I'm sure, here at the end of the day as it was when the first racers crossed the finish line earlier. The volunteers at the aid stations were usually the ones leading the efforts as they supported athletes all day long and handed out kudos just as much as water.

Another key point about the aid stations that only a back of the packer would recognize and revel in was cold water. Even at the last water stop and late in the day, the water at the aid station was cold. Usually by the time folks like me reach that last aid station they are lucky if there is any water let alone water that is nice and cold. It gives you that little extra boost to handle that last mile plus to the finish. All the aid stations were fully stocked with water, sports drinks, gels, and bananas. This was also something unique to a race of this distance in my experience — having a great selection at the aid stations.

The final stretch of the run can be a bit of a good news/bad news situation for some folks. As runners hit Pennsylvania Avenue the finish is in site but not within reach. Athletes made a right turn on the Avenue and ran away from the finish before turning at 3rd Street and running back up Pennsylvania to the finish at 7th Street. Throughout the entire morning and into the early afternoon, the finish area was packed with athletes, friends, families, and spectators. All finishers received a nice medal and got to enjoy various food and drink vendors as well as other tents set up for equipment suppliers, much needed massages and other community groups.

As the day was something rare for Washington, DC, at this time of year — warm, not hot and little humidity — it was a great opportunity to replenish fluids, grab a bite, and chat with other racers. This turned out to be a positive as waiting for shuttle buses back to the transition area was longer than most expected. But considering this is the nation's capital and you are trying to move several hundred people halfway across the city on a beautiful early fall afternoon it should have come as little surprise. I took this time to talk with several racers as we discussed where else we raced during the year, which races we liked and didn't and our general thoughts on the Nation's Triathlon.

Race organizers have been diligent about receiving and acting on feedback and suggestions from racers and have already made several changes to the race including new routes for all three events. In 2008 there was a new transition area, a triangular swim course and a single bike loop. With this type of support and response, it can be expected that the race may change many times over the course of the next few years as organizers hope to perfect the experience.

Even before the first wave of swimmers heads out, the Nation's Triathlon offers a unique experience for participants. Starting with the expo that preceded the race, athletes are welcomed to the city and have an opportunity to shop and take home the token freebies after attending the safety briefing. At the expo athletes had a host of booths and suppliers to visit and purchase those last minute needs for the big day. The relative ease of the registration process was accentuated by the organization of check in at the expo and set up in transition.

Many of the standard race day procedures applied including bracelets for entry into transition, colored swim caps for waves, no packet pick up on race day. But there were some extra features that made this race stand out. There were seminars on racing and wellness issues at the expo. Bike racking was done by individual number as each athlete had a specific spot and not just random placement along the rack. Beyond the usual race day photos, video of the event was taken and could be purchased by participants.

Although I am a local athlete, the city and surrounding area offer a plethora of accommodation options as well as dining and tourist activities. The city also offers plenty of travel choices, whether you are coming from far away (airport and train) or have shorter transportation needs (taxi and Metro).

While my race history is limited (about a dozen races over the last three years), the Nations Triathlon will be the first repeat race I will do. My experience at the race made this decision an easy one—great venue, great organization, and a great way to finish a season. I am looking forward to the new routes and new challenges in the coming years and I hope you'll consider being a part of the unique event.

About the Author

James P. Toner Jr. (J.P.) got started in triathlon as a goal he set for himself to complete an intermediate distance event for his 40th birthday. Two months prior to his first daughter being born (he now has two), he had major back surgery. J.P.'s doctor told him that the main reason patients ended up back in his office was because they were afraid to go and do the things that they used to do before having back problems. He wasn't going to let that happen and so with incredible support from his wife and family he decided to take things one step further and do something he had never done before. J.P. had a strong background in swimming but needed help with biking and running. He hired an amazing coach and completed his first intermediate distance race in 2005. After that he was hooked and has continued to race and volunteer at events. Although J.P. tells people he would never do an ultra distance race, he is now training to do one for his 45th birthday.

Best of the U.S.^{SM} Triathlete Competition

v a r i o u s

Race Distance: Intermediate
1.5K Swim, 40K Bike, 10K Run
Month: October
Race Web Site: www.bestoftheustriathletes.com

Author: Krista Schultz
Racing Category: Age Group 25-29

I feel honored to write about a prestigious race such as the Best of the U.S.^{SM} Triathlete Competition. This race promotes the hard earned accomplishments of amateur athletes from all over the nation by bringing top athletes from each state together to compete for the honor of being the best amateur triathlete in the country.

Each state provides a USAT sanctioned short or intermediate distance qualifying triathlon to designate their top amateur. This race provides an opportunity for the future professional triathlete and/or top age grouper to show the U.S. their talent and compete amongst America's best. The unique competition is held in a different location each year and is comprised of 100 talented athletes, one male and one female representative from each state.

I attended the Best of the U.S. Triathlon (BOUS) for the first time in 2006. I will never forget the excitement I felt one warm summer day when Jerry MacNeil called. Jerry, the race director for the BOUS, told me I was runner up at the Maryland state qualifier, the Columbia Triathlon, and that the winner would not attend the BOUS that year. I remember the enthusiasm in his voice when he asked if I would be interested in representing Maryland at his race. Jerry made me feel important and he sounded proud when I said I would definitely take on the challenge. Jerry immediately put me in touch with my teammate Philippe Kozub. Philippe and I made travel plans together, and we spent hours on the phone discussing our excitement about competing and trying to win an award for our state.

The 2006 BOUS race took place in St. Paul, Minnesota. Philippe and I met at the airport the day before the event and even though we had

never seen each other it was not a problem connecting. After we were acquainted and settled it was time to get to the race location.

The race was well organized and provided a group to take us out on the bike course for a preview. The course was set up like a professional International Triathlon Union (ITU) style event, with a spectator friendly double loop route.

After getting a detailed bike course tour all the competitors attended a race meeting like no other I had experienced. It was a small field compared to a normal age group race, and we were treated like professional athletes. They took our pictures, fed us, and honored each athlete by announcing our names and the state we represented at a ceremony. That night we were inspired and nervous but definitely glad to be there amongst such talent.

The vivid memories I have of race day still make me smile. I can recall the excitement and happiness I felt just like it was yesterday. The weather was great for racing and the water was cool enough for a wetsuit. There was a short course race for the town before our event so there were good crowds for the race. Even the guys we met from the local bike shop were there to support the race and cheered us on.

As the athletes prepared to race, Jerry announced everyone's statistics as if he were actually present for all their accomplishments. I even heard him say, "Krista is racing in her Pink bathing suit again." Jerry has a way of making everyone feel important and he sparks excitement amongst the crowd.

I felt nervous as we lined up in the water to prepare for an intense start to a competitive race. As I looked around all I saw were extremely fit men and women with very serious looks on their faces. I was extremely nervous until out of nowhere Philippe grabbed me so tight I couldn't breath, and we exchanged a hug and a good luck. Best of the U.S. is about the team concept and racing to win for your state not just yourself. I felt like I was part of a team and all the selfishness was taken out of the sport that day. All the activities we had taken part in prior to the race made it more team oriented and a lot more fun. This helped my confidence level immensely because it took the focus off me and made me feel happy to be there. I was ready to race for a higher purpose, which was for others.

It was a windy day and the swim was rough. The buoys were blown around so much that part of the men's field went off course. The bike leg followed with rolling hills and a few flat stretches that made it a fast course but I remember all too clearly the harsh winds. I had to fight to keep my speed up so I could catch the girls who beat me out of the water.

I saw Philippe on the bike course once, and he yelled for me. I could also hear Jerry as I reached the transition areas proudly announcing all the athletes' progress. I remember seeing Philippe on the run course and everyone told me I needed to step it up to match my teammate's top overall male performance. I finished with a strong sprint and a personal record that day, and Jerry congratulated me.

I called my dad and coach immediately after the race to tell them how I did. My dad gets so excited about his childrens' accomplishments so I was happy to share this with him. It is always nice to do well at a race but it is much more rewarding to share your perspective with those who care about you.

Philippe was 2nd overall, and I was 10th so we won fourth place for the state of Maryland. We both received beautiful crystal awards for our state and ourselves, and Jerry wrote me up as breakthrough athlete of the year. The race results were very close for both the men and the women.

After the race all the athletes and their fans were taken on a great cruise. We all ate, drank, and talked about the highlights of the race. It was a terrific bonding experience, and we all got a chance to just have fun and relax. I actually felt a little sad to see it all end but it gave me incentive to go back the following year. I gained so much experience from that entire weekend and found a new favorite race.

I enjoyed the event so much in 2006 that it became a top priority for me to qualify in 2007. Philippe and I both placed top amateur at the Columbia Triathlon to secure our spots at BOUS for 2007. The 2007 race took place in Cypress Gardens Adventure Park in Winter Haven Beach, Florida on October 6.

One of my best friends, Kristin, flew from New Orleans to watch me race and we met up at the airport in Florida and waited for Philippe to arrive. When we were all there we traveled to our hotel not far from the race site. Philippe and I enjoyed telling Kristin about the prior year's race, and she seemed to get excited as we told her the nations top amateurs would be competing. I remember her encouragement that night and for someone who knew nothing about the sport she was very interested and supportive.

The next day the athletes met at the adventure park for the race meeting. Jerry introduced many of them and their extraordinary race accomplishments for the year. His speech also made us realize very quickly that race day would not be a walk in the park. In addition to the level of competition I was worried about the day. The heat was so extreme and the water was so warm that the race was not wetsuit legal that year. The bike course was extremely flat and the run course was in the park and had many turns. Both the bike and run would be two quick laps.

The night before the race was stressful because one of Philippe's race wheels was damaged and he couldn't get it fixed in time. He found an athlete doing the short course race held before ours and he said he could use his wheel when he was finished. This was great but still stressful for my teammate because he would not be completely prepared until minutes before the start of his race.

Preparation is so important for a competitive triathlete since equipment, nutrition, and a clear mind can make a huge difference in race placement especially in such a short race where seconds matter. That night we didn't sleep well because of the stress and anxiety.

It was still dark as Philippe and I drove to the park on race morning. We were ready except for the race wheel. I went for a warm up run and Philippe just waited. As I ran through the park I realized how many turns there were and knew this run course would be a challenge because it would be hard to keep a steady pace.

When I made my way back to transition for the final preparations I saw Kristin and another friend who came to cheer for me. It made me happy, and I felt like their support gave me strength. They took pictures and pumped me up for the start. Jerry was excited as usual and celebrating the resumes of all the special men and women racing that day. He asked to see my race attire and was jokingly disappointed that I didn't have a pink uniform again. He knew I had new sponsors and was proud to say it is important to represent those who support you. Again, Jerry has a way of making every athlete feel important and his encouragement and excitement about the athletes is a large part of what makes Best of the U.S. so unique and special.

The race start came too soon. I was worried that Philippe did not get his race wheel, and I saw him run to the start. I didn't get to talk to him much, and we didn't hug this year before the start.

A yell from Jerry started the race! We were swimming so fast I couldn't sustain the pace and fell back with the second group of girls. When I finally exited the water I could see a girl I beat last year ahead of me. The distance from the water to the transition was far but I could hear my friends yelling for me as I gained speed up a gradual climb toward my bike.

The bike loops went fast and before I knew it we were running, and I was done with my first loop. As I ran past the finish for the last run loop Philippe called my name and yelled, "Finish!" He thought I was on my second loop but I had to yell back that I still had three miles to go. Jerry noticed this and announced that I still had one more lap even though the heat was making me want to stop that instant.

It was so hot that overheating was a problem for many people. There was not enough salt available to replace what the athletes sweated out that day. I cramped badly as I turned through the park. I managed to pass one more girl before the last mile but almost felt like I had to crawl to the finish.

I crossed the finish line and found out the great news that Philippe had won! He was named Best of the U.S. and it was well deserved. I was amazed at how he pulled it all together to win especially with the level of competition that year. I did not place as well but was still glad to have competed and shared in the entire experience.

The awards ceremony was nice, and we all went out to celebrate that night. The season was over for me, which gave me a reason to just have fun in Florida with my friends.

The Best of the U.S. is my favorite race of all time for many reasons. It has a great race director, it provides a team experience, and it is a challenging event. I had a great race in 2006 and another great new experience in 2007. There is no other event that can compare and it deserves to have great athletes attend because it helps the sport grow. It also gets amateurs excited to be the top in their state with the hopes of being the Best in the U.S.

About the Author

Krista Schultz's triathlon career began in 2000 when she lived in New Orleans, Louisiana. She comes from a large family of four boys and three girls and all are into sports. In Krista's words, "My family is the most important thing in my life, and my father has always been my hero." Krista played team sports most of her life but ran the 800 and 400 events in track and field when she reached college. Her coaches at the University of New Orleans pushed her to run cross country, and she grew to like the longer distances.

Krista has competed in many triathlons including two ultra distance races, five long course races and around 40 short and intermediate distance events. She is presently an Elite triathlete gaining more speed every year. Krista's goals are to improve in the ultra distance and compete all over the world. She loves to travel to races and gain new perspectives from other cultures.

Superfrog Triathlon

coronado, california

Race Distance: Long
1.2 Mile Swim, 56 Mile Bike, 13.1 Mile Run
Month: March
Race Web Site: www.superfrogtriathlon.com

Author: Donald Carl White
Racing Category: Age Group 40-44

The sport of triathlon is said to have been born in San Diego in 1974 with the Mission Bay Triathlon, a place where the pioneers of the sport clashed. Not far from Mission Bay is a quaint little suburb of San Diego called Coronado. Located within the city limits of Coronado is the Naval Special Warfare Center, better known as the training grounds of the United States Navy Seals and home to the Superfrog Triathlon.

The Hawaii Ironman® was first held in 1978 in Honolulu with just 15 participants. Some of those pioneers were Navy Seals and those Navy Seals wanted an edge on the competition. To get that edge a Navy Seal named Moki Martin came up with the idea of cutting the race distance in half and adding some SEAL flavor to the event. Thus the Superfrog Triathlon was born. 2008 brought the 30th consecutive running of the event, making the Superfrog the first and oldest long course triathlon in the world — and you have probably never even heard of it.

In 1985 I entered my first triathlon. I had the triathlon bug and I had it bad. A few months later at the height of the Cold War I enlisted in the United States Navy. So my triathlon career was put on hold. In November 1985 I entered boot camp in San Diego, CA and followed that with Basic "A" school and my first permanent assignment on the USS DIXON (AS37) home ported in San Diego. I began training again and competed in both military and civilian triathlons in and around the Southern California area.

At a local triathlon in San Diego in 1987 a friend asked me if I was planning on doing the Superfrog. I had never heard of the Superfrog Triathlon and began to question him in detail about the race. It did not

take long before I said "Yes, I'm in, where do I sign up?" Twenty two years later and hundreds of triathlons/duathlons later (including six Hawaii Ironman finishes) I can honestly say that the Superfrog is my favorite triathlon. My eight finishes at this race have included both my fondest and worst racing memories.

It is often said that a diamond is hidden in the rough. Superfrog is that diamond, and it is very rough to finish. Born in an age where triathlon was an extreme endurance competition only for the well trained and arguably fanatic athlete, Superfrog emerged as a stepping stone for Navy Seals and other military triathletes preparing for the famed ultra distance course in Hawaii. It is no different today. If you want a race that will prepare you for the challenge in Hawaii the Superfrog is the race for you. Likewise, if you always dreamed about being a Navy Seal this race will give you a nano second in the life of a Navy Seal.

The race is and always has been located in Coronado, CA. When Supefrog began it was located at the Navy's Special Warfare Center. It has moved several times to nearby areas and is now held at the Silver Strand State Beach. The race was traditionally held in September. In 2008, however, the race was moved to the late March, early April timeframe, which is sure to make it a spring classic in the San Diego Triathlon race schedule.

The race is a circuit style competition with multiple loops of each event. As you stand on the beach and look out at the ocean in front of you before the race, think to yourself as the Seals do and say "The only easy day was yesterday." The swim is in the Pacific Ocean, and it consists of two, 1,000 yard loops with a 100 yard run in between. Some like the amphibious run but many hate it. One thing is for sure, the water will be cold; usually around 60 degrees and the waves will be big. Wetsuits are allowed and encouraged. But not everyone will wear one. The big cold surf makes our Navy Seals who and what they are today — warriors.

After the cold brisk swim, athletes run up the beach to T1. Bikes wait in the transition area surrounded by Basic Underwater Demolition School (BUDS) volunteers. Once on your bike you peddle south down the Silver Strand Highway 75 toward Mexico. The bike course is a flat four-loop route that is very spectator friendly. It is on a nicely paved highway down one side and back up the other, a triathlete's dream course.

The wind is usually a factor. It could be a headwind, side wind, and/or tailwind depending on the day. There will be aid stations on each end of the looped course. Race founder Moki Martin always says if you're not sure of how many laps you have done than take another lap and we will sort it out in the end. Most racers today have computers and GPS so it is usually not an issue.

Upon completion of the bike course, the real fun begins — the dreaded Superfrog run. Like the first two legs of the race the run consists of loops. Over the years, the various routes that made up the Superfrog run course have had one constant — sand. Not just hard packed sand, but dry sand that is often ankle deep.

You now have your running attire on and are heading out for the beginning of your 13.1 mile run. The air temperature is probably in the 80s or low 90s. San Diego is known for cool temperatures, but it is now late in the morning or early afternoon for those who wish to get more for their money by spending more time on the course. A typical run might go something like this: You head out on your wobbly legs; the pavement beneath you is asphalt, blacktop radiating the heat that you will get to know all too well. Soon you turn onto the beach where dry sand greets you, the ankle biting stuff that make Navy Seals tough. This portion of the dry sand will only be about 100 yards before turning into wet sand. The cool breeze will be priceless so enjoy it, you will only feel it briefly as you run by spectators lounging on the beach with their refreshments.

Before hitting the pavement again, the sand will make you feel like you have never run before. All your training miles will seem like a waste. As you take a breath you will be passed no doubt by a Navy Seal racing at breakneck speed. He lives in this stuff, don't worry he will be out of sight in no time. He has a smile on his face, and you think to yourself why is he smiling? The answer is he is not wearing his 50 pound pack on his back, and no one is shooting at him.

No top brass will be at their desks at the Navy Seals headquarters. They will be ahead of you in the race or on the sidelines volunteering to make your Superfrog experience one of a lifetime. The Admiral is usually at the awards ceremony to help hand out the very unique trophies or plaques to the winners. One year the overall champions were awarded director's chairs with the race logo printed on the back rest. My first age group award was a triangular piece of wood with a small clicking frog dangling on a chain — unique indeed. When you get to the finish line you can say that you are a Superfrog! You will have completed the oldest and one of the most challenging long course triathlons in the world.

Post race activities usually bring together stories of the day which might even earn you an award that you were not expecting. You must race Superfrog to find out how to win that one. Other awards are given for the fasted splits in each event, each named after Superfrog finishers from the past that have inspired us. Refreshments are always available and racers usually spend time hanging around and sharing their day out on the course. The race also offers a relay version for those that don't want to go it alone and it also has a physically challenged athlete division for those seeking the ultimate competition.

There are no qualification standards to enter the race, just sign up via mail or the website and pay your entry fee depending on your military rank. At $135, it is the best bargain in the business for a long course triathlon. Register early if you want to save a few bucks, the price goes up if you wait too long.

My personal assessment of the Superfrog is that it is a top notch, high quality competition. It is a great race because it has it all, history, tradition, location, competition, the US Navy Seals, and of course all the sand you could desire. Considered a grass roots event, the race director and staff do an outstanding job with all aspects of the event. The athlete's safety is always the first priority.

The race expo is usually small and not the focus of the event but it has grown over the years and is worth attending.

Hotel accommodations are available in all price ranges from the local Motel 6 to the world famous Hotel Del Coronado. San Diego is a well known tourist destination and is certainly worth a trip from out of town. For military competitors NAS North Island has a Navy Lodge right on the beach.

The entire race is a unique experience. Once only available to the elite military traithletes and special invited civilian competitors, the Superfrog is now open to anyone who is willing to accept the physical test brought forth by the United States Navy Seals. Proceeds from the Superfrog event go to the Naval Special Warfare Foundation, a non-profit (501c) organization established to honor all who have served in the sea commando services from World War II to today's Seal teams.

About the Author

Donald Carl White is an Active Duty Navy Senior Chief Hospital Corpsman stationed on the USS KITTY HAWK (CV63) forward deployed in Yokosuka, Japan. He has more than 22 years of active duty service. Donald has competed in triathlons since 1985, competing in course distances from super sprints to ultra. His age group competitive racing resume includes races in Europe, Asia, and North America.

Donald first took up the triathlon challenge in the summer of 1985 after seeing a poster in a bike store for the USTS Baltimore, Maryland Triathlon. His $200 Panasonic ten speed bicycle served him well for his first few years of racing. Competing in eight Superfrog triathlons over the years has been a highlight of his triathlon career. In 1991 he finished 2nd overall finishing a mere 29 seconds behind the winning time. After a three year lapse in competition due to a tour with the US Marines in Kaneohe Bay, Hawaii he returned in 1995 to compete again. He is an All Navy triathlete and seven-time ultra distance finisher. His greatest triathlon accomplishment came on September 23, 1995 when he finished the 17th Superfrog triathlon in 4:29.40 placing him 1st overall and placing him in the history books

Auburn World's Toughest Half Triathlon

auburn, california

Race Distance: Long
1.2 Mile Swim, 56 Mile Bike, 13.1 Mile Run
Month: May
Race Web Site: www.auburntriathlon.com

Author: M. Tilden Moschetti
Racing Category: Age Group 30-34

There is perhaps no more aptly named race in the sport of triathlon than The World's Toughest Half. This race is my favorite, yet the course is so challenging that I repeatedly ask myself what I am doing out there.

I chose to do this race after volunteering in 2005. Many of my friends did the race that year and it was clear that the focus of the event was on having a great time and a great challenge. This race is set in Auburn, California, in the foothills of the Sierra Mountains. The race is normally held on the last Sunday in May. Sometimes the weather is amazing, other times it's a little toasty.

This is not your typical race. This race is about taking risks, pushing your level of endurance, and discovering what it means to be an athlete. Everything works well but the event is not hyper-organized. Registration is easy, problems are quickly dealt with, but at no point do you see officials running around on walkie-talkies ordering athletes around.

One thing that makes this race so great is the amazing volunteers. They are mostly high school students and they are full of enthusiasm and friendly words of encouragement. The entire atmosphere is like this. Everyone is very friendly and they help make the athletes feel relaxed. It is all about the athletes having fun, the organizers having fun, and the volunteers having fun.

The two transition areas create the only logistical challenge. They are about six miles apart. The swim start is at the Diamond Bar area of Folsom Lake and the transition area is located at the Auburn Overlook.

Some choose to park at the overlook and ride down to the start. You'll be on your bike plenty, so I'd suggest dropping your stuff off at the overlook and then driving down to the swim start to park. There is also a shuttle bus that can take you, your bike, and transition bag back to the start.

The swim is the only stage that is flat. Taking place in Folsom Lake, the water can be perfect. The year I raced, it was 65 degrees (wetsuit legal and actually mandatory) and smooth. The lake is big enough that there is not a lot of jockeying for position, but plenty of opportunity to get on someone's feet. While my best swim wasn't here, it was certainly my favorite. I love fresh water, and the lake just begged to be swum in. There is also plenty of support making the whole swim experience great.

But alas, all good things must come to an end and the swim finish melts into the toughest stage of this race—the bike. The bike course had, by my altimeter, 6,500 feet of climbing. Yes, that is a lot. When I first went to noodle around on the course before riding for real, it took me and a friend about 5 1/2 hours to ride the course. We took our time and stopped often, but I knew then we were in for a challenge. The pavement is all good quality. The roads are open to traffic but most of the route takes place on lightly traveled streets. Police are stationed at major intersections along the route to allow athletes to pass freely.

I found the first six miles to be the most difficult. Athletes ride out of the park and through rolling farmland. Challenging hills make it challenging to find a rhythm. It is well worth the time to look around though. It is beautiful countryside. I mean, really, really beautiful. Toward the end of the six miles a giant vista to the left displays the dam on the lake. Don't spend too much time looking at it as there will be plenty of time to see it from the run course in a few hours.

The next segment begins as you pass the second transition area on your right. Very quickly you will pass the Maki Heating and Air building who very graciously gave permission for the race to pass through their private road and for the city to pave the road. Before the paving occurred, athletes had to get off their bikes and walk through a very narrow and rather dangerous path. You then ride through some residential areas with a few very short but steep climbs. You'll soon find yourself alongside the freeway. This area is fairly flat so live it up because it will change.

The first aid station is 13.6 miles into the course and is at the top of "LeMondWalked Hill," which I will explain later. Don't worry about this climb yet, you are descending it at this point. It is a nice downhill, nearly straight and fast. In fact, this section is filled with them—long climbs and long descents. Nice trees line the roads and a small pond will be visible on your right. You'll soon cross over the freeway and ride through Applegate and hit the second aid station at 21.3 miles. The next segment is very challenging. It requires a lot of concentration as you descend a super steep hill for 1.2 miles to a campground. This area is stunning. You are in a forest with a river and if it were not for the painful climb you know is up ahead, it would be most tranquil. The climb back out is definitely challenging and continues for 1.2 miles. Yes, it is beautiful, but those darn pretty trees shield any breeze and you are climbing for dear life. Finally you make it, and the worst really is over.

Or is it? You go back the way you came into town and repeatedly ask, "Where did this hill come from? I don't remember it from the way out." But this direction is faster with a net descent. Once through Applegate again and on the other side of the freeway, there is an out-and-back section to tack on some extra miles. This area is tough as it is a little more exposed and windy. You'll be very anxious to see the turnaround, but don't fret, the turnaround is there, it is just about two miles further than you wish it to be.

Ahead is the infamous "LeMond Walked Hill," a punishing four mile climb with a 12 percent grade. Greg LeMond allegedly once walked this climb in one of his many training sessions in the area. This tidbit was even spray painted on the road at the base of the climb. Really, this climb is not too bad, but the legend is nice. At the top of the climb is an aid station and just about six miles to go. It is a fairly nice ride back to the transition area over the same territory you rode on your way out.

Finally, you turn into the Auburn Overlook after 56 long miles and see your nice running shoes waiting for you where you left them. The run is a brutal half marathon, mostly on trails, with a 1,300 foot elevation gain. The first aid station is at mile two. This section is really nice with good footing. The trail continues to the 3.25 mile mark where you turn around. The trail then splits at mile five where there is a long steep descent. At the bottom of the descent you begin a 1.5 mile climb (with a gain of about 400 vertical feet) to the Auburn Overlook. During this stretch you will make up all the elevation you lost from the starting line. You make your way around a dirt road that leads to the next few aid stations. Finally you are at mile seven, but the challenge has yet to begin on the run course!

After running alongside the finish line you woefully head back out on the course. This is not a second loop, it just starts that way. Soon you are running on the area used for the dam's construction. This area is not too bad. But, near mile nine you come to The Pit. This area is a steep descent that you know you are going to have to run (or maybe crawl) up again. It may only be about a mile downhill, but with each step it is clear that it is madness. Around the 10 mile mark you sadly turn around, knowing what doom is in store. It is a very slow slog back out of The Pit. It is hot, exposed, and steep, and you are totally worn out.

At the 11 mile mark you turn onto another climb called the Cardiac Bypass trail. This punishing climb is another .4 miles. When you hit the next aid station, you are almost home. The rest of the run is along a very nice canal trail. More likely than not, you will contemplate jumping into the canal, but probably refrain as it would just delay the relief of finishing the race. The trail dumps you a half mile from the finish line. The rest of the run is completed in a haze of sweat and tears.

Take your time around the friendly folks at the finish line. The food is fantastic and the spirit is definitely fun.

About the Author

Tilden Moschetti has competed in triathlons for approximately six years. He is very active in local triathlon clubs and has even served as president of the San Francisco Triathlon Club. In Tilden's words, "I signed up for my first triathlon (Wildflower) because I was bored going to the gym. The night before I wrote out my will and I considered it a good possibility that I would die on the course. In a sense that was true, a part of me did die that day, the boring and lazy part." That year he signed up for six additional races, hired a great coach (Hypercat Racing) and has been training hard since.

Black Bear Triathlon

pocono mountains, pennsylvania

Race Distance: Long
1.2 Mile Swim, 56 Mile Bike, 13.1 Mile Run
Month: May
Race Web Site: www.cgiracing.com

Author: Jim Epik
Racing Category: Age Group 45-49

The Black Bear Triathlon is a challenging long course race located in the Pocono Mountains of eastern Pennsylvania. It is held in late May or early June and is currently the largest long course triathlon in Pennsylvania and New Jersey. The nonstop elevation changes of the inaugural 2007 course were designed to test the mettle of even the fittest triathletes. If you are looking to explore your personal limits or are preparing for a hilly ultra distance race, this should be a race you consider.

Personally, I put this race on my calendar in 2007 because it was the inaugural year (it's the only way I get to use the word "first" in the same sentence as "race"). For those looking for something a little tamer, Black Bear offers a short course distance that is held on the same day. Fortunately, the short course leaves out many of the strenuous climbs found on the longer route. For those racers who will be bringing family members as their own personal cheering squad, there are plenty of facilities and activities at the race site to keep everyone entertained during your time on the road.

There are no qualification requirements for entry in the race other than registering online through the web site. With that said, I strongly recommend having good bike handling skills for the extremely fast down hill portions of the course that are staged on rough roads. Completing a flatter long course prior to attempting this event would be advisable.

There are monetary incentives for early registration. The race is held in a location about an hour and a half from Philadelphia and New Jersey, and within two hours of New York City, so flight scheduling for those of you who need to fly in should be relatively easy.

I personally try and make racing events mini-vacations and take a couple of extra days off to drive and sightsee along the way.

Packet pickup is held on the standard afternoon prior to the race and was held in Beltzville State Park. This afforded participants a great opportunity to look over the transition area, check out the bike course, and double-check the drive time from the area hotels (20 minutes). A pre-race meeting held the same day covers the basic information on the course, logistics, and changes to the event schedule—nothing new, but worth attending for any last minute changes to the bike route. A small expo of vendors was located at the site and was well stocked with last minute items you may have forgotten. Several mechanics were also standing by to make bike checks or minor repairs. I had never had to use these services in the past, but these guys at Black Bear saved me when a bike gnome punctured my rear tire on the drive up.

The Black Bear swim is a one loop in-water, wave start, in Beltzville Lake. Summer temperatures in the Pocono Mountains can be fickle with morning air temperatures ranging from the upper 40s to mid 50s. I would recommend being over prepared with a number of different outfits for the conditions. Water temperatures can vary (62-76 degrees) making this a wet suit legal race. The lake is one of the cleanest I have ever been in to date. I saw many athletes in sleeveless long john wetsuits at the start, but I opted for a full sleeve suit for comfort.

As is normal, a light mist hovered over the water prior to the race and then burned off by the start. The swim course was well marked with large bright buoys making the course extremely easy to sight while swimming. For those who get jittery in open water swims, the start was in small waves. The course took me a little over 35 minutes to cover which is typical for me at this distance, so I believe the course was accurately marked. After making it around the first buoy I spotted several packs of swimmers from the earlier waves and was able to draft on them thereby conserving my energy for the hills to come.

The race director was on his toes with the competitors' needs in mind. There were sports drinks available immediately upon exiting the water—what a great move! The combined T1-T2 transition area was well marked and laid out with short course racers on one side of the corral and long course athletes on the other. The configuration made the normally hectic activities associated with changing a breeze. Volunteers located in the transition area were well coached and provided excellent guidance in navigating into and out of the park. Again the race director was on his toes providing bottles of water at the entrance point.

Once on the bike, the two loop 56-mile course provided a level of misery I have not experienced since living in the mountains of northern Alabama. The route had virtually no flats, so if you are the type of athlete that enjoys climbing, this race is tailor made to test your resolve. Each loop takes the participants up two major climbs, after completing the climb, an immediate U-turn is made and you head back down the mountain. I overheard several racers saying that this was a little unnerving after having exhausted themselves on the climb. The grades are in fact steep and fast. Be forewarned, hold on tight and make sure your bottles and other equipment are well secured.

As the race website states: "…a scenic yet challenging bike course; with elevations of more than 650'." I can assure you, the course lives up to the full meaning of the word, "challenging." Having driven the course the day before, I knew to hold off on going out too quickly and risk burning out before finishing. Personally, I tried to remain seated as long as possible on all of the uphill portions. Fortunately, this strategy provided ample opportunity to spend quality time talking with the other athletes in my pack. Everyone gave positive encouragement as we slugged out the climbs.

Near the end of the ride, just when you think you've got the course whipped, there is a particularly nasty little climb. Mercifully, it is short, although it did not feel that way at the time. The ride is through heavily wooded rural roads and the local traffic was extremely respectful of riders. Enjoying long glimpses of the water during the ride was clearly the best part. The bike aid stations (passed twice) were well stocked with bottled water, Hammer Gels°, and Gatorade°. And again, all the volunteers proved to be well versed in their jobs and readily offered the goodies.

The 13.1-mile run is also two loops conducted over a combination of gravel roads and wooded dirt paths. Again, don't expect much relief from the climbs and descents experienced during the bike course. If you've never completed a race that traverses a dam, it's an experience you won't soon forget. The dominate feature in the route was a deceptively gentle slope down the side of the dam. As a confirmed middle-of-the-pack racer, I was reduced to walking up this long gradual climb on both loops.

Fortunately, the race director purposefully placed the two primary aid stations at strategic choke points at the top and bottom of the dam. This positioning worked extremely well providing the maximum number of opportunities to rehydrate and fuel up on the way down, at the bottom, on the way up, prior to beginning the long flat traverse across the top of the dam, and then again prior to beginning the next loop.

The one flat section of the race comes while crossing the top of the dam on a service road. Views of the lake and the valley from this vantage point are magnificent. The structure of the loops provided many opportunities to see friends, exchange a few high fives, and give words of encouragement for finishing. If you are looking at making a bid for a podium position, the loops give you many opportunities to size-up your competition. Aid stations were well stocked with formula, water, gel, cola, cookies, jelly beans, and salty pretzels.

After a long day of racing, the best part definitely comes as each racer crosses a wooden covered bridge just prior to finishing. The backdrop makes for memorable photo opportunities.

Besides all of the activities the park offers, competitors can also shower in the large bath house before heading home. Post race activities were as good as I've seen anywhere with complimentary massage, food and drinks, raffle prizes, and great music.

I highly recommend driving the bike route a day or two before the race. After seeing the hills you will be climbing, try out one of the local eateries. I ate at Platz's Restaurant, conveniently located on the road between the race site and the hotel and found the meal quite good. The town of Lehighton has several restaurant options, so everyone should be able to find something to fit their tastes.

There are numerous over night accommodations near and around the race site with family owned facilities, mid-level chains, and camping options. The area is also a popular vacation area, so don't forget to check out the local fishing, kayaking, and camping.

About the Author

Jim Epik races in the 45-49 age group. He has completed more than 25 triathlons, ranging from the short course distance through the ultra distance. The Black Bear Triathlon was his third long course event.

St. Croix Ironman 70.3®

st.croix, u.s. virgin islands

Race Distance: Long
1.2 Mile Swim, 56 Mile Bike, 13.1 Mile Run
Month: May
Race Web Site: www.stcroixtriathlon.com

Author: Eric Goetz
Racing Category: Age Group 35-39

St Croix is in the United States Virgin Islands just east of Puerto Rico. The island is small and has numerous secluded beaches. The St. Croix Ironman 70.3 (a.k.a. Beauty and the Beast) takes place during the first week of May, starting and ending in downtown Christensted, the largest town on the island.

The beauty of this race is defined by the spectacular ocean swim. The water is so clear that you can see tropical fish, wave to scuba divers, and keep track of your progress on the ocean floor. The bike leg is equally impressive, not only visually as you peddle along seaside cliffs, but it also offers challenging terrain including the much dreaded climb called the "Beast." The run continues with a rolling primer and a route that takes you through a golf course and along the coast for a series of amazing vistas and brutal hills.

This description is one you will likely find online or in triathlon magazines since this race is commonly sited as a "must do" and one of the most challenging long course races in the country. So what is it really like to compete in this race? Let me share an insider's perspective.

It has become a tradition for a group of athletes from the DC Triathlon Club (in Washington, DC) to visit St. Croix each year for a week to race and then enjoy the island as we recover. As a two-year veteran of the race, I returned for a third time in 2007. All of the talk in the weeks leading up to the race was about the rum drinks, sun, and beach time. But the challenge of the 70.3 was sorely overlooked. Thinking about having a Lime-n-da-Coconut while you sit back and fry yourself into a "tan" was far more appealing than the thought of running in 90-something degree weather with 90-something percent humidity. Go figure.

Stepping off the plane after a short flight from Miami, I immediately smelled the salt air and got slapped with a rush of humidity. As in years past, complimentary rum drinks were served as I waited with my fellow club members in baggage claim. It wasn't a short wait despite the fact that the plane I arrived in was the only one on the ground and sat about 50 yards from the bar. But my mind quickly floated into island time and the humidity soaked in as my shoulders dropped into relax mode. After all it was a taper week right? As I waited for my bike and luggage to make it off the plane, there were a host of taxi vans waiting to shuttle us to our destination while the drivers offered the lay of the land.

There are many options for accommodations on the island, from small B&Bs to world renowned resorts. Having stayed at a few places throughout the island, I've come to appreciate the convenience and amenities of Hotel on the Cay which sits on its own little island about 100 yards from the heart of Christensted. A three minute ferry ride takes you to and from the Cay. While the well known Carambola Beach Resort and The Buccaneer are beautiful, lavish, and great places to vacation, being right in town and literally at the race start is a big benefit. Transition is in town but the race is actually a beach start from the Cay. Additionally, if you stay at the Cay you get to set up transition and then go back to your own room, just steps from the starting line. There are plenty of other in-town options as well that vary in cost as well as esthetics.

Registration is simple. Everything is right in town and there's a great street festival to commemorate the weekend. There's a small assortment of race gear and goodies available, slim pickings compared to other events, but then again most people are out lounging next to the pool rather than walking around town in the days leading up to the race.

There's also a mechanic crew ready to fix equipment and handle reserved bike rentals that are available for racers not wanting to ship their own bikes to the island. The rentals that I saw were brand new entry level Trek road bikes.

In the days leading up to the race I kept thinking about that brutal run. Don't use it all up on the bike I told myself. Think nutrition, patience, strategy, and pacing.

Race morning begins early. With a 6:30 a.m. start time, I was up by 4:30 a.m. and headed down to transition. I laid out my transition in the dark as the buzz of athletes steadily grew. The mandatory swim warm up was a short dip to get to the race start at Hotel on the Cay, about 100 yards away.

Everyone gathered on the beach tweaking their goggles and itching to go. A few port-o-potties were lined up on a barge at the waters edge and the sun rose over the east end of the island. As the first glimpse of the day was illuminated, broken clouds moved slowly overhead and the pending heat could already be felt. We lined up in age groups on the beach and watched the ceremonial start of the pros kick off into the bay. The water is warm, salty and buoyant all year long so it's a no-wetsuit race. All were eager as the start approached. Then, "Ready, Set, GO!"

The swim is a beach run-in start that soon turns into a mass of arms and legs that churn the water. It's a fight all the way to the first turn about 100 yards out. There's no real option to stay on course at the beginning, as everyone feeds for the first buoy. At the buoy you make a sharp left hook turn where the punishment of condensed bodies quickly dissipates.

After the first turn the athletes slowly thin out on a straight shot toward the ocean. The ocean floor, always in sight, is deepest at the turnaround which is about halfway through the course. The water is relatively calm on most days but can get choppy at the farthest point where the swells are also more apparent. There is a wide range of tropical fish and sea life to distract you as you swim, not to mention the security and filming scuba crews below you. The hardest part is staying focused.

On the return stretch the current tends to be behind you guiding you back to shore. Sighting becomes easy having a range of building and land forms to set your course. There is also a fort tower on shore that is great to sight off. Don't assume you're finished once you make it back to the dock. The last portion of the course follows the shore for about 200 yards to an exit ramp and for some reason it always seems like there's a current working against you. When you make it to the ramp reach up to get a helping hand into transition.

The first transition is a soft grassy area that you enter as soon as you're out of the water. There really aren't any bad bike rack locations and there is plenty of room between rows.

After rolling out of transition along a short gravel path, the first few miles of the bike course are pretty easy rollers out of town to get you warmed up. There are also some shallow grades and rough patches of pavement that slow you down. The first large climb is at mile six before a nice long descent back into town. This completes an eight mile loop from the start of the bike leg (also used as the bike course for the short course race).

As you cut through town you begin a 48 mile long loop. Some technical riding takes you around the "hot corner"—a tiny 90 degree turn. The crowds pump you up as you head toward the Beast, the headwinds on the south side, and the rest of the loop around the island. The ride along the coast is one the nicest parts of the course and there are many sections of new pavement. Still there are some rough patches but the view is gorgeous. Make sure to stay on the left hand side of the road (traffic drives on the left).

The jokes and chatter among athletes grows as you get closer to the Beast—the notorious three quarters of a mile long climb. Around mile 20 you make a sharp left turn and within a few feet you're already in your lowest gear. Heart rate, watts, cadence and speed—none of it means a thing. With an average grade of 14 percent or more and sections reaching 24 percent it's all you can do to keep the pedals going forward. A 39/27 is highly recommended by the race organizers but even that doesn't stop competitors from bringing flip flops strapped to their saddle bags in order to walk up. At an average speed of five mph it's easy to see the markings painted on the pavement, showing you how far you've gone in tenths of a mile and how steep in percentage grade.

As you near the top the cheers grow louder and are peppered with coaching tips like, "Pull up with your legs!" which of course is good advice if you haven't already tried that. A well placed aid station at the top of the climb is a great place to refuel and take photos of the Caribbean Sea. Quickly over the crest you begin a winding descent that takes you through quiet farm roads.

Before you know it you're sharpening your BMX skills on a series of speed bumps through a neighborhood that leads you across the island to the south side. At this point you've reached the southern plains which are open to the air whipping in from the sea in a stiff headwind. The course is mostly rollers until the last 15 miles when the terrain becomes tougher. Once you make it to the tip of the island you climb over to the north side once again. The last eight mile stretch and final notable climb is the same as the first climb on the small loop that began the bike leg. The upside to this is that you get a nice three mile descent into transition.

There's a great network of local police making sure all the road crossings are clear and this event essentially shuts down the entire island. The crowds are out in force like sun dancers asking for more heat.

You come into transition the same way you left and before you know it you're on the way to your run.

The run is a lollipop two loop course that takes you out on a two mile stretch leading to a two mile loop within the Buccaneer Resort and golf course. You then return back to town. Sharing the route for a couple of miles with the bike course allows you to keep tabs on your competitors and friends. The heat can be devastating and swamp-like with partly cloudy skies letting the sun in on the damp and humid course. At times you can feel the vapors rise from the ground. Aid stations are an oasis of support, staged about every mile.

The run course is hilly with some trail running and one steep climb on the resort grounds. This is a common walk section where you get to meet athletes from all over the world. Many racers including Kona veterans walk side-by-side on this grueling section of the run.

The first loop is tough but the second is a test of will. The heat cranks up as the sun reaches its height. The hills become less forgiving and the miles seem to stretch out. The hardest part of the race is often misconstrued as the Beast when in reality it's the intense heat of the run, especially on the second loop.

Cheering crowds signal that you're nearing the final half mile as you race into town weaving through historical side streets. The route drags you around town for another six blocks and gives you one last jab before you cross the finish line.

For those who aren't ready for the long distance, the race also offers an awesome short course version. You get to experience all the heat and revel in the encouragement of the huge crowds.

After taking a breather, the massage tent is a common stop. I fell quickly back into island mode and was ready for some time off. Thoughts of rum drinks and soft sand mixed with clear waters became my main focus. From there it all got better. Even the heat was forgotten in the tropical paradise.

The following week was a recovery week and luckily we had our share of beaches to enjoy. Carambola, Buck Island, Jack's Bay, and Sandy Point were some of the highlights that eased the pain away. A few Lime-n-da-Coconut drinks at Cheeseburger in Paradise also did their part. Did I mention a bottle of rum costs $2.75?

There is a range of quality restaurants like Savant and Bacchus that merge island life and international flare. It's easy to fill your days on St. Croix with adventures including hikes to far out tidal pools, snorkeling along Buck Island (a national wildlife refuge), and scuba diving the "wall."

The St. Croix Ironman 70.3 is a great race and an awesome destination event. It will continue to be on my roster for years to come. It is brutal in many regards but also offers many rewards. Weeks later you'll find yourself suffering from island withdrawal. Slowly, reality will settle back in and you'll start looking ahead to next year.

About the Author

Always on the hunt for adventure, Eric Goetz dreams of his next challenge before his current one ends. The two-time ultra distance triathlete in the 35-39 age group, has biked from San Diego to Washington, DC, Rome to Barcelona, Glacier Park to Yuma, Vancouver to Mexicali, and Toronto to Rhode Island (the former on a mountain bike with only a sleeping bag, cash, and a tool kit of essentials). These incredible experiences have fueled a lifetime of memories: Screaming downhill at upwards of 55 mph; climbing continuously for over 25 miles; tracing 136 miles of the Blue Ridge in a single day — fully loaded with gear; riding eight centuries in as many days; covering countless miles and meeting even more personalities. All in pursuit of the important truth: What is his limit?

This year Eric is coordinating a team to do the Race Across America (RAAM), training at the Tour of California and racing Ironman Arizona® and the St. Croix Ironman 70.3. Then after hammering across the country in six days, Eric has his sights set on organizing Total 200 v4 (total200.com), a one day 200 mile ride and Endure 24 (endure24.com), a 24 hour road bike race. Eric resides on Capitol Hill in Washington, DC.

White Lake Triathlon

white lake, north carolina

Race Distance: Long
1.2 Mile Swim, 56 Mile Bike, 13.1 Mile Run
Month: May
Race Web Site: www.setupevents.com

Author: Doug Marocco
Racing Category: Age Group 40-45

Triathlon is recognized to have originated in San Diego and continues to flourish on the West Coast with the traditional season opener, Wildflower Triathlon. The East Coast has its own version of Wildflower in the White Lake long course triathlon which is held simultaneously on the first Saturday each May. For the past six years, I have made the pilgrimage five hours south from my Virginia home to White Lake, North Carolina in order to participate in what has become one of the biggest weekends of racing east of the Mississippi.

Although not as well known as Wildflower or some of the more established races in the east like Eagleman, the White Lake races are ones that athletes continue to put on their calendars each year. Since North Carolina State Park rules limit the number of race participants, beginning in 2009, the race is held on the first two consecutive weekends in May, each with the same long course race on Saturday and the short course race on Sunday. This addition allows for many more athletes to participate in the event. There are no differences in events between the two weekends and awards are given out for all races individually.

White Lake is part of the North Carolina Triathlon Series which are all managed by Set Up Events. In addition to the North Carolina series, Set Up Events also has ownership of the Virginia Triathlon Series and the South Carolina Triathlon Series. The nice thing about participating in any one of these events is that you know you will always get the same high quality race production at an affordable price. An additional perk for White Lake competitors is that they all receive a technical running shirt and socks.

The festival atmosphere of race weekend gets started early on the Friday prior to race day when the site is swarmed by those athletes wanting to preview the course. Many of the northern athletes have only trained outside a few times and want to test their bodies and equipment for the first time since the previous fall. They welcome the opportunity to wear shorts and actually ride a bike that is not hooked up to a trainer. Shaving legs is still optional at this time of year, so don't be surprised if many people still have the hairy look. Race registration and packet pick-up begins at 3:00 p.m. for the USAT sanctioned event, so have your membership card ready. Later in the evening, Counterpart Coach, Doug Marocco (that's me) often presents a clinic on race execution that is especially useful for first time long course triathletes. I would not normally recommend a dramatic change to an athlete's execution plan so close to the event, however, many athletes have no plan at all for a race that could last up to eight hours. Over the years, it has been extremely gratifying to have people tell me after their race that they used some advice from my clinic and it made a positive difference.

The races sell out in less than 24 hours once race registration opens in January. A wait list is started and you do have an option for charity slots if you missed out and didn't register the day after New Years. While you are registering for the race, you may also want to try and reserve one of the air conditioned/heated lodge rooms on the grounds. Other lodging options that make the race so welcoming are climate controlled dorm rooms that sleep 20 or screened in barracks that sleep up to 24. They are a little more primitive, but still have access to a shower and are so close you can roll out of bed and set up your race equipment in your pajamas. In fact, all of the sleeping options including putting up you own tent or sleeping under the stars are between the swim start and the transition area.

If a race expo is important to you then you will be happy to know that experienced professionals are on hand to provide technical bike support or take care of any last minute needs.

The long course event attracts a mix of elite, age group and novice triathletes. The flat course is appealing to first time racers, but also draws the best in the sport primed to set a PR. A special feature for those age group athletes looking to compete for the overall places is an Open and Masters Open Category that goes off as the first wave.

The long course is as simple as a race can be at this distance. It's a glass-like lake swim, pancake flat bike course, and two loop flat run combined with a spectator friendly venue that has places for children to play and a lake to splash around in. All these things make the experience ideal for families as well as the racers.

On race morning the sun rises with a glimmer across the crystal clear lake that has a visible sandy bottom and a maximum depth of about nine feet. The race uses an in-water wave start with a water temperature that hovers close to the USAT threshold temperature of 78 degrees. The race is usually wetsuit legal and has actually been in the mid 60s, however there have also been times that a warm spring will raise the temperature to a no wetsuit status. If you have a full suit and a sleeveless, bring them both as well as a speed suit in case neither of them are allowed.

The swim course is a long triangle that is approximately 600 meters out, 800 meters across, and 600 meters back with a visible marker to site off at the finish line. Large orange and yellow corner buoys help keep everyone on track to swim fast. With a quick exit onto a wooden boardwalk that frames the start area, you proceed another 100 meters on grass to a smooth in and out flowing transition area. Once you've mounted your bike you can start hammering the 56-mile cycling portion of the triathlon.

The bike course is flat and fast with only seven turns. With no measurable elevation, the bike course is so flat that you could literally stay in the aero position for the entire course. Not changing positions eventually wears on your back, neck, and legs so it is important to stand up out of the saddle occasionally to break up the monotony. The first few miles of the bike circles the lake and then at mile four takes a right hand turn out to smooth and open country roads.

Although the course is not closed to traffic, it is extremely rare to see any cars other than several mechanical support vehicles. The initial 25 miles fly by and for those riding a disk, the unique sound at 25 plus miles per hour is awesome. It is even better when you are the one making the noise. Once you reach the 30 mile point many riders will come to realize that they didn't pace themselves well and will pay the price. Although there may be some prevailing winds out of the southwest from mile 30-38, most of the course is protected and can make for a personal bike record. The swimmers that made the first leg of the race look so easy inevitably give way to the more powerful cyclists along this stretch and the race starts to take shape. This is an ideal course for large riders that want to push big gears. The pursuers that are bent on making a charge for the lead often times drag riders with them. The packs that do form throughout the course are heavily patrolled by the USAT course marshals. This is evident by the volume of race numbers on the pink violation sheets after the race. Drafting at the long course distance is an eye opening four minute penalty.

In order to have the proper distance, the course does a short two mile out-and-back at mile 38-42. This is a great place to check your competition. If you can keep count to the turn around you know that you are in good shape. It is time for you to down some fuel for the battle over the final 10 miles of the bike course before transitioning to the run.

The bike finish is just a few meters from the transition area, which makes for a quick change. Without breaking stride, cyclists turned runners sprint with helmets on and bikes in hand to their designated rack, slip on their shoes and go. White Lake like all other North Carolina Triathlon Series events has individually numbered rack spots so that you do not have to worry about finding a spot to park your bike race morning. That alone is good enough for 15 more minutes of sleep the night before the race.

The run course is a flat, two-lap, out-and-back figure-eight with aid every mile. There is some shade in a nice neighborhood section that you pass on four occasions but other than that, the temperatures are often unforgiving. One consolation is that you will see all the other athletes along the way and so you can judge your effort and place compared to your friends and competition. If you are running strong the course layout is your friend because you can really see what kind of ground you are making up.

After completing lap one and running back within site of the start/finish area, you may have a very strong inclination to skip lap two and jump into the lake. In fact, in 2003 close to 40 percent of the field didn't end up finishing, and I think the lake temptation got more than a few of them when temperatures soared near the 100 degree mark. With half the run to go, it seems like the fast swim course and flat bike course have given way to a hot, flat run and what was once the goal to PR, has now turned to just getting to the finish line. Make the most of it and trudge on. Running, shuffling, or walking, eventually you, along with hundreds of others will arrive to the voice of the announcer as he calls your name and brings you to the finish line with another triathlon achievement.

Once you have made it through the course and cooled down with a dip in the lake, be sure to take advantage of a post race massage and your pick of grilled burgers, chicken, or rice and beans. As a typical triathlete, you are proud of you accomplishment, but inevitably talk of what could have been. Thoughts immediately turn to thinking about how you will be better prepared next year.

The White Lake weekend has a special place in triathlon and is a "must do "race. In six attempts at the course, I am fortunate to have experienced the thrill of victory winning the race in 2004. Since moving to "the other coast" from California, my off-season training has focused on being ready by the first week of May for White

Lake. The opportunity to compete at a spectator friendly course that is convenient to get to and is supported by a professional organization is why hundreds of triathletes keep coming back to White Lake year after year.

About the Author

Since doing my first triathlon on a borrowed bike while stationed in Japan with the Marine Corps in 1986, I am fortunate to have competed in more than 300 triathlons. The sport has been the primary reason that my family and I have been to such incredible locations around the globe as Australia, Belgium, England, Estonia, France, Honduras, Italy, and Thailand as well as Hawaii for nine Hawaii Ironman® World Championships.

Living in Southern California during the infancy of the sport, I was able to train alongside some of the best endurance athletes in the world and have a hand in the development of equipment that has become a mainstream part of triathlon. After enjoying what is often considered the mecca of triathlon for the majority of my 21-year Marine Corps career, my final change of stations landed me on the east coast in Quantico, Virginia. I expected a real change in the triathlon scene, however, surprisingly the race schedule is full of events within driving distance every weekend and the competition from top to bottom is fierce.

Wildflower Long Course Triathlon

Race Distance: Long
1.2 Mile Swim, 56 Mile Bike, 13.1 Mile Run
Month: May
Race Web Site: www.tricalifornia.com

Author: Brandon Del Campo
Racing Category: Age Group 30-34

I was in the process of discovering triathlon and had done a few intermediate distance races. My excitement for my new found hobby was clear as I told anyone who knew me all about it. My father was on the receiving end many times and had informed me about a rather large race about five minutes from his house that he and my mother had just moved into up in Bradley, California. The race was called "Wildflower" (as part of the Wildflower Triathlons Festival) and was considered to be the "Woodstock" of triathlon.

My dad found out about the race one day when he was out on his Harley and stopped for lunch at a local coffee shop. He was talking to a woman who had done the long course race and was commonly referred to as the "Swiss Miss." She had apparently won the Hawaii Ironman World Championship® about five times, so she said. Obviously this was Natasha Badmann but I had not heard of her or Wildflower. My dad asked her if he could get a picture of her on the Harley. He thought the photo would be pretty cool since she was in her cycling kit. She agreed and later my dad wrote "How Natasha wins all her races!" as a caption for the photo. He had told Natasha that he had a son just starting to do triathlon and he told me that she said I must come and do this race.

I decided the following May to do the long course at Wildflower. Unfortunately as May rolled around I was hit with a stress fracture in my foot. I wasn't able to race but I still decided to go watch and see what it was all about.

The race takes place at Lake San Antonio, in Monterey County, California. Having my parents only 10 minutes from the race start made it very easy for me. I was able to sleep in a nice warm bed while most

WILDFLOWER LONG COURSE TRIATHLON

of the competitors and spectators camped in tents and RVs in a full service camp ground at the race site. That is part of the lure for Wildflower. You can see that the camping atmosphere adds an element to the race that other races don't have. How often do you get to camp out the night before with all the people doing the race?

Wildflower is spectator friendly if you are a fit individual. Since it starts down in the lake which is surrounded by hills there is a bit of a challenge to see large portions of the race. For me, hobbling around in my stress fracture boot proved to be quite hard but I still managed to watch the start and T1. Then I climbed up the hill for parts of the run and then hobbled back down to see the finish. The bike is like most races where you really don't get to see any of it. Luckily there is plenty of food for spectators to buy while waiting for the bike to finish. A "long course burrito" is a must for anyone there.

I had been told that the course was very challenging and it doesn't take a genius to figure out the race is not flat. Plenty of hills on the one loop bike course and then heaps more for the run. I feel that during my spectating I got a taste of what they were talking about as I scampered up and down hill all day. Watching the race had me sold! I wanted to do it so badly and knew that the next year I would be free of injuries and ready to give it a go.

The following year rolled quickly and suddenly I couldn't believe that I was less than 48 hours away from my first Wildflower long course triathlon! I had brought about 20 people with me to do the race as well. We decided that since my parents lived in the area that we would not camp but use their house instead. We also rented another house down the street and realized that many of the homes in the neighborhood were rented by racers. So there is definitely an alternative to camping if that is not your cup of tea. However, staying in a hotel is not really an option. I suppose some do, but the drive to the race would be about 45 minutes to an hour.

We were all down by the race start for packet pick-up. The race organizers obviously know what they are doing as the process was very simple. There was even a shuttle that you could take up and down the hill. They also allowed you to take your bike on it. That was key as doing those hills the day before may not be the best for your performance.

There are not many restaurants near the race so the night before you have to make sure you are prepared to cook some dinner. My crew was fortunate enough to have my mom cook up a nice pasta dinner for everyone. I would assume that everyone camping has the BBQs going. Maybe one year I will suck it up and camp out to see what that is all about.

On the morning of the race we all piled into a motor home that we borrowed from a friend of my parents and headed into the park. I had some concern that it was going to be complete chaos and take forever to get in since there was only one road down there but as it turns out the process was very quick and the RV was parked in a great place to act as a home base for all of us. All we had to do now was get down to transition. You had the option of taking the bus but most of us just rode our bikes.

T1 and T2 are the same location, so it makes it very convenient for the athletes. Spectators get a great view of all the action and the pro field is placed right up front so all can watch the super fast transitions. It was then that I knew I really wanted to try and get good enough to hold a pro card. I wouldn't be able to watch the pro race this year as my age group wave was going off right after the pro women. They launch everyone in waves five minutes apart. Some of the age groups have so many people in them that they require two starts. That just shows you what a huge race Wildflower really is.

The swim start is a bit narrow so it can be rather chaotic until you hit the first turn buoy. At least the race is wetsuit legal so you have a bit more buoyancy during the washing machine portion of the swim. The course is one giant rectangle that takes you through the boat harbor on the lake. The swim can have some chop but won't be anything like swimming in an ocean unless of course a boat gets away with making some large wake which was the case for me at the turn around point. You know you are approaching the end of the swim when you start to see the giant poster cut out of an athlete exiting the water. It looks like "attack of the killer triathlete" and can throw you for a second if you are not expecting it.

You will get to transition rather fast as the run up the ramp is not very long. Getting out on the bike can be a bit discouraging as you are thrown one massive hill to start. You basically have to climb out of the park before you get rolling. Having a high heart rate from the swim can make the transition from swim muscles to bike legs extra challenging.

After you get out of the park you can start to find a rhythm but don't get too excited as you will hit some pretty decent rollers rather quickly. There is a nice treat after the rollers with some smooth down hill and then gradually flat sections with small climbs for a while that allow you to get the pace up. Don't get too comfortable in your groove because Wildflower has another massive hill in store for you. For me, the hill proved to be everything that was said about it. The road surface is a bit rough and you will see a good section of eight percent grade. When you make it to the top you may think you are hallucinating because you see a giant Energizer Bunny beating a drum. Don't panic. That is one of the traditions of this race.

From the top of the climb you might feel relief but save it for later. This is where Wildflower starts to get its reputation. You are pretty spent from the climb and now have to carry on for more torture in the form of large rollers. If you paced yourself properly you will for sure see detonated cyclists that seem to be standing still. Hopefully one of the well run aid stations will have something to help them bounce back.

There is a nice downhill that takes you back into transition so you can take a moment and stretch your back and get your legs ready to run. Most years the sun will be getting ready to beat down on you pretty hard if it hasn't started already. If it is an off year with rain, plan on a good romp in the mud!

The run is a combination of pavement and trail. You will climb as many hills on the run as you did on the bike. There is a section on the run that is so steep most people would move faster by briskly walking rather than running. I would say that while Wildflower is known for its hard run course, it will play well to someone that is strong and able to run downhill very fast. You are going to make up more time screaming down the hills than you will powering up them.

The run course is mentally tough too as you go downhill only to hit the 10 mile mark where you flip a U-turn and go right back up. It isn't so bad as the hill is only a mile long. Once you crest the top you can start to turn your legs over as the rest is flat and downhill. The last 3/4 of a mile is so steep that it will make you never want to run downhill again! You can guarantee that you will have some angry quads come Sunday and Monday.

The finish shoot has stands and plenty of spectators awaiting you. The announcers are great at calling everyone out and making each athlete feel proud of their accomplishment. Everyone gets a finisher's medal and they have plenty of water and post race snacks.

The awards ceremony takes place just meters from the finish on a nice grass area that is in the shade and surrounded by food to buy. They give out awards to the top five in each age group and top 10 for the pro field. The awards move along pretty quickly so you won't be stuck sitting there for hours on end if you choose to stick around or were fast enough to receive one.

The following day you can head back down to the race start and watch the intermediate distance race. If you are feeling extra peppy you may even be crazy enough to do that one too. They have a category for fastest combo so if pain is you game I say go for it! You will find me in the stands watching.

I think that the race gets better each year, and I see why people come back. For anyone who is looking for a fantastic race that offers something a little extra then I suggest you plan a trip up to Bradley, California the first weekend in May for one of the best long course triathlons around. Word of caution: It sells out fast so sign up early!

About the Author

Brandon Del Campo was a former cross country runner for UCLA. He began competing in triathlons in 2004 with no swim or bike background. He focuses on long course and ultra distance triathlons and currently competes in the 30-34 age group.

Eagleman Ironman 70.3®

cambridge, maryland

Race Distance: Long
1.2 Mile Swim, 56 Mile Bike, 13.1 Mile Run
Month: June
Race Web Site: www.tricolumbia.org/Eagleman/

Author: Stacy Fitzgerald Taylor
Racing Category: Age Group 40-44

It was late 2005 when I first heard about the Eagleman Ironman 70.3 Triathlon, I was sitting at my computer one day and a thought came to me out of the blue: "Stacy, you are turning 40 next year." Oh my god. I told myself, "Don't panic, just stay calm." What am I going to do? Well, I knew I needed to do something challenging. Over the years I ran five marathons and while I still love running, I didn't want to do another. I also knew I didn't want to do anything crazy like climb Mount Everest or jump out of an airplane. What to do? I remembered a sprint triathlon I did a few years ago and thought, "Yes, that is it. I will do another triathlon!"

So, I began my online triathlon search and looked up triathlons in the Baltimore/Washington, DC area. I found many shorter distance triathlons but remember, I was looking for something "big." Eventually, I came across the Columbia Triathlon Association website and clicked on the Eagleman button. The race looked interesting and challenging and race day was the next June in Cambridge, Maryland. While I had never done much swimming and didn't even own a road bike at the time, I signed up right then. I then asked myself, "Stacy, what the heck have you just done?"

I trained hard over several months for the 1.2 mile swim, 56 mile bike and half marathon of 13.1 miles. Come race day in June, I completed the race. It was the hardest thing I had ever done; none of my five marathons even came close. While packing up my gear in the transition area after the race I cried tears of joy and amazement at what I had accomplished. Right then and there I fell in love not just with the Eagleman race, but with the sport of triathlon. I was hooked and knew I would be back

to complete Eagleman another year. "Happy 40th birthday, Stacy," I told myself.

I signed up for Eagleman again in 2007. In April I learned that I won a lottery slot to compete in the Hawaii Ironman World Championship® and I was going to use my race at Eagleman to validate my lottery slot. Come race week in early June, I was so excited to be going back to Eagleman where just one year before, I discovered the amazing sport of triathlon.

There are some really great things about Eagleman. First, there are several slots awarded to the top finishers to compete at the Hawaii Ironman World Championship in Kona it and attracts some of the best pros and very fast age groupers. Next, the bike and run courses are very flat and very fast, which is great for nearly everyone. The bike course also includes several miles through the Blackwater National Wildlife Refuge.

Eagleman is a very large race with over 1,550 entrants. Even so, the atmosphere is really laid back. I think this is due in large part to the good people of Cambridge who are very welcoming to the triathletes and also provide great volunteer support.

Cambridge, Maryland is accessible by car from several airports including Baltimore/Washington International (BWI), Reagan National, and Washington Dulles. There are many hotels and motels available in Cambridge, but these fill up quickly (there is a great list of hotels and phone numbers on the race web site). There are also other lodging options in nearby Easton, Salisbury, and Annapolis. Camping is available for race weekend at the local high school with shower facilities available at the nearby YMCA. The race website provides plenty of information about lodging in the area.

I have stayed at the Holiday Inn which is right on the main street in Cambridge and is close to the race start. The best thing about this hotel is that although you have to check out Sunday morning, the management opens up a few rooms so that guests can come back after the race to take a shower, which is great for those who are driving home that day.

The Eagleman expo and packet pick-up are located at Sailwinds Park. The expo opens on Friday afternoon until early evening and then again all day on Saturday.

Registration includes a nice expo with many well known regional and national vendors in attendance.

In the past there has been a pro forum on Saturday afternoon where pros racing took questions from the audience. After taking many questions from the audience, some of us took the opportunity to go on the stage to get autographs and had a chance to talk with the pros one on one.

I left the expo and drove the short distance to the race site at Great Marsh Park. At Eagleman, all bikes are required to be racked on Saturday. I made my way through transition and racked my bike in the designated area. As I was leaving transition, I walked by the pro racks and recognized professional triathlete, Miranda Carfrae. I stopped to introduce myself and to chat for a couple minutes. She was very nice, and I wished her good luck on race day. I then headed back to my hotel to rest up for the afternoon and evening.

In the morning, the temperature was cool and the sky was overcast which are always welcome race morning. The nicest surprise was that the water was as calm as it can be on the Choptank River. This was a relief for all those racing because on Saturday afternoon we all groaned in despair as we watched the Choptank live up to its name. The winds were blowing at 10-20 mph and there were large swells and whitecaps on the water. But come race morning, we were relieved that it was going to be a fast day for everyone.

The water temperature was in the low 70s and was wetsuit legal. Speaking of wetsuits I hadn't been nervous all morning until it was time to put on my wetsuit then it suddenly hit me. The excitement I felt all week changed to anxiety. I'm not sure why. Maybe it was because I was using Eagleman to validate my Kona lottery slot or because I was thinking about the pain from the previous year. In any case, I got into my wetsuit, grabbed my pink swim cap and goggles and walked to the swim start. I was in the 40-44 women's age group which was the largest swim wave of the day. There were 91 of us, and I had not been in a swim start with that many women before. This only added to my anxiety. We waited onshore while several other age groups started their race. Finally, it was our turn.

By the time I finally got into the water I wasn't nervous anymore, I became surprisingly calm. It was kind of weird. Since I am a relatively slower swimmer, this allowed me the luxury of being perfectly happy to start near the back of the pack, where it's usually less physical. We had to swim about 20 yards out to the start which gave me the chance to make sure my goggles were secure. Once at the start, we treaded water for a couple of minutes and watched the previous swim wave head out into the Choptank. Then the gun went off and the 91 of us started swimming.

There is a large bridge that connects Cambridge to Easton on the opposite side of the bay. With the bridge in the distance and several yellow buoys along the way, sighting is not a problem. It took me quite a while to get out to the turnaround and when we turned back to shore at the orange buoy, the current was practically pushing us along. It was awesome. This was a much better experience than the previous year, when there were one to two foot swells and stinging nettles. Nettles are tiny little jellyfish that you can't see. They sting a bit and bother some people more than others. For me, I didn't even notice anything until I was on the bike. I had some itching on my neck and upper arms but it didn't last long.

After 1.2 miles of swimming, it is always a relief to get out of the water. There is a short run to T1 and the crowd support and cheering along the way is really great. I actually enjoy transitions and this one went very well. I sat on the ground next to my bike and peeled off my sleeveless long wetsuit. I pulled on my socks, shoes, helmet, and sunglasses, and I was off with my bike. As you leave transition, the bike heads out through a neighborhood. This provides a great chance for spectators to see the competitors and their cheering and words of support are so encouraging. Soon you find yourself riding along country roads with little or no traffic, and eventually you make it to the Blackwater National Wildlife Refuge.

At about mile eight on my way out on the bike, I saw the eventual men's winner TJ Tollarkson, who was on his bike heading back to Cambridge and there was no one else even close. At about mile 10, I saw Desirée Ficker leading the women's race. Natascha Badmann was closing in behind her. They were really battling it out, it was amazing to see the pros race like this. Natascha ended up with a women's world's best long course time. As an age group competitor, you just don't get many chances to see the pros racing right on the other side of a small two lane road.

What makes this bike course so great is the Blackwater National Wildlife Refuge itself. It is a beautiful place. It is very quiet and peaceful. There is only nature out there, no homes, no cars, no people (except for us on this day). The refuge was established in 1933 as a haven for migrating ducks and geese and includes 26,000 acres of tidal marsh, freshwater ponds and evergreen forests. While you probably won't see them during the race, the Blackwater refuge is also home to the largest population of American Bald Eagles on the East Coast north of Florida. Approximately 20 miles of the 56 mile bike course travels through the refuge.

This year on the bike the wind was very calm until about the last 10 miles heading back into Cambridge. I began to recognize some landmarks so I knew I was getting close to the bike finish. I was tired but feeling pretty good. At this point, I was looking forward to the run.

I made it back, dismounted my bike, and ran through transition to rack my bike. I took off my helmet, changed my shoes put on my race belt and headed back out for the half marathon. As with the bike, the run starts from transition into the neighborhood but makes a right turn and follows a road north along the Choptank River. As with the bike, spectators have many chances to see the competitors and cheer them on. This year, my legs were feeling pretty good by about mile one (the previous year it took me about three miles before I felt my "running legs"). At about mile two there was a guy holding a sign that simply said, "Go Faster!" I found this both funny and inspiring and so for a short time, I did just that.

Most people love a flat run course, but at Eagleman it can be very hot. While there is some shade from trees while running through the neighborhood, once you get off the main road and all the way out to the turnaround, there is no shade at all. If it is a hot day, the run can be brutal. This year however it was still slightly overcast and not too hot at all. Perfect.

There is a long stretch from about mile three out to the turnaround just past mile six where you can see everyone running up ahead as well as those heading back in for their finish. It allows the pros and competitive age groupers a chance to see how their competition is doing. It also gives a chance for people like me to see some of those faster people (well, those who hadn't already finished anyway), but also to see some triathletes who are inspiring for other reasons. One of these people I saw was a man who lost a leg in Iraq and raced Kona in 2006. I saw him twice and the first time I couldn't resist yelling "Great job!" as we passed by each other.

At about mile five you come to a fork in the road at the Long's Grocery store, which is a great sight to see. As you head to the right past the store, you know you have just about a mile to the turn around at the halfway point in the half marathon. There are many spectators cheering you along this stretch, which really helps as you pass back by at about mile seven. It was at this point that I thought again about how much better I was feeling than the previous year. I know that a full year of training and race experience played a role but the conditions were also much better. I was still feeling pretty good until about mile eight, when I began to slow down my pace. I wasn't in any pain but was just getting tired. I simply kept putting one foot in front of the other and continued to move forward toward the finish.

That's the key to the sport of triathlon of any distance in my opinion. Just keep moving forward in order to finish. It doesn't matter your speed or where you place in your age group. Each race is always about finishing. Today was no different.

The cheering and encouragement at the end of any triathlon is truly amazing and Eagleman is no exception. As I made my way that last mile back to the finish,

I couldn't help but pick up the pace. Finally, I made the left turn to the finish chute along a stretch where the crowd is huge and all are cheering like crazy. That's yet another great thing about this sport, at any distance the cheering and encouragement from the spectators is the best. All of them are cheering for YOU. It doesn't matter your finish time but for that one moment you are a winner and a rock star! As I finished for the second year in a row, I knew that I would be back. I was again amazed at finishing this great race called Eagleman.

About the Author

Stacy Fitzgerald Taylor is 41 years old and has been racing in triathlons since 2006. She has been running regularly since competing on the cross country team in high school. She has completed a total of 13 triathlons including one ultra distance (Kona in 2007), five long course races, five intermediates and two short courses.

Staying fit has always been important to Stacy, but even more so since being diagnosed with a heart problem at the age of 33. She had Ventricular Tachychardia, a life threatening problem that involves the electrical connections in the heart. She was lucky to have a procedure to fix the problem, because otherwise she would have had to wear a pace maker for the rest of her life. The doctor told her at the time that if she didn't have such a strong heart from running, she probably would have had a massive heart attack and maybe even died.

An article was published about Stacy in the Winter 2008 edition of *TriDC* magazine. The article tells her story of getting a lottery slot to Kona and her experience there. The story is titled, "Never Say Never."

Ironman 70.3® Buffalo Springs Lake Triathlon

lubbock, texas

Race Distance: Long
1.2 Mile Swim, 56 Mile Bike, 13.1 Mile Run
Month: June
Race Web Site: www.buffalospringslaketriathlon.com/bslt.php

Author: John Shafer
Racing Category: Age Group 45-49

Of the long course triathlons, one race stands out as my favorite, the Ironman 70.3 Buffalo Springs Lake Triathlon. This race tops my list for three reasons: challenge, support, and atmosphere.

The Buffalo Springs Lake Triathlon (BSLT) is held annually during the last weekend in June, in Lubbock, Texas at the Buffalo Springs Lake State Park. The BSLT leaves you feeling as if you raced an ultra course but in half the time and distance. The best advice I can give anyone considering this race is to be prepared for heat, wind and hills, and also to train as if you're headed to an ultra distance race. I've heard many compare the conditions there with those in Hawaii, and I'd agree except that it can be much hotter in Texas.

Mike and Marti Greer, owners and organizers of the BSLT put on a first-class event. The race celebrates 20 years in 2009 and enjoys a reputation of being one of the finest courses in the 70.3 series. The host hotel, the Holiday Inn Lubbock-Park Plaza, is located close to the city's edge with easy access to roads leading directly to the race site five miles away. With registration and a multi-vendor expo available at the host hotel two days prior to the race, everything required for a worry-free race is available on-site.

An incredible all-you-can-eat pre-race pasta meal is offered in the host hotel the night before the race and is often followed by keynote speakers and/or athletes' forums. Distinguished speakers in the past have included Dave Scott, Chris Leigh, and Joanna Zeiger, just to name a few.

Race morning comes early. Parking is at a premium and the narrow road leading into the park can get substantially backed up with athletes and spectators, so of any race to show up early for, BSLT is certainly one.

The transition area sits at lakes edge in a parking lot at the bottom of a steep hill leading in from the park's main entrance. At max capacity, the transition area can be tight; however, it's always possible to set up for a fast and organized transition. The layout and entrance and exit points make for short transition legs and fast T1 and T2 times. Bring a flashlight as you'll be setting up in the dark.

The swim course is held in spring-fed Buffalo Springs Lake, always pleasantly clean and cool, permitting a wetsuit swim. The first wave starts soon after first light, likely to minimize exposure to the heat and sun while on the bike and run.

Of the four times I have done the race, the swim has been a single-loop counter-clockwise course. It has an in-water start from a sandy beach and finishes on a carpeted ramp with just a few short steps into the transition pen. Several buoys' and a narrow lake width make it virtually impossible to swim off course. Several waves spread athletes out nicely, but leave enough swimmers in close proximity for drafting and easy navigation. Nestled in a canyon and protected from wind, the lake is always calm and current free. All this adds up to exceptionally fast swim times.

The bike course is a one lap, out-and-back type course with several significant climbs and screaming descents. Immediately after leaving transition, you are in your small-front-ring/big-rear-cog combo, climbing the hill back towards the park entrance. My experience has been that if you overwork that first hill, it seemingly takes forever to get your heart rate back where it belongs and you'll pay miserably for your early ambitions while out on the run.

The bike leg includes mid-Texas' best scenery, with everything from farmland, wooded areas and open prairie with sage brush, to cattle, coyotes, birds of prey, and even the occasional tarantula on the road.

Regardless of where you are on the bike course or in what cardinal direction you're pointed, the wind always seems to be almost in your face or definitely in your face. The reprieves come during the several long descents, or on the numerous climbs. Of note is one particularly cruel climb (and subsequent descent) known as the "corkscrew," a steep section of road with several hairpin turns on it.

My first year after completing the race I asked an official why there were hay bales on the curves of the corkscrew. His answer? He said they keep the less cautious athletes from plummeting off the road and into the canyon when they overshoot the curves. The next year I got to see a competitor first-hand test the hay bales' stopping power along with Trek's® bike crash replacement program. I was on the way up; he was on the way down and lucky for me, in the outside lane.

The run follows along the lake's upper end and winds its way through a residential area shaded by trees, but absent of wind. Several spectators line the route encouraging athletes on with cheers and multiple other methods of espousal. Towards the third mile, the first substantial hill introduces itself, and boldly so if you overworked the climbs on the bike. Atop the hill, you find yourself facing Texas prairie and the blazing sun, which often drives temperatures in the upper 90s or 100s on race day.

Conquering the second major climb, runners embark on what I call "the longest mile," a straight and very long section of road where runners can see the halfway point and run turnaround. A large factory building stands out against the horizon in the distance, which measures your progress for you as you head towards the turn.

On the way back, after facing a final menacing third climb occurring at about three-quarters of the way through the run leg, competitors drop back into the lake canyon, to the welcome relief of shade from a few trees and the fervent cheers of spectators. The music and finish line announcers can be heard closing in two miles from the finish, and at mile 12, the finish area becomes visible momentarily; compounding the desire to finish and end the race-pain this course is renowned for.

Finishers cross the line and are congratulated by enthusiastic catchers and a significant finisher's medal. From there it's only a few short steps to the aid, massage and refreshments tents. Being Texas, the race naturally offers ice cold beer and a variety of other drinks and eats to replenish fluids and calories lost during the race.

Of course, there's no excuse to go nutritionally deprived when running the BSLT race. Both the bike and run legs have substantial aid stations located smartly along their routes, which are amply stocked with all the race-day essentials. I have yet to see run aid stations exhaust their supply of ice which for me is a much needed commodity essential for cooling during the run.

The BSLT provides distinctive finishers awards for the top age group finishers and professional athletes, and offers qualifying slots for the Ironman World Championship in Hawaii. It also is a qualifier for the World Championship 70.3

in Clearwater, Florida. The BSLT race t-shirt remains one of the best designs out there, and it always draws comments from fellow triathletes and wanna-be's as well.

This gem of a race rarely fills up until just prior to the event, so you don't have to worry about solidifying your race calendar a year in advance just to secure a spot on the starting line. And not least to mention is the big Texas hospitality and enthusiasm extended athletes from locals and race supporters throughout race weekend. I've witnessed just about every type of imaginable athlete encouragement on the BSLT race course, contributing to why this race will always remain one of my favorites!

About the Author

John Shafer is an active duty career Marine Corps infantry officer who discovered triathlon in early 1998. That spring, after nearly 20 years of competitive running, his need for cross-training developed out of necessity as his knees just couldn't keep pace with the high mileage running routine he had developed over the years. Coming from a multiple marathon history, having on-and-off again affairs with a mountain bike, and having served as a Marine Corps water safety and swim instructor; triathlon seemed to be the logical progression.

John soon developed an insatiable desire to train and compete, registering for 10-12 races a season much to the chagrin of his wife and family. As an older age-group athlete, he migrated toward the longer course races, finding that the long and ultra course races were the distances where his slowing cadence seemed to be most competitive.

Having to date completed nearly 100 triathlons of all distances, with 18 ultra course races (including four Hawaii Ironman races) and over 50 long course finishes all across North America, he has found the long course to be his preferred distance.

Not a day since has passed where triathlon has not been of influence in John's life. Whether training, racing, coaching, or utilizing his multisport experience to inspire others to accept mental or physical challenges, triathlon and its many parts have had a positive impact on him and those around him. In John's words, "Triathlon is truly 'my sport,' and the BSLT is truly 'my course!'"

Spirit of Morgantown Triathlon

Race Distance: Long
1.2 Mile Swim, 56 Mile Bike, 13.1 Mile Run
Month: June
Race Web Site: www.spiritofmorgantown.com

Author: Jennifer Ragone
Racing Category: Age Group 35-39

I was preparing for my first ultra distance triathlon. I felt good about my training, and I was looking for a long course race to test my fitness level about a month prior. So when I found out about the MedExpress Spirit of Morgantown Triathlon, (formerly known as the Mountaineer Triathlon) a long course race in Morgantown, West Virginia (home of West Virginia University) I immediately signed up.

The MedExpress Spirit of Morgantown Triathlon takes place in late June. The race promoter, HFP Racing, is known in the triathlon community for both the high quality of its races and the difficulty of its race courses. The web site for this race specifically stated that the MedExpress Mountaineer Triathlon would be a perfect "final tune-up for those racing in Ironman® Lake Placid four weeks later." In HFP terminology, I knew that meant, "Get ready to climb some major hills on the bike!" This event also had a prize purse of $25,000, so I knew it would attract some stellar athletes, which always makes my race experience more exciting.

Driving into Morgantown with my friend, Aaron, two things were evident, there was no flat terrain anywhere nearby, and the area was a typical college town. The host hotel for the race, the Waterfront Place Hotel, was located in downtown Morgantown and was extremely close to the swim start and the transition area. It was an easy quarter mile walk from the front door of the hotel to the transition area.

The hotel had all the amenities we could need. Check in for the race was located in the hotel and as always, HFP was very organized. The entire check-in process took less than 10 minutes and the volunteers were

very very knowledgeable about what needed to be done the night before the race — such as racking bikes — and what could wait until race morning. Aaron and I racked our bikes in the transition area, which was located in a parking garage 20 meters from the swim exit. Knowing the transition area would be covered made setting up hassle-free; we did not need to worry about anything getting wet if it rained.

The low key nature of this event and the surrounding area certainly made me feel stress free, with the only concern being, "Where can we get some good food for dinner?" Aaron and I met up with our friend, Hope (who was also in town for the race), to find some food. We ended up eating at a typical college bar — the wobbly tables and the smell of stale beer came at no extra charge.

The food was great, especially the onion rings! However, we learned not to expect fast service in that part of town. The server apologized for the long wait for our food, but we didn't mind. It was a nice summer evening, and we enjoyed sitting at our table outside, looking over the Monongahela River. We topped off our evening with some dessert as we stopped at a gas station, where the three of us promptly loaded up on Junior Mints®, Twizzlers®, Reeses Pieces®, and the infamous Now and Laters®, just to name a few goodies!

Race morning arrived in the form of a wake up call from the front desk. The weather forecast called for sunny skies and temperatures in the mid 70s. But forecasts are so rarely correct that it should not have come as a surprise when I walked out of the hotel to cool temperatures, cloudy skies and a light drizzle. While walking to the transition area, I couldn't help but think, "Nothing like swimming, biking, and running in the rain to start off a Sunday." I enjoy racing in the rain, for me, it was a relief to know I would have cloud cover rather than the scorching sun.

After double checking my transition area, we headed down to the swim start, which is a quarter mile beyond the transition area. The swim takes place in the Monongahela River, known locally as the "Mon River." Morgantown and HFP had arranged for the Mon River Dam downstream and the Mon River Lock upstream to be closed during race morning. This eliminated the current in the river and allowed for a narrow rectangle course to be used for the swim.

Wetsuits were allowed, since the water temperature was in the low 70s. Before the race director starting asking the athletes to enter the water, I couldn't help but notice how relaxed everyone was. Knowing the Type-A personality of most triathletes, it was refreshing to see most of the competitors standing around in the misting rain, joking with one another, as if we were all hanging out at the beach for the day with our family and friends. Even though everyone was there to race hard — there were even a few internationally known pros in the crowd — there was none of the high-strung nervousness that I see at so many other races. I have come to realize that the friendly, low-strung atmosphere is not just a characteristic of the MedExpress Spirit of Morgantown Triathlon; it's a signature of all HFP events.

I entered the water with 30 other women in my wave. We waded out to the starting line to tread water until the gun went off. When the gun fired to signal the start of the race, I began swimming in the upstream direction (upstream, that is, if there had been any current), toward the first buoy. I thought to myself that I couldn't believe how clean and calm the water was. Because my wave was so small, I had all the room in the world to swim. I didn't have to worry about getting caught in the melee that can sometimes erupt at the start of a race.

The swim course forms most of a rectangle. We started by swimming a small distance upstream to the first buoy. At the upstream buoy, we turned left to swim to the middle of the river, before turning left once again, to reach the long, downstream part of the course. Another left turn brought us close to the shore again, where we swam a small distance upstream to reach the swim exit (which was downstream from the swim entrance). I had some trouble getting into a rhythm with my stroke early in the swim, but by the time I reached the downstream stretch, I had settled in. Once I started to relax, I began to appreciate the calm water, the lack of current, the small size of my wave, and even the large size of the buoys, which made them easy to site!

Exiting the swim involved climbing up a ramp to reach dry land. There were volunteers on each side of the ramp to assist the athletes out of the water in an organized fashion. The exit went smoothly for me, and once I was out of the water, it was a short, 20 meter run to the transition area.

It was still raining, so having the transition area in a covered parking garage made a big difference. I was pleasantly surprised to see that many of the bikes for the women in my age group were still racked. I knew that during the bike ride, I could catch some of the faster swimmers, so I was eager to start riding.

In a well-rehearsed, precision dance of transformation, I stripped out of my wetsuit. Hardly more than a fraction of a second later, I had donned my helmet, sunglasses and bike shoes, and I was heading out of T1. Spectators who had the good fortune to not have blinked at the wrong moment couldn't help but comment on the speed and grace with which I performed my transition.

The bike course started in downtown Morgantown. While riding through Morgantown, it seemed like every few seconds I passed a volunteer telling me which way to go, controlling traffic, pointing out particularly slick spots on the road or simply cheering for the athletes. Within the first mile, I took a left turn, as instructed by a volunteer, to cross a bridge over the Mon River and to leave town. Across the river, there weren't many spectators. The rain began to fall a little harder, so I took off my sunglasses, and put them in my jersey pocket. It was time to settle in and ride.

The bike course had a distance marker every five miles. I passed the first five mile mark on a flat section of road along the Mon River. I was beginning to wonder where the hills were. I thought that I might not get my money's worth of climbing during this race. I had only started to have those thoughts when Fort Martin Road took a turn away from the river. I looked ahead of me, up a long, steady grade, and saw a string of racers sitting up and trying to spin, or out of the saddle and grinding gears, just trying to make it to the top. I wanted to shout, "Now THAT'S what I'm talking about!" I came to Morgantown for the hills, and I finally found them. I shifted down the gears, and spun up the hill, occasionally telling the big guys who were huffing and puffing, "Keep it up!" or, "Good job!" as I passed them with a smile.

To my delight, the hills continued, but so did the rain. It was not terrible rain. In fact, with the rain to keep us cool, the day was quite comfortable. However, there were some sections of the bike course where the road surface was somewhat rough. To the credit of HFP and the race volunteers, the sections of road that had some hazards had been meticulously marked with orange surveyors' paint --- every pothole or significant crack in the road was marked bright orange and visible from a distance. So the rain and markings on the road provided a slight distraction from my main goals for the bike ride: climbing hills and passing people.

The course meandered along country roads that tried to follow the general contours of the landscape. A map of the area shows long ribbons of road cutting through empty spaces. There were not many turns on the course. But even if they had not been well marked and staffed by volunteers directing cyclists, there would not have been many opportunities to get off course. There just are not many intersections on those roads.

I followed the volunteers and other cyclists. I passed the first aid station at mile 14, near the point where the bike course crosses the West Virginia-Pennsylvania border. They had a full assortment of water, electrolyte replacement fluid, ice, and gel. I didn't need anything yet, so I continued to ride. A two mile, relatively flat out-and-back section gave me an opportunity to see who was just ahead of me, and who was just behind me. I was excited to see my friend, Hope, ahead of me during this section. We gave a smile and a cheer to each other in passing. Then I put my head back down, and continued to work. I arrived back at the river, near the beginning of Fort Martin Road. I had completed the large loop of the course; it was time to head back to the transition area on the same road we had ridden out of town.

I pushed myself back to the bridge over the river, I crossed into town, and I arrived at the transition area. As I approached the entrance to the transition area, a volunteer directed me to turn around, and head back out. I was only half way through my ride. Now that I knew the course, it was time to do it all over again! The second loop of the bike was just as much fun as the first. I had been riding as many hills as I could find during training. All of those hills paid off during the second loop of the bike course. I almost had a perfect ride... almost.

I spun up Fort Martin Road, I thanked the volunteers who staffed the turns on the course, I cruised through the out-and-back section. But a mile before finishing that second loop of the bike, for the first time during the ride, another woman passed me. When a guy gets passed by a woman, they call it, "getting chicked." When I get passed by a woman, I call it, "incentive to pick up the pace!" After all, we still had a half marathon to run.

Like the bike, the run is a two loop course. The first half of each loop is an out-and-back along the river, downstream of the transition area, and the second half of each loop is a loop through neighborhoods upstream of the transition area. I had another spectacular transition, then I left the transition area to start my half marathon. Volunteers directed me along the course, past an aid station fully stocked with cookies, bananas and pretzels in addition to all the usual aid station treats. I worked on finding my rhythm as I ran on the pancake flat path along the river, and I thought about the advice my friend and coach, Brady, had given me before the race. "Run a swift pace and find your rhythm. Give 110 percent. You should have nothing left in the tank when you cross the finish line."

About five minutes into my run, I saw Aaron running in the other direction. He was a mile or two ahead of me, and almost done with the first half of the first loop. He was flying, and as usual, he was having fun while doing it. I heard him say, "Alright Jenny-J!" Then, within seconds, he was gone. Not long after that, I saw Hope, also running in the other direction. She was smiling as usual, and picking off the men, one by one. "Getting chicked" is taken to an entirely new level when Hope is racing! We exchanged a high five as we passed, then she was gone.

By the time I reached the turn-around, the rain has stopped (momentarily, at least). I noticed that many of the athletes had some white cake-like film on their shirts, so I made sure I took some extra electrolyte fluid at the mile two aid station.

Heading back into town, I started to notice the number of spectators had increased dramatically. They were mostly college students who looked as if they had just woken up.

I completed the first part of the course — the out-and-back that was downstream of the transition area. After passing the transition area and then the finish line, I began the upstream half of the course. Whereas the downstream half was a flat out-and-back, I knew that I had to look forward to something called "Devil's Hill" in the next few miles. The trail along the river became a dirt path, and I wondered when The Hill would come. When I finally reached the right turn that was at the bottom of the hill, I didn't just see the hill, I came face to face with the devil himself! The hill is a steep grade, with an aid station at the top. But to get there, you have to pass the devil. Or, at least, you have to pass someone dressed up as the devil, welcoming you to his hill and encouraging you not to walk.

At the top of the hill was another right turn to continue through some residential neighborhoods, and then some city blocks. There were a few low grade climbs before I got to the short downhill that brought me back toward the transition area where I found the sign that said. "Finish to your right, Second loop to your left" So off I went to start my second loop. Again, I saw Aaron and Hope along the course, smiling contently.

I continued to hold a decent and consistent pace and started to notice that many of the competitors had slowed down. That meant that I could just focus on passing other racers. There is nothing like passing some people to build your confidence and make you think that you are invincible. But it couldn't last. My world started to shatter as I realized that the second time up Devil's Hill would require a bit of walking, much to the dismay of the devil (or the costume-wearing college student). Once that hill was behind me, it was smooth sailing back to the sign that said, "Finishers to your right, Second loop to your left." This time, I made a right and felt great as I ran down the finish chute and crossed the finish line.

There was a large crowd of spectators at the finish. As I turned around and starting approaching the food table, I witnessed a great moment. A woman was about to cross the finish line. As she came cruising along, I realized that one of her legs was a prosthetic device. Immediately after finishing the race, both of her children ran up to hug her. I overheard her daughter say, "Mom, one day I want to be able to run as fast as you and have as much fun as you do when you run... And, it's really cool that you passed so many boys!" I walked away with a smile on my face. What a great way to spend a Sunday: swimming, biking, and running on the hills and in the rain!

About the Author

Jennifer Ragone is a Senior Human Resources Consultant with a Global Information Technology Company. She lives in Ashburn, VA with her dog, Lucy. She began racing triathlon seven years ago, and competes in ultra distance trail runs during the fall and winter months. She enjoys long distance triathlons and ultra runs and has finished three ultra distance triathlons, several 50K trail runs, and a 40 mile trail run in Uwharrie State Park, North Carolina. When not working, swimming, biking, or running, Jennifer is usually baking and spending time with her friends and family.

Tupper Lake Tinman Triathlon

tupper lake, new york

Race Distance: Long
1.2 Mile Swim, 56 Mile Bike, 13.1 Mile Run
Month: June
Race Web Site: www.tupperlakeinfo.com/tinman

Author: Debi Bernardes
Racing Category: Age Group 45-49

I'm riding along on the Tupper Lake Tinman Triathlon bike course at a comfortable speed, or as comfortable as one can be for a hilly 56-mile race, when all of a sudden I feel like I'm driving one of those big cushy Cadillacs. You know the kind I'm talking about? The two-tone paint job, big rubber wheels that look like marshmallows, where you feel no bumps, but just the gentle wave over the rough roads?

I look behind me at my rear wheel…is it flat? Say it isn't so! CRAP! Well, that really wasn't the word that came out, but I will pretend to have some consideration for others of finer sensibilities. I quickly get off the bike, feel the rear wheel, and again confirm to myself that yes indeed, I do have a flat. I had just gotten past the halfway point of the bike course and I was in the top eight when this flat sidelined me. At this point my husband rides by me and yells out, "Are you okay?"

All I can yell back at him as he zips past is a big loud, "Yeah, I'm flat!"

Let's go back to the beginning.

We are competing at the Tupper Lake Tinman in upstate New York, Tupper Lake is located about 45 minutes west of Lake Placid, home of the 1980 and 1932 Olympics, and some really great scenery. The race is a 1.2 mile swim, 56 mile bike, and the run is a hellacious 13.1 mile course. The weather is absolutely freaking perfect!

I had decided to try this race as it gave me a chance to check out the Ironman USA course, and it would be a perfect long weekend vacation for my husband and me. We signed up in early January because the race has a history of closing pretty quickly, but not as fast as some of the more famous long course races on the East Coast. The cost of the event is very reasonable, and I knew that there would be some great competition because of the prize money that is awarded.

This is an event that is managed by the home town, and I mean the WHOLE town is in support of the race from start to finish. It's one of those races that you feel honored to compete in as everyone makes you feel like a super-star when you show up.

We had decided to forgo the usual hotel stay as there weren't that many places within a short driving distance for an early morning start, and instead chose to stay at the local campground about two miles from the race start. Since we are also cheap, we also didn't want to pay the higher prices in Lake Placid. Staying in Saranac Lake is also an option as it is about a 30 minute drive from there to Tupper Lake.

There is also a lack of dining facilities in this small town. So don't expect to see a Starbucks® unless you are staying in Lake Placid itself. But the local grocery stores more than fulfill your needs.

Race morning comes, and the local crow wakes us up. Who needs an alarm clock when you have a bird "croaking" away at 5:00 a.m. right above your tent? We make our coffee and oatmeal and then head over to the race. After setting up my bike in transition, I head over to the porta-potty line for the millionth time, only to see this one guy trying to figure out which potty he should go into.

He had two open ones in front of him, a big line behind him and he is standing there like he's on Let's Make a Deal trying to decide which one he should enter. At this point I yell, "Pick the one on the left Bob!" Yes, it is the world-famous writer Hurricane Bob! He quickly gives me a hug and goes into the potty on the left. Did he win the grand prize? Only Bob and Monty Hall can tell us.

My job today was to run past Bob on the course. I know he's a decent swimmer; he's a much better cyclist than I am, and he would have a 10 minute head start on me. I decide that I will have to swim as well as him, and hope that he doesn't go 15 minutes faster than me on the bike if I want to run past him later in the race. Game on!

The swim consists of a straight out-and-back on a lake that is clean and has a perfect temperature for a sleeveless or long sleeve wetsuit. Unfortunately, the swim course has the sun right in your face as you head back to the finish. I was able to find some poor guy's feet to draft off of on the outward bound portion of the course. I kept poking his toes, and then I tried to stay away from him to give him a break only to find him again as I headed back home to transition. It's a good thing that we had all those other waves of swimmers in front of us, because you know you're on course if there is a whole pack of swimmers you are passing from 1-3 waves before you. They are always very careful about sighting, and usually stop frequently (maybe every five strokes it seems) to make sure they stay on course. So I was able to use them to stay on course versus poking my head up and getting blinded by the sun.

The bike course is made for cruising with a capital "C." I'm having a great time, riding faster than expected. This is a fun course! Sure, it has hills galore, but they are fun hills. You leave Tupper Lake proper on flat roads, and very soon you are going up and going down. Before you know it you are at the turn around point, and it's time to fly back home. And just where was my husband? I expected him to pass me before the turn around!

Back to the flat: I hook my bike up onto the guardrail so that my fluids don't drain out of my "sippy" cup. I quickly put it in the small ring of the back cog set to make it easier to remove the tire, and put back later on. I'm a NASCAR® pit crew in operation! I open up my repair kit; grab everything out of it and search and search and "ARGHHHH!" Where are my freaking tire pry bars? They must be hiding somewhere in the little four inch bag. I know they were in here the last time I helped a friend with a flat. (Note to self: Check repair kit before you race.)

Finally, I give up and see what I do have that can help me get the tire off the rims of my 404s. I have an Allen wrench I try to use, only to get one part of the tire off. I need another object to help finish removing the tire. I start walking up the road towards a parking lot about 75 meters from where I'm parked. As I head up there I keep my head down and look at the road debris hoping I will find something else that can help me out. Think "MacGyver" an old 80s TV show. Ah-ha! I find a large piece of metal solder wire. I hope that it is stiff enough to help me out. I trot back to the bike, and within seconds I have my tire off! The first challenge is out of the way and I wasn't going to think about how I would get the tire back on.

I get the new tube in place and I am able to roll the tire back onto the wheel easily. Believe it or not, I get the whole thing back on by hand using the Zen method. Slow, steady, with no pressure, breathe in, breathe out…patience Grasshopper. I then quickly try to remember how to work my CO_2 cartridge, and before you know it, I'm back on the bike riding with the rest of the crowd. Estimated time in the pit is ten minutes. Not a record, but then again, if I hadn't spent so much time swearing and pretending to pull my hair out, and looking like someone who's lost her brains, I would have saved at least three minutes.

Now I just need to get my head back in the game. I had passed a ton of people on the way out, and all of them passed me while I was sitting on the side of the road. This has got to be the hardest thing to do in a race, especially if it's your "A" race of the season. This was my "A" race, of all the races for this to happen, it had to be this one.

You know there is no way you can make up that lost time. It's gone, over, history and "yes, we have no bananas." I almost want to quit right then. I figure I can do a long run the next day instead. But then I think about Karen Holloway at the race I DNF'd at back in April. That fun-in-the-snowstorm long course duathlon in Richmond where we had to knock the icicles off the seats, race. Karen was in the lead; she had a flat, changed her tire, and believe it or not, got back into the game to finish second. If she could do it, so could I. Sure, I wasn't going to get second (and I wasn't a pro) but at least I would give it the old college try. In other words, it wasn't over until the generously proportioned woman SANG!

Get off the bike in 3:02 (went from 46th overall to 348th overall).

The run course is interesting, and there is never a dull moment on this course. The run portion of a triathlon is something that I always look forward to every time I get off the bike. Before I forget, my motto for the day was to be "I love hills" to keep things positive. So yes, I love hills. Especially hills that basically last three miles long. And they are the first three miles of the race. Did I say, "I love hills?"

Just to let you know, I never pay attention to my mile splits during a race as this helps to keep my anxiety level down. If you don't know how fast you're going (or not) it's never going to hurt you. Relentless forward pursuit and you've got to love those hills.

It's right around mile two that I go past Bob as he is headed in the opposite direction. I'm thinking, "Oh good, he's only about a mile in front of me." Wrong! It turns out there was a big loop I still had in front of me and Bob was just cruising past the six mile mark at that time. It became apparently clear to me that he would have to do a lot of walking if I were to catch him, and I knew this wasn't going to happen as he looked way too coherent.

My plan for the run is to follow the 10 minute run/30 second walk routine. I would pop a Cliff Shot Block® into my mouth at that time, suck on it and try not to choke on the little bites that accidentally went down my throat. Then I grab some water at the aid stations.

I spent the remainder of the race passing about 100+ people on the run, and basically enjoyed myself as I managed to keep my heart rate under control. This is a tough course with a wide variety of changing terrain. From the sand on small trails as you cross abandoned train tracks, to the trail in the woods that is just plain fun. There is some good news though, as the last three miles are pretty flat. I continue to keep my momentum going, and feel great until we hit the final 200 meters which is on a sandy field with a lot of bumps in the terrain. At this point I was just sort of numb as I crossed the finish line about 12 minutes slower than my goal time, but with that flat tire I will take it gladly. And Bob beat me.

Would I do this race again? In a "New York minute!" (I couldn't resist!).

About the Author

Debi Bernardes is a professional multi-sport coach, athlete for over 35 years, mother of two and wife to only one guy. In Debi's own words, "I used to be slow, but through determination and pleasure I have improved as I've aged. If I can do it, so can you!"

Muncie Endurathon

m u n c i e ,   i n d i a n a

Race Distance: Long
1.2 Mile Swim, 56 Mile Bike, 13.1 Mile Run
Month: July
Race Web Site: www.muncieendurathon.com

Author: Marc A. Nester
Racing Category: Age Group 30-34

Who would ever think that one of the oldest and best run triathlon races would be set in the small, rural town of Muncie, Indiana? The Muncie Endurathon is just that race! The history of this race began on September 13, 1980 and is considered to be the oldest long course race in the world. At one time, this fantastic race was the host to the International Triathlon Union long distance world championship and numerous USA Triathlon long distance nationals. Although the race was originally held during the month of September, it now takes place in the balmy month of July.

Athletes can expect warm and humid race day conditions. Although the race is wetsuit legal, the scorching July weather warms the serene Prairie Creek Reservoir where the swim take place, to temperatures that skirt on making wetsuits illegal on race day. Although there are not any qualifications for this race, the rolling hills on the bike and the challenging reservoir run makes for a arduous day, even for highly trained athletes.

While putting together my racing schedule for the year, I consulted my triathlon coach who gave me a few ideas for races that would not only fit into my schedule, but also prepare me the best for my ultra distance race in August. After a few discussions we decided that Muncie would be the best long course race for me. The Muncie Endurathon was similar to the ultra course I'd be racing in terms of terrain and race day conditions. Therefore the race was going to provide a great way for me to test my fitness, race and nutritional strategies that I would be using later in the season.

Signing up for the race was easy and took very little time. There were no extra fees for signing up online, which is nice compared to many races. Also, any updates and important information about the race was emailed to registered athletes up until race day.

After taking a quick flight from Washington, DC, I arrived safely in Indianapolis, Indiana. Following the flight, I had an easy one hour drive to Muncie. Upon arriving in Muncie, I proceeded to check into my hotel, which was the Holiday Inn Express. The Holiday Inn Express was the sponsor hotel of the race and was close to the race site. The hotel itself wasn't a five star establishiment, but it did provide a comfortable, clean place to sleep each night and the people working there were very helpful and friendly. There appeared to be other options for housing within the city, but I prefer to choose the sponsored hotel if possible. The race also offers free indoor housing to 50 athletes at the Harris Chapel, which is located on the actual race course. The church donates their facilities and provides cots for the athletes to sleep on. Also provided is breakfast, consisting of bagels, fruit, and juice for all staying on their grounds. In order to secure indoor accommodations at the Harris Chapel, athletes need to email muncieendurathon@yahoo.com and provide the number of people needing lodging.

The pre-race meetings and race expo take place at the Horizon Convention Center. After arriving at the convention center, check-in was very easy and well organized. The Midwest charm of the volunteers was evident throughout the check-in process and carried over to the race. The pre-race meeting was mandatory for those people who haven't raced Muncie before and is recommended for everyone so that they are informed of any race changes.

The pre-race meeting was very informative and was very professionally presented. They went over the course in extreme detail and even explained where each aid station was going to be placed on the bike and run courses. In addition, the head USAT referee for the race provided information about the rules and expectations of each athlete. He went into each facet of the race and explained the common penalties and how to avoid them. He also informed all the athletes participating in the race that he and his staff would be inspecting each individual helmet to ensure that everyone had the proper USA safety certification. He made a big deal about athletes trying to use helmets that were only approved in Europe and not in the United States. We were informed that we would be disqualified if we tried to race with a helmet that was not sanctioned by USAT. Unfortunately I was one of those athletes who had a helmet that wasn't approved yet in the United States so I had to either buy a new one or risk getting disqualified. Actually a fellow participant overheard my conversation with the race director and head referee and offered to lend me an extra helmet that he had.

At the race expo there were a variety of vendors that sold the basics needed by a triathlete on race day, but I thought that it could have been better. I think that the apparel selection was slim and that the vendors could have provided more selections overall. I would have liked to have seen some of the race sponsors at the expo. One of the "cool factors" of the expo was that they had FitTech, Inc. (now T3 Multisport) available to answer questions regarding bike fit and performance testing. They also gave exclusive deals to Muncie participants for their services.

Race day was very well coordinated and happy volunteers helped direct athletes and spectators to parking and to the transition area. The transition area was located in the grass and there were plenty of portable toilets for the athletes to use. The area was clean and there was ample room for racking bikes and all the other gear needed for the race. It was nice to see that the referees did verify with everyone to make sure that they had racked their bike in the correct place or risk a penalty.

The transition area was also secure and the volunteers were very strict about only allowing athletes in and out of the area. The race director was very diligent about providing time updates to let the athletes know how much time they had before the race began. He announced when the transition area was going to close numerous times, which provided athletes enough time to venture on down to the swim course.

The race course was very challenging, yet rewarding. The swim was in a picturesque body of water that was very clean and calm. The most challenging part about the swim wasn't the distance, but locating the buoys for navigation. The warm sun bounced off the water making accurate navigation nearly impossible. After making the last right turn to come back to the start of the swim, the sun shone directly in my eyes, making it difficult to see. Many participants had longer swim times because of the sun. I know that I had to stop a few times and take off my goggles to ensure that I was still on course.

After the swim, there was a short jaunt up a hill to the transition area, which made my heart-rate spike. Once on my bike, I immediately noticed the gently rolling hills. The roads are mostly well paved and felt particularly smooth, except for the last few miles of the ride where the roads were a bit bumpy. The ride itself is challenging because it is on wide open rural roads, so even if there is the slightest breeze, you feel it.

All of the intersections were properly manned by the local police department and volunteers. The race was also properly marshaled and athletes were not able to draft off one another without receiving a penalty. Aid stations on the bike course were located approximately every nine miles and they were properly stocked and maintained by the volunteers.

Much of the bike course is on local highways, so it isn't very spectator friendly. However, the volunteers always made sure to scream out words of encouragement, providing at times a much needed boost of energy.

Although the bike course had some rolling hills, the most challenging part of the Muncie Endurathon is clearly the run. The run course around the Prairie Creek Reservoir tests the most seasoned triathlete. The run takes place on very smooth road surfaces, but is not shaded at all. So not only do you have to worry about all the hills to go up and down, but also the sun beating down on you for 13.1 miles.

Because of the challenge, the run course is very well marked and very well staffed with volunteers. The run is an out-and-back course, so there are good opportunities for spectators to watch their favorite athlete on the run. Once again, I noticed the Midwest charm and much appreciated it at the aid stations and throughout the entire run. The volunteers were great throughout the race but most notably on the run.

Aid stations were located about every mile or so and were stocked with plenty of fluids and cold towels.

At the end of a daunting run course, there is one final, long up-hill at mile 13 before crossing the finish line.

The Muncie Endurathon was my 18th triathlon and 4th long course race. On race day, the weather cooperated very well and cooled off the reservoir water to a manageable 77 degrees, making wetsuits legal race morning. Luckily the "wind gods" were feeling friendly, because the winds were very light during most of the bike; allowing me to stay within myself for the bike portion of the race. However, by the time the run started, the heat had set in and the temperatures were in the upper 80s. I noticed the heat on the run right away.

By mile six of the run, my feet hurt with every step. Even though I was wearing socks, I managed to acquire severe blood blisters on both feet. I attribute this to the humid conditions that made my feet extremely moist. After crossing the finish line, I went straight to the medical tent to be tended to. The medical staff was more than friendly and very accommodating in order to treat my minor injury.

This race is a must do for athletes who enjoy a first class race and a challenging course. The grassroots feeling and the Midwest charm are hard to beat qualities in any race, not to mention that this race is said to be the oldest long course race in the world. From the race director down to the volunteers, all are willing to help in any way they can to make an athlete's experience the best that it can be. The course provides a formidable challenge to any athlete, but first timers should not be afraid or deterred from signing up. The entire staff makes each athlete feel at home and their words of encouragement throughout the race will help all athletes dig deep in order to cross the finish line. I know that my name will be on the list of participants for the race in years to come!

About the Author

Marc Nester completed his first triathlon in 2001 and has been hooked ever since. At the time, he thought that a short course race was long enough and that he would never have the desire to compete in anything longer. Boy was he wrong! In his own words, Marc feels that "training and racing in triathlons has provided me with a healthy outlet to life's stresses, and has provided me with unique goals to strive toward." Marc is a member of his local triathlon club (DC Triclub) and will be a mentor this year for their New Triathlon Program. For the 2008 season, Marc was selected as a sponsored athlete and team member of Team Aquaphor.

Musselman Triathlon

geneva, new york

Race Distance: Long
1.2 Mile Swim, 56 Mile Bike, 13.1 Mile Run
Month: July
Website: www.musselmantri.com

Author: Christopher Martin
Racing Category: Professional

Entering only its 6th year, the Musselman Triathloquickly moving to the top of triathletes' "must do" lists thanks to word of mouth advertising from past entrants. The event comprises a weekend of activities that will keep you busy and entertained during your entire visit to the town of Geneva in New York. The race itself is challenging, scenic, and fun. It is one of the few events that truly has something for everyone whether you are a newbie or pro, recreational triathlete or masochist, nutritional health nut or oenophile, budget-conscious or luxury traveler. Race director Jeff Henderson is an avid top-level triathlete who has created this event to showcase the best that his hometown has to offer.

Geneva is located at the northern end of Lake Seneca in upstate New York's Finger Lakes region. This region is popular among Northeastern ers and Canadians for its lush rolling hills, beautiful lakes, and bountiful supply of vineyards. Perhaps not as well known as other Finger Lakes region towns such as Watkins Glen and Ithaca, Geneva boasts a vibrant small town community complete with a historic downtown from the town's prior standing as a center of regional water and rail trade in the early 20th century.

Geneva is a reasonable five to six hour drive for city slickers in Boston, New York City, and Philadelphia. Destination triathletes will find Geneva an easy hour drive from the Syracuse Airport.

The event consists of a short course distance event on Saturday morning and a long course distance race on Sunday. These races are staged out of Seneca Lake State Park, which offers ample parking, well-maintained facilities, and beautiful lake front views. Competitors with superhuman

MUSSELMAN TRIATHLON

recovery powers are encouraged to sign up for the DoubleMussel which honors the fastest combined time for both races. On Saturday afternoon, many of North America's up-and-coming professional triathletes take the stage in the fan-friendly draft-legal International Triathlon Union (ITU) Pan American Cup race that winds through the town's lake front park and downtown.

Registration is quick and painless and chamber of commerce personnel are on hand to answer any questions you have about the region. The expo is located on the campus of Hobart & William Smith Colleges and features a small handful of local retailers in case you forgot to pack anything on your way to the race. Check-in for lodging in the colleges' dormitory home stay program is also handled at registration.

The biggest challenge for Musselman competitors is to find the time to pack race day gear before the race. The afternoon is a non stop slate of activities starting with the trip downtown to watch the constant flow of triathletes sprinting by at top speed in the multi-loop course of the ITU race. After the conclusion of the ITU race, entrants can partake in the pre-race pasta banquet which is included in the entry fee. The banquet typically features a talk from a guest speaker from amongst the professional elites proceeded by the award ceremony for the ITU race.

Before heading to bed, competitors can hustle back over to the college campus to listen to last minute pre-race instructions from the race director, always presented in an entertaining manner while utilizing the lecture hall's audio-visual capabilities.

If Musselman has a weakness, it is the swim course. While the lake is beautiful and inviting, it is also very shallow at Seneca Lake State Park. Wading out 200 to 300 yards only gets you to a waist-deep water depth. The long course swim is set up as a two loop triangular course with an in-water start, but the long walk in waist deep water from the end of the second loop to the swim exit is a major hindrance to fast swim times. To further slow your swim split, the prevailing summer winds blow from west to east, creating a chop and current that needs to be navigated. The wetsuit-legal swim portion of the race is a test of persistence and navigation tactics.

The Musselman Triathlon is named for the razor mussels that populate the lake. However, don't be scared off by tales of past competitors getting cuts on their feet by the mussels. The mussels only live in the rocky areas of the lake floor, so as long as you only step on the sandy bottom which extends from the shoreline out several hundred yards, you will be fine.

Any limitations of the swim course are quickly forgotten once your trusty stead is mounted and rolling through the scenic bike course. The bike course heads south along the eastern shore of Seneca Lake, then turns east toward the shore of neighboring Cayuga Lake. After a brief respite on a flat stretch northward along the lakeshore drive on Cayuga Lake, the route returns westward back to Geneva across rolling farmland.

While traveling the roads that run along the lake shores, competitors are faced with the tough choice of sitting up and enjoying the pretty views or putting their heads down and hammering at top speed. When crossing the Mennonite farming communities that separate the lakes, competitors are treated to occasional obstacles in the form of horse and buggies to break up their rhythm. Due to the prevailing west to east wind, the toughest section of the bike course is typically the final 12 miles back in the headwind as they roll up and down back towards Seneca Lake.

Five fully stocked aid stations complete with water, nutrition products, and fruit serve the bike course. If these choices are not to your liking, you can take advantage of the special needs bag drop, an option not usually found outside of ultra distance events. Competitors seeking additional replenishment beyond officially-sanctioned options (or those seeking solace from a poor race) can stop at one of the five wineries that line the course.

Overall, the bike course is attractive to both beginners and experts alike. The course is not sufficiently difficult to deter anyone from doing this race as their first long course triathlon, but the mix of terrain and conditions will challenge those athletes seeking fast splits and top placement.

While the bike course provides an excellent variety of terrain and scenery, the run course goes above and beyond. It includes everything from flat lakeshore paths, winding downtown streets, quiet neighborhood roads, and rolling gravel trails. A few short, steep climbs and descents mark the halfway point of the run to further separate competitors leading to the homestretch. True to form, the course offers a mix of shaded and non-shaded portions, which can become a significant factor as the heat begins to build on some of the more exceptionally warm days. The run is a true test of one's abilities to run in any and all conditions.

As with the bike course, the eleven aid stations on the run course are well-stocked with refreshments and enthusiastic volunteers. If the official race-provided nutrition is too healthy for your palette, the ice cream shack along the waterfront two miles from the finish line has been known to offer complimentary cones to competitors as they struggle through the final stretch of their race.

The finish area is a bustling hub of activity after the completion of the race. Immediately after finishing, competitors can minimize the soreness they will experience the next day with a relaxing soak in an ice water bath followed by a massage. Recovery is further aided by plentiful quantities of food that include the classic cornerstones of the American diet—pizza and ice cream. The wait for awards is made shorter by watching and cheering on the next generation of triathletes in the Musselkids race. The faster competitors are rewarded for their patience for the awards ceremony with specially labeled bottles of wine from area wineries.

Musselman has not yet sold out, but there is one compelling reason to sign up early—to reserve a room in the dorms of Hobart & William Smith Colleges. Besides being the perfect accommodations for the budget-minded triathlete, living in the dorms with other athletes provides a wonderful social opportunity to make new friends. The college allows the use of its newest dorm, de Cordova Hall, which comes equipped with air conditioning and lounges with televisions tuned to Le Tour de France®. The dorm rooms come with linens for the beds and the college campus is the center of many of the pre-race activities such as registration, the expo, and pre-race meetings.

For more luxury-oriented travelers, the Finger Lakes region is heavily dependent on the tourism industry and thus boasts an extensive repertoire of accommodations from chain hotels to delightful family-owned bed and breakfasts. The recently opened Ramada Inn on the Geneva waterfront will put you right at the center of the racing action and will permit you to roll out of bed and straight into the transition area on Sunday morning.

Jeff Henderson's greatest strength is his ability to recognize that being a triathlete is more than just swimming, biking, and running. It also includes fellowship in a community of athletes. The Musselman weekend brings newcomers and top triathletes together on the same playground and provides a wide variety of activities to allow individuals with diverse backgrounds and histories to meet and forge new friendships. The pre-race banquet, post-race activities, and dormitory-style living all successfully contribute to this open and friendly culture.

The race was created to showcase Geneva and Jeff has successfully convinced the local community to stand up and enthusiastically throw its support behind the race. Local businesses generously provide financial and product support, highlighted by the title sponsor Red Jacket Orchards and their line of unbelievably good juices and fresh fruit that are served at all of the pre and post-race meals. The local townspeople generously come out to staff aid stations and line the streets in town to cheer on competitors. The proceeds from the race are used to support local charitable organizations such as the Geneva Boys and Girls Club. Race organizers even take the time to address global issues such as environmental sustainability by choosing to provide bamboo race t-shirts in lieu of traditional cotton fabrics.

Musselman's greatest strength is that it has the personality of a grassroots event managed on a professional level. Hopefully, this race manages to hold on to its humble and idealistic character as the race continues to grow in stature and size.

About the Author

After six years as a top level amateur triathlete, Chris Martin is trying his luck as a professional triathlete. Realizing he shouldn't quit his day job, Chris continues to work as a full-time chemical engineer, researching areas of heavy oil refining at Headwaters Technology Innovation in Lawrenceville, New Jersey. Chris' goal is to tackle as many of the famous and iconic races in triathlon's young history as he can before his wife Tara makes him grow up and settle into a more traditional lifestyle.

5430 Long Course Triathlon

boulder, colorado

Race Distance: Long
1.2 Mile Swim, 56 Mile Bike, 13.1 Mile Run
Month: August
Race Web Site: www.5430sports.com

Author: Brian Daniel
Racing Category: Age Group 35-39

The third in a triad of progressively longer summer triathlons offered by Boulder, Colorado's 5430 Sports, the 5430 Long Course Triathlon offers a fast course, beautiful scenery and a world class field of competitors.

I have been an avid triathlete (although a mid-pack racer) for many years and I had already competed in the Boulder Triathlon Series once before. The series consists of the 5430 Sprint Triathlon in June, the Boulder Peak Triathlon in July and the 5430 Long Course in August. Thus, I already knew that this race was a classic taking place in my own backyard.

There are no pre-race qualifications that must be met, but the number of competitor spots is limited to the first 1,000 athletes to register. The race normally sells out many weeks prior to the event. One thing to keep in mind, however, is that 5430 Sports offers a great discount to those who register for all three races up front. This is an incredible deal considering the venue, the quality of the races and the swag with which everyone receives. To make registration as easy as possible, 5430 Sports offers an online option, or you can print, fill out and mail in your registration.

The Saturday before the race, everyone convenes at the Boulder Reservoir in order to pick up packets, peruse the expo, attend pre-race meetings and chat with each other before the big day. The pre-race meetings offer an array of information including the latest conditions of the course, a recap of the USAT rules governing the races (the actual referees discuss passing, being passed, what constitutes drafting, penalties, etc.), and an opportunity to ask any questions of the referees and the race directors. In addition, a small intimate gathering always takes place after the main discussion where newbies to the sport or to the distance can

discuss nutrition, training, and pre-race preparation in order to shake off some of the nerves that always accompany competing in your first long course race.

Then race day finally arrives. Even before sunrise, with the transition area open to the athletes at 5:00 a.m., and with a field of approximately 1,000 racers arriving mostly between 5:00 a.m. and 5:30 a.m., the feeling of electricity in the air can be felt as soon as you turn into the gate at the Boulder Reservoir, which is located just north of Boulder. The atmosphere at this race is a mixture of relaxed excitement and extreme professionalism. Owner of 5430 Sports, Barry Siff, has directed more than 40 multi-sport events and, as a competitor, is a four-time ultra distance finisher, has completed over 30 marathons, and also participated in numerous adventure races as the captain of Team Salomon North America. Armed with a distinctive background of racing and directing, Siff leaves virtually nothing to chance when putting on 5430 Sports events. Registration and packet pick up are always smooth, the shirts are always top notch athletic wear (that you can actually use in the gym or on a run or hike), the race set-up and transitions flow easily and without flaw, the course is challenging but fair, every finisher receives a "finisher" item, and the post-race expo is attended by hundreds (who are all treated to free beer, many free samples and exhibits by many of the top vendors related to the sport of triathlon).

Once at the reservoir and out of your car, you pack up your gear and take a short walk down the paved drive to the transition area which is set up in a large parking lot near a pavilion at the swimming beach. Parking at the reservoir is plentiful and is free to competitors and spectators alike until 7:00 a.m. After that time, be aware that your friends and family will be charged in order to get in to watch the race.

The transition area is roomy enough to comfortably allow the athletes to set up gear with just the right amount of elbow room. Free standing four-bike racks line the parking lot and are segmented by age group designation (the race's wave start is delineated by age group). Within the transition area, you get to choose where you want to set up your transition space (again, within your particular age group's designated area), but there is no unfair advantage to any competitor since all the same age groupers (and the pros too) set up their gear within about 70 feet of each other. Announcements are made about every 10 minutes letting the racers know the time, and the amount of time remaining until the transition closes in order to set the timing devices and mats. This usually occurs about 15 minutes before the pro wave start.

After your transition space is prepared and you are ready to race, you can stop for a moment and look around in order to really appreciate what a great venue the Boulder Reservoir provides for triathlons. As the sun begins to rise, you can see many hot air balloons launching in the area, and you can begin to make out the foothills of the Rocky Mountain region beginning to take shape in the West. A short walk then takes you to the beach for the swim start. Don't worry, if nature calls at any time (as it most always does), 5430 Sports provides about 50 port-a-potties all set up facing into, and out of, the transition area. So, even when everyone has the same idea at the same time, the lines for this pre-race tradition at this venue are rarely longer than about five to seven minutes.

Down at the beach, the swim course is set up with good sized orange balloon buoys about every 100 meters and giant yellow triangle buoys about every 500 meters; therefore, sighting is usually not a problem during the swim. Standing on the beach, you can look directly to the east and see that the swim goes out about 700 meters before taking a big 120 degree left turn and heading northwest for about 1,000 meters and then turning left again to head southwest for the final 200 meters before ending at a giant red finishing arch. Seeing the other athletes beginning to gather near the start, you take a deep breath and mentally prepare for the day.

As the time for the pro race nears (6:30 a.m.) you might see notable professional racers either toeing the line or simply hanging out to cheer all the competitors. Boulder is a hotbed of triathlete activity and many of the world's best pros live in or around the city.

Next thing you know, it's finally time to get started. As the minutes count down, the national anthem begins to play, skydivers bombard the reservoir, and a group of white doves is released just as the final skydiver nears the swim finish pulling a huge USA flag. Then the only thing left is the sounding of the starting horn.

Separated by five minute increments, all of the seven waves of athletes enter the water by just after 7:10 a.m. about the same time the pros reach the bike portion of the race. Pursuant to the USTA rules, racers are allowed to wear wetsuits for the swim portion of the race. Some do not; however, the water is usually around 70 degrees no matter what month it is or what the outside temperature is.

The first athletes finish in just under four hours and the last ones finish in just over eight hours. On the faster end, and in an effort to acquire one of the annual one-of-a-kind trophies associated with placing in your age group (individually hand made by Barry Siff's wife, Jodee), racers from every walk of life and of almost every age push themselves to the limit and show that swimming, biking and running are indeed a great way to spend a Sunday.

The professionals go head to head for a generous purse that pays both men and women 1st - $6,000, 2nd - $3,500, 3rd - $2,500, 4th - $1,500, and 5th - $750. There is also a $250 prize for the first pro man and woman out of the water, the man and woman with the fastest bike split and the man and woman with the fastest run split.

Triathletes, whether first timers or veterans of the sport, can all rejoice that such a great series of events exists, especially since they all take place at the same venue. Having the chance to participate in progressively longer events at the same locale is very rare and the racers living in or near Boulder, Colorado are extremely grateful and excited to have this unique opportunity.

For the spectators, it's also an incredible venue at which to watch a triathlon and keep up with the family. The entire swim is viewable from the beach (where kids can play and swim), and the bike and run loops also give people more than one chance to see their favorite racer. In addition to keeping up with the competitors, there are areas for picnicking, sand volleyball, boating, and generally laying around (there are many trees where you can rest in the shade while the racers battle the sun and heat).

For the out-of-town racer or spectator, accommodations are fairly easy to come by. Boulder, Colorado is the backdrop for this event and the city and the surrounding areas offer many hotels from which to choose. The race also designates an official host hotel (which offers discounts to racers until about a week before the race).

All in all, the 5430 Long Course Triathlon is a great race and 5430 Sports pull it off with style and with great professionalism and respect for every racer in attendance. What's not to like about a group of people who spend countless hours preparing for and creating a great atmosphere, organizing vendors who provide great food and drink, and who present a race where one can enjoy high competition and great friendships at the same time? In short, 5430 Sports has created a fantastic series of triathlons and the Long Course Triathlon is a challenging, but wonderful way to finish out your season.

About the Author

Brian Daniel is an attorney who works in the Denver area and has been involved in the triathlon lifestyle for many years. He is a mid- to back-of-the-pack racer who truly enjoys the training and the competition. He is married to Katheryn Daniel and they have a beautiful daughter, Providence, who is a challenge to keep up with.

Brian has battled numerous life-threatening medical conditions for over a decade and finds that training and racing give him not only peace of mind and confidence, but also provide him with much better health than his doctors could ever have expected. In fact, the directions he receives from numerous physicians over the years is to "Absolutely, keep it up!"

In Brian's own words, "Triathlons have given so much to me (better health, increased athletic confidence, and terrific friendships), that I look for every opportunity I can find to give back to the triathlon community or to help other racers train and compete. With me, it's truly a lifestyle that I absolutely love."

Barb's Race

Race Distance: Long
1.2 Mile Swim, 56 Mile Bike, 13.1 Mile Run
Month: August
Race Web Site: www.vineman.com

Author: Diane Hill
Racing Category: Age Group 50-54

"I'll have you doing a triathlon by the time you're 50."
                                    - Linda Gagnon, May 12, 2002.

Thus the seed was planted…and watered. Six weeks later it blossomed. I became a triathlete, having successfully completed my first Tri-for-Fun, at age 46. I wouldn't exactly say I had fun. Nor would it be fair to say that the triathlon bug bit me. Even the thought of doing another triathlon would not enter my mind until months later.

The following spring, when my cousin's wife, Lynn, was diagnosed with metastatic cancer, I began thinking about Barb's Race. Linda had competed in Barb's Race the previous year. I knew it was a women-only long course event that raised money for local cancer charities. I also knew I wanted to do something for Lynn. On the morning of May 30, I committed to participate, not to compete, but to complete Barb's Race. Sadly, that same day, Lynn succumbed to cancer. I shared with my cousin that I had chosen to do Barb's Race to honor Lynn's life. Ironically, the race would be held on Lynn's birthday.

Eight of my friends, all seasoned TriChics, had already signed up for Barb's Race. The incredulous looks I got from these same friends when I told them I, too, had signed up, puzzled me. "What other races are you doing this season?" It never occurred to me that you're supposed to gradually work up to the long course distance. This was not an indication of newfound confidence; it was purely ignorance on my part. Ah, to be a newbie.

Over the next several months, we trained together, as best we could, despite our variable schedules. I took advice and tips from everyone.

181

I also borrowed a road bike, bike shoes, and even a wetsuit. Yes, this was going to be a group effort.

The weekend before the race, my dear friend Karen died suddenly and unexpectedly of complications from various cancers she'd been fighting for years. Imagine my conflict when I learned that Karen's memorial service was scheduled for the same day as the race. Her husband insisted I keep my commitment to Barb's Race; that Karen would have wanted it that way. However, he had one request of me — that I write her name on the back of my hand and take her with me. My husband and children attended the service in my absence, although this meant they would not be out on the course to support and encourage me.

So, with a heavy heart, I headed to Guerneville without my family. Linda and I decided to carpool. Actually, Linda took me under her wing, ensuring that I had packed all the necessary gear. I checked my bags and then checked them again. Triathlons, particularly destination triathlons, are logistically much more complicated than marathons. Some triathlons, including Barb's Race, even have two different transition areas. Would I really have all the right gear when and where I needed it?

We met up with the rest of the TriChics at the race expo. I suddenly felt like an undergraduate in a graduate class. What was I thinking? Who was I kidding? Why didn't somebody try to talk some sense into me? Oh, yeah, they did. I didn't listen.

The race expo was surprisingly low-key, relaxed, and friendly. Ditto for the registration process. Like other events, the pre-race seminar provided all the race specific information needed, including any last minute course changes. I looked around. Two hundred experienced triathletes surrounded me. A few had already completed a long course race. I felt I was the only one who truly had no idea what I'd gotten myself into.

We were then all introduced to Barb Recchia, a longtime Vineman Triathlon volunteer and race committee member. A two-time cancer survivor, Barb is the reason, the inspiration, for this race. One feels peaceful and calm and capable in her presence. Her race, although physically challenging and as competitive as you want it to be, unites women as they race together in honor and in memory of others and in hope for a cure. The focus is on others, even as you race to the finish. My goal for the day was to enjoy the spirit of the event, rather than the outcome.

A good night's sleep would have been nice. So would a forecast of early morning fog, cool temperatures, a slight breeze and high clouds. This was not the case. As I arrived at the race start at Johnson's Beach, the sun was already peaking through the fog. This didn't bode well. The fact that I didn't feel chilly as I waited to get body-marked was not a good sign for me.

In addition to the required body marking, I asked the volunteer to write "Lynn" on my right arm and "Karen" on my left.

I racked my bike, squeezed into my borrowed wetsuit (thankfully, wetsuits are allowed per USA Triathlon guidelines), put on a purple age group swim cap, grabbed my goggles, and followed others to the shore to "warm up." This made no sense to me. I had never swam 1.2 miles before, and I certainly didn't want to add to the distance by warming up! Besides, by that time I was so nervous, I could barely get myself near the water, never mind in the water.

It was time. I positioned myself in the back of the pack to avoid being in anyone's way. Then the unexpected happened. I had a panic attack. I know this is not uncommon for open water swims, but it was new to me. Then I heard a voice (Lynn? Karen?) say, "Just put your face in the water and you'll be fine." Whoever it was, they were right. I guess I should also mention that the swim is held in the Russian River, which is shallow, shallow enough to stand up if need be. Ah, reassurance to even the most nervous of swimmers.

I found my stroke (breaststroke), got comfortable, and headed upstream. I am way too slow to draft, but I caught myself laughing as I visualized the butterflies in my stomach pulling me along. After a few minutes I realized it wasn't so bad. In fact, I found myself actually enjoying the swim. Slow, steady, relaxed. Forward motion. Did someone just bump into me? "Sorry. Excuse me." Wow, polite swimmers! I had heard horror stories of chaotic, almost violent swims. You won't find that to be the case at Barb's Race.

I couldn't believe how quickly the turnaround came! Slow, steady, relaxed. I passed by one of the lifeguards in a kayak and thanked him for being there. I was now close enough to the swim finish to hear cheers. Even though some swimmers were sprinting to the finish, I kept my heart rate low, my pace controlled. This was not really my race strategy; I have only one speed. As I climbed out of the water, a school-aged boy shouted, "Hey lady! Can I have your swim cap?" This was one of the highlights of my day. I wondered what he'd do with it? Another highlight quickly followed. As I turned around, there was Barb, all smiles, exclaiming, "Diane, I knew you could do it. I'll see you at the finish!" I could be wrong, but I bet not all triathlons are so nurturing.

I continued up the ramp to find my bike. Being in the last swim wave and being a slow swimmer means it is *very* easy to locate your bike. Finally, off with the wetsuit (easier said than done). On with the bike jersey, helmet, sunglasses, bike shoes, and socks. Arm warmers? Well, I didn't really need them, but I wore them anyway. Psychologically, I wanted something to take off later. I quickly walked the bike through the transition area. Spectators lined the street, shouting encouragement. The bike leg starts with a short, but steep hill. I choose to walk it and started the 56-mile bike adventure at the top.

The bike course is a self-guided tour through one of California's most beautiful wine countries. This is perfect for families and friends of those racing. Be sure to pick up a bottle or two of a Chalk Hill variety; it will make a great conversation piece. Trust me. This will make more sense later.

The first five miles were deceptively easy, riding through the quaint town of Guerneville. Woohoo! Only 51 miles to go. Then I realized I hadn't seen any other riders yet. I was alone, but not lonely. My thoughts turned to Karen and Lynn. I felt their presence.

The first hill (at mile five) was a reality check. My denial was fading. The course description does mention the ride has rolling hills, 1,600 feet of climbing, is technically demanding, and challenging. No mincing of words here. I found it hard to focus on the magnificent beauty of the landscape while sucking air on those lovely rollers. God help me when I reach the dreaded Chalk Hill, but that will be hours from now. Hey, look! I've caught up to some riders.

Aid stations are strategically located along the course, about every 10 miles. The volunteers are a welcome sight. Cheerful. Smiling. Encouraging. I made a point of thanking them for their help. It was the least I could do; without them there is no race.

The website clearly states temperature highs could range between 80 and 95 degrees. Just my luck—we were in for a hot one. I had no doubts this race would be hard, but the heat ups the ante. Oh, well. If I keep in mind the old Team In Training® mantra of "pace, fuel, and hydration" I know I will be successful. Eventually.

The heat and the hills began to take their toll. Fortunately, after each climb, there was the reward of the downhill and the cooling breeze that accompanies it. It was hard to stay present, to focus; my mind was preoccupied with Chalk Hill. And Chalk Hill was close, very close. I planned accordingly, insuring I was properly fueled and hydrated in preparation for the big climb. Words of encouragement were scrawled in chalk across the road. "You go, girl!" "Breathe!" My pace slowed so much I thought I was going to tip over. Imagine my surprise (horror, really) when I reached the top and realized that this wasn't THE hill. Chalk Hill was yet to come! Again my thoughts turned to Karen and Lynn and the challenge I faced was put back in perspective.

I was petrified as I began the slow climb up Chalk Hill. My self talk changed from "Just keep going" to "Get off before you fall over." I stopped, only to discover the hill was too steep for me to begin riding again. Humbled, I walked to the top. The kind spectators assured me I was not the only one the hill has conquered. (Over the years, Chalk Hill would repeatedly prove to be my nemesis.)

There is a tremendous and much unexpected benefit to the "strategic" walk break up the hill. I was refreshed! I felt recovered! Then, "Whoa!" I was flying down hill faster than I've ever ridden before. I passed women, the same women that provided encouragement on Chalk Hill. I felt great!

The rest of the ride was uneventful. Well, sort of. Nowhere in the race literature did it say anything about passing a cemetery. I was caught off guard and overcome with emotion.

Heading into the transition area at Windsor High School was a thrill. It was quite a festive atmosphere. The streets were lined with enthusiastic spectators who cheered the athletes as they finished the ride and began the half marathon. This is the perfect place to relax and enjoy the culmination of a hard day's work. I would get that chance later.

It felt so good to get off the bike and into my running shoes. Pleased at my foresight to wear a visor rather than a running hat, I doused my head with water and slathered on more sunscreen. Although it was sunny and hot, I felt amazingly good, especially considering my race started so many hours ago. The half marathon is my favorite part of the race. This is not because I am a more experienced runner than swimmer or cyclist, but because of the social factor. I get to chat with the volunteers and spectators, to encourage other participants, and to enjoy the catered aid stations that are available almost every mile. Since the run is an out-and-back course, I saw some of the same people more than once, including my TriChic friends. There goes another one! "You are awesome!"

As I turned the corner toward Windsor High, I saw my family! They made it in time to see me finish.

Barb greets all the athletes at the finish line. As she put the finishing medal around my neck, I promised her that I will return. And I have, every year since.

Barb's race isn't for everyone, it is part of the Vineman series even sharing their website. It covers virtually the same course as Vineman 70.3, one of the most fiercely competitive triathlons in the country. Passion. Endurance. Dedication. Perseverance. That should tell you something—it's not easy! A very important distinction, however, is that Barb's Race welcomes women to try something extraordinary. There is a unique camaraderie. You can sense it. It is a privilege to participate in this physically and emotionally challenging event with an inspiring group of women, in support of a truly important charitable cause.

About the Author

Diane Hill's athletic endeavors began at the age of 40. She is currently a veteran of more than 20 marathons and ultra distance marathons, which she credits to Team in Training coaches for the Leukemia and Lymphoma Society's endurance sports training program. An unfortunate (non-sports related) ankle injury and subsequent rehab on a stationery bike opened the door to triathlon training.

Diane's community involvement and volunteerism earned her the privilege of carrying the Olympic Torch for the 2002 winter Olympics. Diane received her B.S. in Nursing from Adelphi University in New York. As an Occupational Health Nurse, she has the opportunity to promote wellness, fitness, and healthy lifestyle choices. Diane and her husband, Jim, along with their two children, Kellie and Eric, live near the American River Bike Trail in Rancho Cordova, California.

"The miracle isn't that I finished...The miracle is that I had the courage to start."
- John Bingham

Timberman Ironman 70.3®

gilford, new hampshire

Race Distance: Long
1.2 Mile Swim, 56 Mile Bike, 13.1 Mile Run
Month: August
Race Web Site: www.timbermantri.com

Author: Scott K. Baldwin Jr.
Racing Category: Age Group 35-39

The Timberman Triathlon Festival began in 2000. The race is held on Lake Winnipesaukee in the middle of the state of New Hampshire. The festival consists of a three day expo, a short course race on Saturday morning, a kids' triathlon on Saturday afternoon, and the long course triathlon on Sunday. The race director has done a great job of turning this local, small town event into a world class race in a short period of time.

The first full year I competed in triathlons I was living in California. My family wanted to take an extended summer trip back to the East Coast to visit relatives. I agreed to take this vacation only if I could find a race that fit into our itinerary. I had only done short races up to this point but decided that jumping into a long course race in my home state while on vacation was a good idea. Since that first Timberman in 2002, I have gone back every year and each time it is a different race for me under different training and weather conditions and with different degrees of success. I have done really well some years and poorly in other years but each year I learn something new. I have seen this race grow from a one-day-no-expo race to a three day event which includes many locals and professional athletes from around the world.

The registration process is painless. There is an online registration process as well as a mail-in option for signing up. The race has sold out for the last several years. Every year it sells out quicker and quicker. Because the race has become part of the 70.3 series, it will continue to be a popular race and it will become more difficult to procrastinate on signing up for this one. There are no qualifying standards, but because it is part of the series, and because it is late in the season, there are final opportunities for those competing to earn a spot to the Ironman® World Championship 70.3.

The race expo has an amazing festival feel and is held over a three day period from Friday to Sunday. Check-in on race weekend is very efficient with many volunteers helping racers get their numbers, chips, and race goodies. It is held at the Gunstock Ski Area in a beautiful setting, usually with bands playing in the background to help entertain you as you stand in line waiting for your number and goodie bag.

There are many booths for athletes to get last minute supplies. While most races have bike companies there sharing their newest bikes, at Timberman, there is a regional carbon fiber bike frame builder that has a very large presence at the expo and has great race weekend specials. With multiple pasta dinners offering professional triathletes as post dinner speakers, many athletes gather together early on before the races begin. To cap off the weekend, there is a lobster and steak feast that is well attended.

Because the area is a resort town, there is a wide range of accommodations in the Lake Winnipesaukee region, from small bed and breakfasts to large resort hotels. The race hotel is within three miles of the race venue and usually sells out very quickly. The lake is a very popular summer destination for people all over New England, so it is important to book a room early on if you know you'll be racing Timberman. Most of the rooms require three to four day minimum stays making it a nice vacation around the race.

The swim takes place in Lake Winnipesaukee. The course is three sides of a clockwise rectangle. To begin, swimmers go straight out to the middle of the lake for about 550 meters, take a right hand turn, go about 800 meters (into the sun), take a right hand turn and then head back to shore about 550 meters away. The swim start is a five minute walk along the beach from the transition while the finish is right at the transition area. The water is 68-70 degrees (wetsuit legal) in mid-August and crystal clear. The lake is shallow the first few hundred yards from shore. Many people run the first 100 yards of the race before starting to swim. The same is true for the last 100 yards as well.

The bike is an out-and-back course and is on a mix of primary and secondary roads. On the stretches where there can be a lot of traffic, there is a shoulder that is at least six feet wide. The first 10 miles are generally uphill including about four good climbs. As soon as you leave the transition area there is a nice two-three minute climb to get your legs warmed up. The next three hills are roughly 10 minutes, 5 minutes, and finally a good steep 10 minutes to finish off the first 10 miles. The next 18 miles to the turnaround are gradually downhill. The course goes by the New Hampshire Speedway in Loudon where NASCAR® races are held twice a year. The course also makes a short loop through quaint Loudon Village. The return trip follows the same path but in reverse.

The slight downhill grade during the outbound portion of the outer 18 miles can mean an average of five mph slower coming back over this section. The last 10 miles of the bike are nice because the serious climbing that was invested at the beginning of the ride pays off with some downhill. There are well supplied aid stations every 10 miles. In general, the road surfaces are in excellent shape but there are a few stretches that are a bit rough. I think the race director must have some influence over the road guys because new stretches of fresh pavement are added each year. I think there is only one more major section that still needs repair and then this will be a very smooth ride.

The run is a two time out-and-back. The course goes along the edge of the lake with shady country roads that weave past many bed and breakfasts as well as lake side condos. As long as the humidity is low the run is beautiful. There is one short steep climb that can be challenging depending on your physical and mental state at that point of the race. The first mile out of each loop is a gradual uphill (which means the last mile of each loop is a nice downhill). There are aid stations roughly one mile apart.

All of the aid stations on the bike and run course compete for a prize for being the most creative. They each pick a theme, wear customs, and decorate the aid station in that theme. This makes the run portion of the race a little less painful because there is entertainment along the way. Every year there is a men's barber shop quartet that is stationed mid-way along the run course. These guys are just amazing and I look forward to hearing them each year. This race is really embraced by the community as can be seen by all the creativity and effort put in by all the volunteers along the course.

This bike course is somewhat spectator friendly if you can get a car outside of the park and have a local who knows the back roads. There are many intersections on the course that can be accessed along the way. There is great access to the run course in and around the transition area and at the turn around. Otherwise, the run course is shut down to all but very local traffic. Because of this, there are spots along both the bike and run course that can be very lonely.

The weather at Timberman can vary greatly, a few years it has been well into the 90s with very high humidity. One year it was pouring rain until about the start time with showers throughout the day. Other years it has been absolutely beautiful with sunny skies, and temperatures in the mid-70s with low humidity. These beautiful days are when I have raced my best in New Hampshire (but don't we all).

Since I have raced Timberman five times so far, I have experienced this race in many different ways with varying results. As with the weather, my physical and mental readiness has varied, and my season leading up to this race has been different each time. I have had PRs on this course and I have had very bad days leading to long walks during the run portion of the race. In 2004 it was a prefect day. The weather was prefect, I was in great long course shape, and I had three really bad long course races under my belt that year so I was due for a really good race.

The day before the race was the very rainy. I spent about four hours watching friends compete in the short course event held the day before. This was probably not the best strategy for the day before my big race but I did it anyway. At Timberman, they have all the long course racers check their bikes into transition the night before the race. This allows time for helmet and bike safety inspections as well as makes race morning a bit less stressful because there is one less thing to worry about race morning. I waited until the last possible moment to check my bike in hoping the rain would go away for the night.

Race morning: I had asked for a 4:15 wake up call. I decided to hit the snooze on the back-up alarm clock until 4:40. I figured that would be more than enough time to get to the race course and get ready for the day. I didn't get to the line of cars outside the park until around 5:20 and by then it was a 20 minute wait to get to a parking space. There are only two ways into the race venue and 95 percent of the participants choose the same way. This has led to long back ups getting into the park on race day and has led to 30-60 minute delays in the race start time to ensure that everyone has time to get race ready and to get as many of the cars off the road as possible.

My warm-up started with a mad dash to the toilet line followed by a more leisurely walk to the transition area to set up my gear. Transition setup went fine. I went for the rest of my warm-up which included another trip to the bathroom and a two mile easy jog.

The swim was pretty uneventful. I took the swim pretty easy since I usually swim between 32-34 minutes regardless of my training or how hard I go in the race. Midway through the race I heard a kayaker yelling at a bunch of people. It turned out I was one of them. We had headed towards shore way to soon and were going to miss a buoy midway through the back stretch. As a result I ended up swimming an extra 200 yards to get back on course. Because the course is so wide open (and the sun) there was no clear group of swimmers. When looking up for my attempted sighting, there were arms flailing all over the place, making it difficult to navigate at times.

190

The swim to bike transition is a short beach run to the grassy transition area. Because of the rain the day before the grass was still soggy with many puddles in between the bike racks. Volunteers were there to make sure we all got through the transition safely, telling us to slow down or be careful. I was sure this didn't apply to me. I took the turn into my row fast and managed to slip and fall on the ground. Next time I'll listen. A few seconds would not have killed me but an injury may have.

I had nearly psyched myself out the day before by driving the hills on the bike course as a reminder of them. I was a bit nervous about the hills because of my reduction of hill training since moving East from hilly California. I remember getting to the 10-mile mark on race day after getting through the hard parts thinking that it wasn't so bad.

In years past I seemed to have gotten in a very congested part of the race during the bike. I don't like this because it seems that the USAT guys have a way of getting my number when this happens. I took the bike pretty conservatively and tried to relax. Every time I started to stress about my pace, position or how I felt, I would close my eyes briefly, take a deep breath and tell myself to relax. The last 10 miles was fun because of the downhills. There are a few uphills on the way back to transition that get me every year, not because they are very steep, but because of their placement on the course. One is about five minutes long with six miles to go and another is about four minutes with about three miles to go. They can be a bit demoralizing at this part of the race, but I was prepared and knew they were there so I just took them easy.

At the second transition, I was a bit puzzled when I picked up my new pair of socks that I sometimes change into for the run and they were soaking wet. So was the pair that I just took off. It took me a few seconds to figure out which pair was less wet.

The run was the best I have ever had for a long course race. I ran the whole race, including the aid stations. I managed to pick off many people along the course. Several people came up and passed me, but each time I was determined to stick with them for as long as I could. The race was very evenly paced for me. I managed to tick off the miles at a 7:10-7:30 pace. My splits for the four segments were 23:39, 23:18, 23:40, 24:06. The run did hurt, but every time I wanted to stop or slow down I would visualize my kids in a race (they enjoy racing as well) and this helped me go a little longer. To date this was my best long course race. Everything fell into place; my training, the weather and the competition. I had no complaints and it kept me excited about triathlon.

Overall, Timberman is a great event. It has races for all ages and abilities. The venue is perfectly located in central New Hampshire on the massive Lake Winnipesaukee. The race organization does an amazing job from the website and registration all the way to the finish line. The race attracts amateurs of all abilities as well as a strong professional field. The course is challenging but a PR is possible with adequate training.

About the Author

Scott Baldwin was a cross country and track runner for his four years of high school. He was a walk-on to the Division I Northeastern University track team his freshman year and ran the 400m hurdles for Northeastern for two years. Overall, he was only an average athlete. Scott finally realized that and spent the next 10 years focusing his efforts on his family and education. While attending Stanford University, he earned a Ph.D. in Mechanical Engineering, had three kids, and got terribly out of shape while gaining around 25 pounds. On a business trip to Hawaii one year, Scott had the opportunity to see the Ironman World Championship® in person and decided that he wanted to participate in that race some day (except he didn't know how to swim). Once the goal of Hawaii is out of the way he would like to go on to other things like completing a 100-mile run and biking in the Race Across America, a cross country bike race.

Whirlpool Ironman 70.3® Steelhead Triathlon

benton harbor, michigan

Race Distance: Long
1.2 Mile Swim, 56 Mile Bike, 13.1 Mile Run
Month: August
Race Web Site: www.steelheadtriathlon.com

Author: Tara Norton
Racing Category: Professional

I am Tara Norton, a triathlete from Toronto, Canada, and as I sit here at my desk to write about the Whirlpool Ironman 70.3 Steelhead Triathlon I am starting my fifth season racing as a pro. My focus is on ultra distance races, but my coach, Scott Molina, has encouraged me to add more long course races to my race schedule to work on my speed. It is because of this that I recently found myself in Benton Harbor, Michigan for the Steelhead Triathlon.

Since 2003, I have been fortunate enough to race in many triathlons throughout the world including 16 ultra distance races. Even with a wide array of races under my belt in a variety of amazing locations, the Steelhead 70.3 race remains a memorable one for a handful of reasons.

First, this race is big, really big. Last year there were over 2,500 athletes registered for this triathlon, making it one of the largest 70.3 competitions around. Having that number of people in one place all with a similar goal in mind lends a great vibe to the event. There are few long course triathlons in the Midwest right now and it draws athletes from across the United States and Canada and from Central and South America as well. Living in Toronto, I was able to drive to the race.

Despite its size, or perhaps because of it, the race is exceptionally well organized. It never felt that busy and you never had to wait in a line for anything (registration, body marking, getting into transition, etc.). If you have any concerns about a mass swim start of 2,500 triathletes, you have nothing to worry about because the start is broken down into very manageable sized waves. As a result, it is far less chaotic than many smaller races, and the chance of athletes with different swim paces getting in each others' way is greatly reduced. Steelhead also has the

option to enter the race as part of either a two or three person relay team.

This is the only race I have ever done in which the location of the start is not actually finalized until race morning. The 1.2-mile point-to-point swim begins either at Tiscornia Beach or Rocky Gap Park, depending on the direction of the Lake Michigan currents. Either way, the swim finishes at Jean Klock Park (where the transition zone is). One piece of advice is to make sure you budget enough time to get to the swim start. You can either walk the 1.2 miles along the beach, or take a bus provided by the race organizers. Based upon the number of people I saw scrambling to get into their wetsuits at the last minute, it appeared to me that many athletes arrived later than they had anticipated.

Being in Lake Michigan, this is a freshwater swim. So, while there is less buoyancy here than in saltwater, the bonus is that there is also less chaffing from your wetsuit. The swim is a beach start, and the beach where we started from is both long and beautiful. I find that the start of a race is perhaps the only place where I have both the time and ability to take in my surroundings properly, and this is certainly a great place to do this. Once the gun goes off, you head out a short distance to a big buoy and then turn to swim parallel with the shore. There are a number of small buoys that mark the swim course and they change color to signal you are getting closer to the turn around buoy. When you finally hit the turn around, you turn and swim towards the shore and the swim exit.

It is interesting to note that there were more marker buoys along the swim course than the race organizers said there would be. Because I counted buoys and I kept passing more than I expected, this made the swim seem longer to me than it actually was. The water temperature was very comfortable and while the water was not smooth-as-glass like you might find on smaller lakes, it certainly was not too choppy either.

One thing about the swim start is that it can be a bit cool in the morning on the beach. My solution was to wear a pair of old socks that I could dispose of just prior to the race. This helped keep me warm and comfortable as I stood on the cool sand before the start. Another thing to remember is that you need to cross a timing mat before entering the water. Doing this properly will ensure that you receive an accurate chip time and save you hassles later in the day, for sure.

Coming into transition from the swim requires a good slog up the sandy beach. The transition zone is well organized, but a bit cramped and muddy. If this race gets any bigger the organizers may have to reconsider the transition set up to ensure it remains smooth.

The 56-mile bike course is essentially a lollipop shape in which you head out about nine miles, do a big loop, and then return along the same nine mile stretch you went out on. There are a couple of short sections of chip-seal road which are a bit rough, but the vast majority of the course is well paved and the entire course is exceptionally well marked.

The cycling course takes you though some nice grassland, beautiful fields, and pastures, though unfortunately I tend to be so focused on my race that I miss this stuff on race day. I did drive the course the day before the race (which I recommend doing) during which I was able to thoroughly enjoy the scenery. Certainly I would consider this course to be very fair in that it does not seem to favor one type of specialized cyclist over another. Its rolling hills make it suited to all around cyclists as opposed to those who prefer climbs or pure flats. From a technical perspective, a 12-25 cassette would be more than adequate for most people, and if you consider yourself a particularly strong cyclist then an 11-23 would work well.

For me it is the run portion of the race that makes this triathlon different from many others. It is particularly enjoyable. After leaving the transition and Jean Klock Park and then going through a bit of the city of Benton Harbor and some subdivisions, the run course takes you along a nice footpath that twists through the Whirlpool Corporation grounds. It is much more interesting than just running on the road.

On the 13.1-mile run you hit a tough uphill shortly after leaving T2, but even though the run is two loops, you actually start the second loop before you get back to the hill. As a result, you only tackle the hill once (which was quite fine with me!).

There is a long finishing chute along the beach which can be tough going as the sand gives away beneath your feet. Carpeting material is placed on the sand, which minimizes this effect, but at the end of the race you certainly notice that running on this surface is tougher than running on a paved road or pathway. The finish is fun though because of the number of cheering spectators lined up along the finishing chute.

The post-race pavilion is a great place to hang out and recover after the race with family, friends, and fellow athletes. The food there is great, and massages are available for a small fee. This pavilion is also where the awards are given out and slots are allocated for the Ironman World Championship 70.3 in Florida. In the 2007 edition of this race, there were 75 age group slots for the top age group finishers, but there were no slots for pros.

From a spectator perspective, this race is as good as any. With the point-to-point swim it is a bit tough to see both the start and the exit from the water, and I observed that most spectators decided to forgo watching the start in favor of seeing the swim exit and transition. As with most long course triathlons, there were fewer people out on the bike course but there were many near the transition and along the run course, in particular through the Whirlpool corporate grounds and along the extended carpeted finishing chute.

The year I did the race, it was hot and dry, but thankfully not as hot as the day before the race. The day after the race was cold and very rainy. Based upon this, I would say that it is a good idea to come to the race prepared for a variety of weather conditions.

The race expo is not very large, but serves its purpose well. There is an Inside Out Sports tent which is excellent for purchasing tubes, CO_2 cartridges, water bottles, and other necessary gear. Andrea Fisher was available at the expo for a question and answer session and there were a number of other scheduled course talks the day before the race to answer any questions athletes may have had. Andrea is a great triathlete and has a wealth of knowledge to share. I imagine the organizers will have a similar set up, whether with Andrea or someone else, each year.

Accommodations seemed plentiful, but a couple of my friends stayed in hotels or motels where the quality was lacking somewhat. I researched accommodation options and learned that The Boulevard is a popular place to stay. It is a nice hotel on the bluff downtown overlooking the lake. There is also the host hotel, The Holiday Inn, and there are also a number of bed and breakfasts to choose from. Two websites to check out are, www.swmichigan.org and www.sjcity.com for a list of all the possible places to stay. I was told that any of the hotels in St. Joseph and Stevensville are good choices. Another cool option to consider is camping on the race site in trailers that are available for rent.

I was fortunate to have a wonderful home stay with the Assistant Race Director, Christine Borah, as did Andrea, so our experiences with accommodations could not have been better. In addition to the comfort and convenience of staying in a home, this also provided me with some insight as to how and why this is one of the best run triathlons I have ever attended. There is flawless attention to detail, and clearly the balance of the organizing staff operated in the same fashion. They have truly thought of everything. For example, body marking is available the day before the race at the expo, thereby saving time on race morning. Likewise, the bike check-in is also the day before the race which is not always the case for 70.3 races. The bike racks are labeled with the names or race numbers of every athlete so that you do not have to fight for a good space on the rack. The all important aid stations are also well placed throughout the course and are all well stocked. As far as "swag" goes, the t-shirt for this race is a technical shirt, not cotton which is great, and even the finisher's medal looks cool.

With its small resort town feel, Benton Harbor is a terrific venue for the race, and if you have some extra time and feel you want to make a vacation out of your trip, there are a number of other towns in the area to explore as well. Even Chicago is a relatively short train ride away. Because there are no qualifications for entry to the race other than being 18 years of age or older, and having the ability to complete this race distance, there is really no excuse not to do this race. So, I hope to see everyone there. I will certainly be going back to race the Whirlpool Ironman 70.3 Steelhead Triathlon again!

About the Author

Born in 1971, Tara Norton is a professional triathlete who lives and trains in Toronto. Focused on long course and ultra distance races, Tara began her pro triathlon career in 2004. She is a 16-time ultra distance finisher and has competed at the Ironman World Championship in Hawaii each year since 2003, most recently finishing in 12th place overall (2nd Canadian woman) in October of 2007.

Prior to turning pro, Tara represented Canada at the Olympic distance World Championships in Mexico in 2002, New Zealand in 2003, and Madeira, Portugal in 2004. In 2003, Tara was named to the prestigious Inside Triathlon All American Team along with other top triathletes from around North America.

In 2004 Tara qualified for the Hawaii Ironman World Championship in her first race as a pro at Ironman Coeur D'Alene, and subsequently finished 25th overall in Hawaii. Tara rallied back from a terrible cycling accident in May of 2005 (in which she broke nine bones in her face, fractured her C7 neck vertebra, and knocked out some teeth), and managed to return to Hawaii for a third consecutive year. Now coached by former Ironman World Champion, Scott Molina, Tara continues to pursue her dream of becoming an Ironman Champion herself. Her 4th place finish at Ironman Lanzarote in 2006 followed by a 2nd place finish in Lanzarote in 2007 and her 9:32 ultra distance PB at Ironman Austria that same season show she is making strong steps in that direction. Now recognized worldwide for her accomplishments in the sport, Triathlon Magazine Canada recently nominated Tara as a contender for Canada's 2007 Female Triathlete of the Year.

Tara can be contacted through her website at www.taranorton.com or through www.absoluteendurance.com.

Big Kahuna Triathlon

santa cruz, california

Race Distance: Long
1.2 Mile Swim, 56 Mile Bike, 13.1 Mile Run
Month: September
Race Web Site: www.firstwave-events.com/kahuna

Author: Abigail Bourgon
Racing Category: Age Group 30-34

I'm a sucker for anything tiki. Tiki glasses, tiki torches, tiki t-shirts, tiki lamps…I love it all. I once convinced my husband to go to Palm Springs for a weekend, just so we could stay in a newly remodeled 1960s motel, restored to its former Polynesian splendor. There were even authentic carved tiki heads surrounding the hot tub. So, when I heard about the Big Kahuna Triathlon I knew it was the one for me. Not for its beautiful location in Santa Cruz, California and not for its ideal long course distance. Nope, I signed up for the finishers' medal. Now, this is no generic metal disc, engraved with race statistics that quickly finds itself lost on the back hook of your closet. When you cross the finish line of the Big Kahuna Triathlon, you will become the proud owner of a large, painted ceramic tiki strung on a leather cord. Truly, how could I pass this up?

But aside from all this tiki talk, the Big Kahuna Triathlon is really a spectacular race. It takes place in and around the lovely, but quirky surf town of Santa Cruz. Located 75 miles from San Francisco, Santa Cruz is justly famous for its many surf breaks, its Beach Boardwalk (circa 1907) complete with carnival rides, and the University of California - Santa Cruz (UCSC) And no, it's not a yellow worm that you see on baseball hats and t-shirts around town. It's the banana slug, the UCSC mascot. Driving down the coast from San Francisco for the race takes about two hours and the scenery is jaw dropping the entire way. US Route 1 hugs the coastline and provides one scenic vista after another. Before you know it, you'll be passing the Pigeon Point Lighthouse. Now is the time to turn your attention away from the ocean and start watching the road, because the rest of your drive into downtown Santa Cruz follows the bike course for the race.

I've been to Santa Cruz many times, and definitely recommend staying in town for a few extra days either before or after the race. Hotels are abundant, and there are lots of things to do besides swim, bike, and run. Rent a long board and take a surf lesson, ride the Giant Dipper Roller Coaster (circa 1924), stop by the Bookshop Santa Cruz on Pacific Avenue, or head to the Bonny Doon Vineyard for some wine tasting. Most activities are centered on the boardwalk or the downtown area, which is also where most of the hotels are located. I would check a review site like www.tripadvisor.com before making a reservation to find out about the current best finds (and not-so-great finds, too). The town of Santa Cruz is fairly small, so pretty much any hotel you choose will be within one to three miles of the race start.

The Big Kahuna Triathlon is held in early September which is a lovely time of year along the California coast. The summer fog that frequently blankets the coast is usually gone, and the temperature is ideal for racing. You can expect temperatures to range from a high of 76 degrees to a low of 53 degrees. The weekend I raced the temperature was in the high 60s, the skies were crystal blue, and the winds were light. Perfect!

As is true of many triathlons, the first impression you get about the race comes from the registration process and race website. If you check out the Big Kahuna website you'll pick up on the beach casual, but still professional feel immediately. The tiki theme is fun and kitschy, but not overdone. I got the feeling that the race organizers want you to have a fun, low-stress race at the beach, but still feel completely supported and respected as an athlete.

This triathlon is definitely not a sprawling, corporate sponsored event with thousands of participants. It feels more like a well organized beach barbeque attended by your close friends. This proved to be true at the Big Kahuna Expo held at Depot Park the day before the race. The expo itself is small, but all the volunteers seemed knowledgeable and very friendly. Depot Park is where the transition area is located for the race, so it's a nice opportunity to check out how bike racks are configured and how the entrances and exits for the bike and run are arranged.

After visiting the expo, picking up your packet, and getting all your gear ready, it's time for some pre-race nutrition. I recommend heading over to Pacific Avenue and the outdoor Pacific Garden Mall. Stretching for several blocks, this street contains many restaurants, shops, coffee bars, and movie theaters. It's a great place to grab a bite to eat, do a little shopping, and some people watching. If you've seen some of the popular bumper stickers around town that say "Keep Santa Cruz Weird," you might now appreciate them!

Race day always begins early. Big Kahuna starts at 7:00 a.m. sharp, and the race organizers recommend arriving one to two hours prior to the start. There is some parking located at the Depot Park (by the transition area), but if this is full there is always plenty of parking just across from the swim start in the Beach Boardwalk public lots for $10 a day. After checking in, getting body marked, and setting up your transition area, it's time to head down to the beach for the swim start, which begins on the beach directly in front of the Santa Cruz Beach Boardwalk.

The swim is a 1.2 mile open ocean swim. The water temperature is about 60 degrees, so wetsuits are highly recommended, but not required. The unique part about the swim is that it follows the Santa Cruz Municipal Pier, a half mile long wharf lined with bait shops, restaurants, and fishing charters. Do you hear a funny barking sound? Yep, it's sea lions. They love to pull out and rest on the pier pilings, and they make interesting companions during the swim. The pier also provides a great cheering location for friends and family (and a spot where they can grab some breakfast while you head out onto the bike course).

One of the few pet peeves I had about the race was the distance from the swim exit to the transition area. I felt like it took forever to exit the water, hit the beach, jog through the sand, exit the beach area, and then run down Washington Street to Depot Park. But I'm not exactly the strongest swimmer around, so maybe I was just a little tired!

The 56-mile bike course has to be one of the most scenic bike legs in triathlon. After exiting Depot Park, the bike course heads across West Cliff Bridge and then passes through a few neighborhoods in Northern Santa Cruz. After just a few miles, the course hits Highway 1 and follows the ocean until you reach Pigeon Point Lighthouse. The course has mostly rolling hills, with no significant elevation change. I was lucky the day I raced because there was only a mild, cooling ocean breeze, but headwinds can make the outgoing section of the bike course a bear.

There are three aid stations (at miles 12, 27, and 44) that provide water bottles, electrolyte drinks, gels, and bananas. Please take the time to get out of your aero bars every once in a while and look around. You'll see surfers, kite boarders, wind surfers, sea lions, sandy beaches, and the beautiful blue Pacific Ocean. The course is an out-and-back route, so when you turn around at the lighthouse you can check out all that beautiful scenery once again.

The 13.1 mile run course (complete with nine aid stations) is mostly flat, but also incredibly pretty. Immediately after leaving the transition area, you'll head out onto West Cliff Drive, which sweeps the Santa Cruz waterfront. The first landmark to see is the lighthouse at Lighthouse Point. Inside is the tiny Santa Cruz Surfing Museum, housing antique surf boards and vintage photographs of the early surfing days in Santa Cruz. Directly to the left of the lighthouse is the famous "Steamer Lane" surf break. This is a great spot to come and relax after the race. It's not uncommon to see a few seals and sea otters jockeying for position on the waves amongst the many surfers.

The run continues to follow the ocean along West Cliff Drive. Look to the left and you'll see tiny beaches, coves, and sea arches that line the coast. Look to the right and check out the multimillion dollar beach "cottages" with the multimillion dollar views. Once you reach Natural Bridges State Beach, the run course heads inland until reaching Wilder Ranch State Park. This 6,000-acre oceanfront park has been designated a "cultural preserve" because of the historic houses scattered across the property. The run course follows the hiking trails that wind through the park providing a Mecca for mountain bikers and horseback riders. Right about now is time to start looking for the turnaround point. What will it be? A small flag? An orange cone? A cardboard sign saying "Turnaround Here?" No, no, no. Now keep in mind the theme of this race. How could it be anything else but a life-sized wooden tiki? Give it a quick kiss for good luck and then head back the way you came.

I have to admit that once I got back to West Cliff Drive the Surfing Museum Lighthouse looked very, very far away. This is when the spectators came to my aid. This area of the course is fantastic for spectators and they are very vocal and supportive. I definitely needed their cheering to bolster my spirits and put a few last bounces in my step, because the last 0.2 miles of the run course are the hardest. You hit the beach and have to run (or slog, in my case) though soft sand to the finish line at the main stage of the Beach Boardwalk.

After grabbing a bottle of cold water, it's time to proudly display your new tiki medal at the post-race luau. While enjoying the live Hawaiian music and eating some healthy snacks, you can watch the throngs of people on the Boardwalk shoveling in corn dogs and elephant ears. You might even be tempted to get one for yourself. I mean, what could be better after completing a long course triathlon than a hot, juicy corn dog?

I know I love the Big Kahuna Triathlon for many reasons — the spectacular scenery, the moderate nature of the course (no difficult climbs on the bike and a fairly flat run), the numerous supportive volunteers, and its proximity to my hometown of San Francisco. But I have to admit that it was also my very first long course triathlon. So, I asked some fellow triathletes with a little more experience for their opinions on the race. Here's what members of the San Francisco Triathlon Club had to say about the race.

"I did Big Kahuna this year and LOVED it. It was my best race of the year and I would do it again."

"I think the best thing about Big Kahuna is that it allows people who want to challenge themselves at the long course distance to do so on a friendly course. For those who have been doing intermediate courses and are thinking of trying a long course, it's a great first one to try it on."

"It is one of the best long courses that I have done within the last 15 years of my triathlon career."

Most people thought the best features of the race were the scenery, including swimming around the Municipal Pier at sunrise, the course itself, and the cheering crowds of spectators. The few negatives mentioned were the 0.3 mile run from the swim exit to the transition area (watch out for small pebbles underfoot), a train track crossing on the bike course causing several blown tires and lost water bottles, and the sand finish. But as one racer stated, "The run finishes on the beach, which isn't easy, but with the finish line in sight and the sound of the announcer clear to hear, you almost forget the sand is there."

Looking forward to seeing you at the start!

About the Author

In Abigail Bourgon's own words, "In my former life I was a well-organized, fashionably-dressed pediatrician. Now I'm a scatterbrained, sleep-deprived mother of a toddler who rarely changes out of jeans. During my spare scraps of free time, I'm attempting to train for my first ultra distance triathlon (along with my husband), while our dog has taken over our couch.

SavageMan Half Triathlon

deep creek lake, maryland

Race Distance: Long
1.2 Mile Swim, 56 Mile Bike, 13.1 Mile Run
Month: September
Race Web Site: www.savagemantri.org

Author: Anathea Carlson Powell
Racing Category: Age Group 30-34

On a cool Sunday morning in western Maryland in mid-September 2007, the SavageMan Half Triathlon was inaugurated. The race was billed as "The Most Beautiful and Most Savage" long course triathlon in the world, with a 1.2 mile swim, a 56 mile bike course, and a 13.1 mile run. The bike course included 5,500 feet of climbing of which a portion topped out at a 31 percent grade and the run included an additional 1,350 feet of elevation gain. The race attracted several world class elite triathletes, 140 age group athletes, 33 relay teams, and a handful of Aquavelo competitors.

Everyone involved in triathlon has raced on uninspiring courses. These often have multiple loop bike courses and out-and-back runs along highway shoulders. At one point, many of us have lost interest in anything other than the master of the stopwatch. SavageMan was the race to return triathlon to its original roots of testing the limits of physical endurance in a gorgeous setting. As one of the organizers wrote in the information for the trial run, invitation-only, "0th annual SavageMan" held at the end of the 2006 season: "If you love swimming, biking, and running and like to challenge yourself, you will love SavageMan. The challenge in SavageMan is not to beat your PR (personal record) because you won't, or qualify for Kona (Ironman World Championship), because you won't, or win your age group because no one cares. It's to conquer a very challenging, beautiful course and enjoy an absolutely beautiful area ideal for swimming, biking, and running."

The Joanna M. Nicolay Foundation, an organization devoted to melanoma research and treatment joined the race as a charity partner. The foundation offered a unique fundraising benefit: For athletes who

raised a minimum of $500, the foundation refunded their race entry fee and gave them tickets to a pre-race dinner. Many of the athletes chose to raise money and fundraising grossed a very respectable $50,000.

Race logistics were handled well all weekend. All events were centered in beautiful Deep Creek Lake State Park. Deep Creek Lake is approximately three hours from Washington, DC and two hours from the Pittsburgh airport by car and is also close to other commuter airports. The park includes a lake with a sand beach (no dogs are allowed on the beach), Discovery Center (where packet pick-up and bicycle check-in were held), and well-maintained campgrounds. Lodging is available in the campgrounds, at local vacation homes, at WISP resort, or at one of the many nearby hotels.

Packet pick-up went very smoothly the day before the race. The athlete's meeting was held in the afternoon and the race organizers stressed safety on the technical bike course over all else. The Nicolay Foundation offered the pre-race meal to all athletes (there was a nominal fee for those who did not participate in fundraising). Although I did not attend the meal, it was well received by other athletes who did.

Several local photographers offered race photos for free on the website after the race. There were a large number of volunteers both from Washington, DC-based triathlon clubs and from local clubs, and everyone seemed excited to be part of the weekend. The weather forecast was in our favor with sunshine, cool morning temperatures, and pleasant afternoon temperatures.

The reality of what I was about to do set in at the athlete's meeting. Most of the participants wore ultra distance finisher shirts and almost everyone brought their triathlon bikes. Although I had run a marathon and raced triathlon for five years, SavageMan was my first long distance course. Due to work constraints, I had only 11 weeks to prepare for the race and almost no base cycling miles in my legs before starting to train on my beat-up road bike. I had never competed in a race longer than it took to run my first marathon.

While I was in training, many people, myself included, asked why I had to do SavageMan. As a general surgery resident, the question on the website, "Are you Savage enough?" was impossible to ignore. Every day at work, we push the limits of biology until biology pushes back, both in our patients and in ourselves. SavageMan spoke to my deepest instinct to find my own limit. Up until the athlete's meeting, I was able to convince myself that the race was doable, but I began to lose my nerve when I saw the field. Sleep did not come easily Saturday night.

The morning of the race dawned cool and foggy. Driving over a bridge to the race, my training partner looked at the lake — leaden with thick fog — and said to me, deadpan, "That will add a level of difficulty to the swim." At that point, I let go of my anxiety and just started laughing. The transition area continued to lighten my mood as it was a bit of a party, with family members, photographers, and athletes mingling in a very small space.

As we were treading water waiting for the gun, none of us could see more than a few feet in front of us and the buoys were invisible in the fog. There was very little fanfare before the race, and before I could get too cold, the race began. We all started swimming, but sighting was more of a figurative process than one resembling appropriate direction finding. We swam like lemmings; very close together and constantly stopped and asked each other where the buoys were. Soon after the turnaround, the start of the wave behind mine began to overtake a group of us. We just hooked onto their feet and tried not to let them get too far ahead. The swim set the tone for the day and reminded me that nature was in control on this course; I was just along for the ride.

It's a bold claim for a race to state it is the "World's Most Beautiful and Most Savage," but the bike course certainly lived up to the billing. After a baby savage warm-up climb out of the transition area, the course followed very gentle rolling hills. This early time was a highlight, with bucolic pastures, friendly police officers stopping traffic at every intersection, and locals cheering. The long descent into Westernport is the coldest I've ever been on a bike, even with arm warmers, leg warmers, and a wind vest. My teeth chattered loud enough to be a subject of discussion among passing riders. We passed some fly fisherman in the Savage River, and it was easy to imagine that we were just out for a morning cruise. This daydream came to a screeching halt in Westernport where the race truly began.

Westernport is home to the beginning of the now infamous Westernport Wall. The "Wall" is the first stretch of Big Savage Mountain and rises 700 feet over one mile with an average grade of 13 percent. It also includes a short stretch of road so steep (a 31 percent pitch over one town block), that it has long been closed to traffic. The climb just begins once the Wall is breached and continues for another six miles as it crosses the Eastern Continental Divide over Big Savage Mountain.

The bike course is the centerpiece of the race and two unusual prizes were offered for parts of this climb. Those who had the mettle to make it up the 31 percent block received a brick engraved with their name to be laid into the Wall for future participants to ride over and admire and to possibly even fall onto. Attempting this block was not required; a more humane way around was offered for those not inclined to force the block. Athletes were also timed over the entire climb of Big Savage Mountain, which was recorded in our splits, and Accelerade gave a year's supply of their product to the fastest man and woman.

After the silence of the long descent into the town, the noise in Westernport was deafening. Westernport was alive with people lining the streets as music played and a bottleneck of bikes slowed at the closed street block. The race organization provided free shuttles so spectators could get to Westernport to witness and encourage the riders over the Wall. By the time I approached the block, my quads were on fire and there were at least 10 other athletes on the wall. Knowing I had less than a 5 percent chance of getting up it, I decided just to go around (a decision shared by many others) and save a couple of quad fibers and my bike.

The pictures afterward were great, and it was easy to see why the townspeople were having such a good time. Regardless of the outcome, everyone who attempted the block fought the good fight, even if it meant landing in the bushes with their bike on top of them. After the fun of Westernport, the climb onto Big Savage Mountain was a true old fashioned grind. Forget the heart rate monitor and the power meter; lose any expectations and just apply foot to peddle.

The signs started to appear around this time. The signs were like traffic accidents; we couldn't look away. Official yellow race signs counted down the miles to the top of Big Savage Mountain with the elevation and percent grade to expect for the next mile, and other signs provided by fans and spectators cheered on and taunted the riders. Signs reading, "What's a little gravity?" "If you can read this, you're still on the bike," "Triples = $300" "Out of Gears? Just Six More Miles To The Top!" were on Big Savage Mountain. At the top, volunteers in red wigs danced to music, handed off water bottles, and screamed support. The party atmosphere was in full swing at each of the four well-stocked aid stations and two men in a Jeep were driving around collecting gear from hot riders and cheering. At the bottom of the descent was a sign that read, "All Savages Safe and Sound? It's Time to Climb!" The course mercifully flattened out toward the end but "Savage Suffering" commemorated a short, especially brutal hill near the course finale.

"What's so bad about this?" I was thinking, and then came the run. After a mile of blessedly flat terrain, my party ended at the short but deceptively painful campground hills. Worse, the "fire tower" hill, a steep, rocky ascent from the campgrounds to a fire tower at the top of the park, lay in wait. It was easy to pick out the relay runners, who were running on obviously fresh legs, and the rest of us watched with envy as they made relatively short work of the fire tower climb.

As on the bike course, the aid stations on the run course were frequent (every mile), well-stocked, and manned by supportive volunteers. My favorite was the aid station at the top of the fire tower which was staffed by a local girls' high school cross country team. SavageMan is definitely in the cards for those girls in the future. The run went relatively well until after the long, two mile descent off the fire tower; I could tell at the end of it that I had almost nothing left. There was nothing to do but keep going, but I was reminded of the "Savage Suffering" sign more than a few times.

The run is a two loop course, and the finish area doubles as the start of the second loop. This was a great mental refresher for me. Volunteers, family members, race organizers, relay team members, and other athletes were having a great time; the post-race party was in full swing with music, food, and great weather. All of the clubs who were there for the club championship were well represented, and everyone seemed to be cheering for all of the athletes regardless of club affiliation. As I passed the finish line, the announcer, Brad Rex, actually said "And there goes Anathea and we'll see her in AWHILE." He swore up and down at a race the next week that he said "A little while," but you heard it here: he said "Awhile!"

It kept me amused until the second fire tower loop when nothing was amusing. As for the second descent, its torture value rivaled the famous 14th Street Bridge in the Marine Corps Marathon. The finish line finally came into view, and with it, my first long course distance finish and the beginning of the road to an ultra distance race. Many of my friends were waiting for me, and many members of my triathlon club, and it made my finish, late in the day, something even more enjoyable. A friend collected my finisher's award, a technical short-sleeved shirt with "Finisher" written below the SavageMan logo, and I gratefully joined the post-race party.

I won second place for my age group (you can look up how many women were actually IN my age group), and the award was the final touch. It was a beautiful print of the SavageMan logo, conceived by one of the race directors, and rendered by a local artist. Once I stop spending money on triathlon training, I plan to frame it. Every time I look at it, I think of the last exchange I had on the course. Running back into the campground for the finish line, another athlete passed me and said, "Can you think of anything better to be doing on a Sunday afternoon?" No.

Useful Links for Information

Deep Creek Lake State Park
www.dnr.state.md.us/publiclands/western/deepcreeklake.html

Lodging
www.savagemantri.org/Lodging.html

Westernport Wall
www.savagemantri.org/Westernport_Wall.html

About the Author

Anathea is a general surgery resident in the middle of her training. She lives in New York City with her dog, Guinness. She began racing triathlon five years ago while in medical school, and has since run two marathons and competed in the 4.4 mile Great Chesapeake Bay Swim in addition to more than 10 short course triathlons and five intermediate triathlons. SavageMan was her first long course triathlon. When not operating, swimming, biking, or running, Anathea is usually skiing with her family.

Ironman Coeur d'Alene®

couer d'alene, idaho

Race Distance: Ultra
2.4 Mile Swim, 112 Mile Bike, 26.2 Mile Run
Month: June
Race Web Site: www.ironmancda.com

Author: Brady DeHoust
Racing Category: Age Group 30-34

Ironman Coeur d'Alene is a late June race that works great for someone like me who lives on the East Coast; allowing plenty of time after the often frigid January and February months to train. Two friends who had done the race in previous years gave me some positive feedback on the venue, and after two consecutive years of racing Ironman USA in Lake Placid, I was ready for something new.

My wife and I arrived in Coeur d'Alene on Thursday afternoon. When I registered, I wasn't sure if we'd have any other friends racing who'd be bringing along their significant other, so we decided to make things very easy and stay at the Coeur d'Alene Resort right on Coeur d'Alene Lake and about 300 yards from the expo village. While this splurge will force me to find a second job, it seemed to be well worth it for the convenience.

The five night minimum stay "included" some food vouchers that were easily used day-to-day at the fine restaurants owned by the resort. The town is filled with great places to eat and excellent coffee houses and cafes. Java on Sherman, a local coffee shop and café, opened at 4:30 a.m. on race morning and was a staple part of my morning routine during my stay.

The community really embraces this race. Each and every athlete out there seems like a hero to the local town folks. They seemed very interested in the lives of people training and racing the ultra distance. The owners of shops that would be inaccessible due to the road closures all seemed in good spirits and used the race to take advantage of a slow work day and do some lounging around of their own.

A few other places that can't go without mentioning: Hudson's Hamburgers, a counter-only diner that has been a Coeur d'Alene institution since 1907 is known to have perfected the art of hamburger making. For those who skip the carbo loading dinner, Tito Macaroni's offers all the pasta and carbohydrates one would need to fuel up for a big race day. Brix on Sherman is considered North Idaho's premier fine dining facility, and is an excellent choice for post race indulgence. And last, but not least, the Coeur d'Alene Brew Pub has fried food and a plethora of beers to choose. You just can't go wrong.

The swim started from the beach near the resort in downtown Coeur d'Alene. The water temperature was in the mid 60s (cool but comfortable with a full wet suit) and visibility was excellent. The course was two 1.2-mile rectangular loops with a short beach section where the athletes ran over the timing mats between loops. Official Ironman races are all mass starts: picture close to 2,000 athletes lined up on a section of the beach about 100 meters long, not much elbow room with everyone standing even before everyone goes prone and starts swimming.

I finally got down to the water with about five mintues to the cannon firing. I jumped in and took some strokes to take care of the initial shock of chilly water. Everything seemed to check out, and I hit the beach and found my spot in the second row in the first quarter of the width of the swim start. Just a minute or so before blast off, the guy right in front of me turned and said that this was his first ultra distance race. He seemed to just want a quick dose of reassurance, so I patted him on the shoulder and offered him the advice to, "Go out there and have fun ... you'll do just fine."

From experience, I know that parts of the first loop of any Ironman swim are quite chaotic and crowded. But with the right attitude and expectations, it's tolerable. My swimming had improved with regular 6:00 a.m. pool workouts with friends who are better swimmers than me. The workouts were often tailored so I wouldn't get lapped or wind up on the bottom of the pool. My aggressive goal was to swim 1:05, but I wasn't going to be discouraged with a swim time of a couple of minutes longer.

The first 500 meters weren't too bad. But around 500 meters in, it was Coeur d'Alene's version of a mixing bowl. Everyone merged in from their free space, all going for the exact same target — the first turn buoy. It was like New York City gridlock. Somewhere in that turn, I took a solid kick and my goggles went from horizontal to vertical. I was able to make the proper adjustment and keep moving without too much difficulty. On the way back to shore, space was more abundant and I was able to settle into a steadier groove. Beginning the second loop, it felt much better to get started swimming again than the short, heart-thumping run on the beach.

The second loop was nice and steady, trying to take advantage of the draft as much as I could. My only mishap came just after making the left turn of the elongated rectangle. The sun was still shining brightly off the waters, making it very difficult to site on the next turn buoy just about 100 meters ahead. After about 15 non-sighting strokes, I lifted my head and had the immediate reaction of "Where the heck am I?" I was swimming directly toward a big boat that was anchored to make sure folks stayed on course — I was not on course. It was a fairly small error, and I was soon back on track and making my way down the final stretch. I was excited with the anticipation of seeing more empty chairs in the changing tent with a faster than normal swim time. I was out of T1 in a not-so-swift 4:21 with everything in order, clear skies, and a great attitude intact.

The bike course is two sections (think figure-8) totaling 56 miles that were repeated twice (two loops) for a total of 112 miles. The first section was a ten mile out-and-back that took us through downtown Coeur d'Alene, then along the lake to a turnaround at a cull de sac. The second section was mostly a loop that took us on hilly back roads parallel to the Spokane River and I-90 into Washington state then back along mostly flat roads through the town of Post Falls. There were lots of rollers in the first 30 miles with two steep, long sections about 20/25 and 76/81 miles into the bike.

The course was fair, with the climbs placed at the right time to (a) break up the packs early and (b) allow you to get them out of the way and set a solid tempo to get back to town. After ten minutes of letting things settle from the swim I began to take in fluids and calories. I don't have a regimented plan for fluids and calories out there because on race day, you just never know how you're going to feel. I try to eat solid food when I actually feel hungry (including gel), and sip on fluids steadily throughout the ride. Unfortunately, it was clear early on that my stomach was not settled. Everything I ingested knotted up my stomach within a minute, and this would last for about 10-15 minutes. It was more of a frustration and annoyance to constantly feel this discomfort. I started to drink more calories than eat and even that left me queasy. On the climbs, I settled into a good rhythm in an easy gear, while others chose to hammer and gain minimal ground. On the stretch back to town, the winds picked up a bit as well as the temperatures. I was a little concerned with my stomach and not being able to ingest the calories I'd need for the rest of the day. Still, things were moving along great, my legs felt spectacular and the bike was rolling smooth.

At about mile 60, I grabbed my special needs bag to get another gel flask and full bottle of Accelerade®. There were a few times near the special needs area where I literally had to sit up and wait for a group to put enough of a gap on me to get out of any potential violation positions. My other option was to ride really hard for a minute to try and find my own legal space. The congestion from the special needs area broke up shortly and I was back through town and on my way out to finish up the last couple of climbs. I felt good on the climbs, a bit fatigued, but still pretty good. I forced down my Accelerade (it certainly didn't go down like it does in training), and tried to get down some gel as much as I could knowing I'd need the calories for the run or I'd be meeting Dr. Bonk somewhere on the run course. At mile 100, I felt strong and pushed by a handful of struggling riders in the final ten miles. I hit town after 112 miles of biking with the uncertainty of whether I'd be able to run well with an unsettled stomach and a slight calorie deficit. I scooted through T2 in a swift 1:45, not allowing myself the time to think of what lay ahead.

The run course is also two loops with two sections each: a quick one mile out-and-back followed by a five and a half mile out-and-back through town then along the lake (same lakeside road as the bike course). The second turnaround ended on a half mile climb. There was very little shade and the entire run took place on asphalt roads.

I had one goal for this race—less than ten hours. If that goal was accomplished, other "reach" goals would be on the radar. I knew sub-10 was in reach with 1:05/5:12, but I also knew that I was perfectly capable of both a 3:25 run, or a 4:30 run—it all comes down to the run or sometimes better named "the struggle."

I felt pretty poor in the first two miles, running along the out-and-back section on the lake path. I tried to keep my game face on and not provide my wife with any signs that I was struggling and have her worrying about me while out on the bigger out-and-back. My stomach was still in knots. I think I was moving along okay, but with some added discomfort. I started with the mile one aid station and made sure to get water and Gatorade at each subsequent station, knowing I'd need it all to keep from dehydrating and/or meeting up with Dr. Bonk.

The community was amazing as we twisted through the neighborhoods. Locals were having parties in their driveways, grilling food, and providing make-shift spray showers to cool off athletes from the heat. At mile three, I started to feel better. My stomach untied itself and I started to feel smooth in my stride. I hadn't checked any mile splits at this point, and decided I wouldn't check at all. Instead, I convinced myself that my motivation to keep moving would be the anticipation of a finishing clock starting with "9."

The run got lonely on the first out-and-back stretch. The skies were clear, and the heat was starting to take its toll. Dry salt was building on my shorts and face. I ate one Fig Newton that took close to two minutes to chew up and didn't go down pleasantly; calories would have to be all liquid based, so I started to drink cola with the Gatorade and water at each aid station.

I welcomed the cheers of the crowd heading back through town to start the second loop. My wife screamed at me a couple of times, and I did my best to recognize her cheering in my daze. This was mile 15, and it was really starting to hurt. This is that point where walking sounds so good, but the thought of being out there longer sounds so bad. "Just move forward," and "You're having a strong race" were thoughts that ran through my head. I thought often of a Mark Allen quote that I didn't remember word for word, but I knew its meaning. The quote says:

"Unless you test yourself, you stagnate. Unless you try to go way beyond what you've been able to do before, you won't develop and grow. When you go for it 100 percent, when you don't have the fear of 'what if I fail,' that's when you learn. That's when you're really living."

Heading up the Degree of Difficulty hill (the hardest spot of the run course), my run became a shuffle. At the turn, mile 20, I started the "There's only 10K to go" reasoning. From hear on out, each step was one step closer to town. I was holding my place well and felt confident about being able to run to the finish. I still had no idea of how fast (or slow) I was running. At mile 22, an age grouper that had passed me earlier, then looked to have blown-up as I subsequently passed him, re-passed me at a pace I could not hold. He stayed in site, but I couldn't move any faster and hold his pace.

During the last wind through the neighborhoods where fans shouted "Bring it home 327!" and "Finish up strong 327!" I started having great thoughts of the finish chute, and a finish clock starting with '9'. I enjoyed the redirected route that said "To Finish" instead of taking the "2nd Loop" route. And finally, the last left turn on Sherman Avenue.

It's about a quarter of a mile stretch, slightly downhill to the finish. Children and spectators lined the finish, well beyond the grand stands and carpeted area. It was time to enjoy a good day. I slapped hands with the kids and pumped my arms. The clock came into focus and read 9:55:xx—solid!

215

About the Author

Brady DeHoust lives in Oak Hill, Virginia with his wife and two sons. He began triathlon nine years ago as a middle-of-the-pack racer in short and intermediate distance races. In 2002, he completed his first ultra distance race at the Great Floridian and his love for the long stuff was born. Since then, Brady has completed 11 ultra distance races, qualifying for the World Championships in Kona in 2005. He attributes his improvements over the years to great training partners, consistency, and a very understanding wife. His two young boys also keep him busy even after a long day training.

Brady has a full time job as an independent financial systems consultant, so training hours come early in the morning and often during his lunch hour to keep the evening open for family time. Some of Brady's interests outside of triathlon include watching college sports and the NFL, snowboarding, cooking, and studying nutrition.

Ironman USA®

lake placid, new york

Race Distance: Ultra
2.4 Mile Swim, 112 Mile Bike, 26.2 Mile Run
Month: July
Race Web Site: www.ironmanusa.com

Author: Aaron Schwartzbard
Racing Category: Age Group 30-34

There is a 20 mile stretch of northbound Interstate 87 that I long for. That ribbon of highway is just north of Lake George in New York state, an hour north of Albany. For 51 weeks out of the year, starting in early August, I look forward to the next time I'll drive on that road. From August to April, it's only a passive desire. In May, thoughts of those 20 miles start creeping into my mind at odd times. By June, as the thermometer strains to reach higher and higher marks, I start to understand the instinctual drive that prompts some birds to migrate thousands of miles during certain times of the year. Through most of July, I sweat through "Code Red" days of 95 degree temperatures with 100 percent humidity and, according to daily news reports, "unhealthy levels of ozone." And as those thick, sweaty days slowly pass, I begin to resent the obligations — social, familial, and vocational — that prevent me from beginning my annual migration just a few weeks early.

Finally, the day in late July arrives, and I hit the road. I drive, anxious but happy, singing with the music on the radio, drumming on the steering wheel, sweating through my shirt and shorts, and the hot, humid air blasts me at highway speed through the open window, I drive and I drive. For eight hours I drive until I pass the sign, "Welcome to Adirondack State Park." Just a few minutes later, I'm driving on those magical miles of highway. The temperature drops from 95 degrees to 75 degrees, the humidity disappears, and the sprawling, continuous suburb that seems to have taken over the entire Mid-Atlantic region of the United States is replaced by mountains, rocky cliffs, and lush forests of conifers. I let out a deep sigh and relax. Everything is right once again. That's just the beginning; I know that in another hour, I'll be in the town of Lake Placid. I can hardly wait.

The first of many times I made that trip was in 2001. I had signed up for Ironman USA, in the town of Lake Placid, New York. Deciding where I would compete in my first ultra distance triathlon was not a task I took lightly. The distances involved thoroughly intimidated me. I had been competing in triathlons for several years, but I was still hesitant to call myself an "athlete" out loud.

I felt that perhaps I should do everything in my power to increase the likelihood that I would finish the race. "Everything in my power" it seemed to me would include "NOT signing up for a race through the Adirondack mountains." The part of me that could consider how difficult the race would be told me to find another race. But the part of me that was formed by a lifetime of choosing trips to the mountains rather than trips to the beach was sure that I was meant to go to Lake Placid. In the end, my id conquered my ego, and I signed up for a trip to the Adirondacks.

In the months leading up to the race, I learned several details about the venue. The swim was in Mirror Lake. A permanent underwater guideline (in place for the kayakers who train in the lake) traced the entire swim course, and could be used as a sort of open water lane line. However, during the race, getting close enough to use that line as a guide would require swimming in the most tightly packed group of swimmers. There would be a fair amount of climbing on the bike course. However, none of the climbing would be very steep; the climbs are all long, sustained medium grades. And the run—I only learned that I would develop a deep relationship with the ski jumps and that relationship would not necessarily be one of love. I didn't understand what that meant at the time. I only knew that somehow, some "ski jumps" would play a prominent role in my run.

I arrived in the town of Lake Placid on the Wednesday before the race. As I drove into town, I felt like I was entering Bizzaro World, where triathlon was the national sport. The sidewalks were packed with toned, fit, athletic families who would gladly make way for runners who weaved through the crowds. Cars would make way for packs of cyclists on multi-thousand dollar race bikes. And the lycra... never in my life had I seen so much lycra in one place!

I reached my hotel, and made some time to get my bearings in the town. The part of town that most triathletes come to know best is the half mile of Main Street, between Lake Placid High School and Saranac Avenue. In front of the high school is the 400 meter Olympic Speed Skating Oval, which serves at the transition zone during the race. Next to the high school is the Olympic Center and the Lake Placid Visitors' Bureau. The rest of Main Street is a nice collection of shops and restaurants. Some of the restaurants have seating that overlooks Mirror Lake, the shore of which runs parallel to Main Street. During race week, you can spend all day watching people swim around the long rectangle of buoys marking the swim course.

The town of Lake Placid has a deep connection to sports. It has hosted The Winter Olympic Games twice, in 1932 and in 1980. The Olympic Center, next to Lake Placid High School, was the location of the defeat of the highly favored Russian hockey team by Team USA in the 1980 Olympics. The Ironman USA bike and run courses pass through the shadow of the 90 meter and 120 meter ski jumps just a few mile outside of town, at the Olympic Jumping Complex. Near the end of the bike loop, the bike course passes Whiteface Mountain ski resort, the venue for the Olympic downhill events. Lake Placid attracts world class athletes all year round.

Race morning... I can never decide whether race morning comes too fast or not fast enough. Either way, once it arrived, there was no turning back. I had some breakfast, then wandered two blocks from my hotel to the transition area. Even though it was just a hair past 5:00 a.m. on a Saturday morning, the town was busy. All the lycra-clad, fit, beautiful people I had seen around town for several days were focused on the last-minute, pre-race details. Do the tires have enough air pressure? Did I pack my transition bags correctly? Have I taken all the necessary precautions to prevent chaffing? I was about to embark on my biggest race adventure to date and I felt... I felt... strangely calm. Relaxed. Focused. I wasn't sure why I felt so relaxed; I had expected that I would be jumping out of my skin on race morning. Then it hit me: Enya. At that moment, I recognized the genius of the race organizers; I realized that they had an unparalleled concern for detail. There would be time later to get the athletes excited. But two hours before the race, the concert-sized loud speakers were blaring Enya across the town. And everyone was calmly attending to their race preparations.

Nearly two hours later, as the rising sun was burning a light fog off the surface of the lake and as I was treading water, battling last-minute nerves, the sound track had changed. "ARE YOU RRRRRRRRREADY to RRRRRRRRRRACE!" yelled the voice over the PA system, with high-energy dance music behind him. "IT'S A BEEEEEEEAUTIFUL DAY IN LAKE PLACID TO SWIM, BIKE, AND RUN 140.6 MILES!" With two minutes left before race start, some of the 1,800 racers were still filing into the lake. Around the shore, spectators covered every patch of ground. Every time my mind started to drift to the enormity of what I was about to do, I would quickly tell myself that I only needed to swim 2.4 miles. I could worry about biking and running once I was done with the swim.

When the canon fired, 3,600 arms began to thrash through the water. My plan had been to swim between 10 and 20 meters away from the buoy line. I had been told how much inter-athlete contact there can be along the buoy line, and I wanted to avoid the melee. After 10 minutes of swimming, I noticed that the swimmers around me and I were packed together like sardines in a can. A few strokes later, I understood why: I had drifted to the middle of the action: I was swimming directly over the buoy line. I tried to move out of the thick of the action, but by that point, I could only ride the current created by the other swimmers.

I finished the first loop, followed the swimmers near me as they climbed out of the water for a short run across a beach, and splashed back into the lake to start my second loop. I decided that the first loop was not so bad, so I decided that I'd aim for the buoy line again. Halfway through the second loop—as I made my way around the buoys at the far end of Mirror Lake, and began swimming back to shore—I reached a state where I had the presence of mind realize that I was doing it. "It"—the thing I had spent so many months preparing for, the thing that I had been anticipating and dreading—was happening, and I was part of "it." I took a brief moment during a breath to look down the swim course. Hundreds of swimmers were swimming toward me along one side of the course and hundreds more were swimming away from me along the other side. More than half a mile away, families waited along the beach to watch their loved ones emerge from the water. Beyond that, mountains rose up to the deep blue sky. In a single stroke, as I gulped in enough air to last until the next stroke, I surveyed the scene, and for the first time, I felt supreme confidence in myself.

At the exit to the swim, volunteers pulled my wetsuit off. I weaved around other athletes as I ran to the transition area, a quarter mile from the swim exit. Entering the transition area was like jumping into the mouth of the beast. Through most of the day, I only had to trust my training, and follow the general flow of traffic. But in the transition area, hundreds of athletes and volunteers were moving in hundreds of different directions. Friends who had done the race before had walked me through what would happen when I entered the transition area, but there is no way to know what it is really like until you experience it.

A volunteer pointed me to a narrow aisle between racks of transition bags. As I ran through it, another volunteer pulled my bag off a hook and handed it to me. Another volunteer pointed me to a tent where I could change from my swim gear to my bike gear. As I finished, yet another volunteer helped me pack my swim gear into my transition bag and took my bag while pointing me to the exit of the tent. I ran through rows of bikes, until I came to the row with my bike, where a volunteer was waiting to hand it to me, then another volunteer pointed me to the transition area exit. I knew I was getting close when I heard the refrain that signals the end of T1 to every triathlete, "Do NOT mount your bike until you have crossed this line!" I found the origin of the call, I crossed the line, I got on my bike, and I started to ride. The transition was a dizzying experience, and I was glad I had 112 miles on the bike between me and the next transition.

I finished the swim and started the bike solidly in the middle of the pack. During the first few miles, most cyclists in my view were riding as if trying to find their rhythm, while a few riders rode past me as if they had been shot out of a canon. I knew that the Lake Placid course, like any hilly course, would reward patience. Only the strongest riders could afford to ride aggressively from the beginning.

The first 14 miles of the bike course is on Highway 73, heading east, from Lake Placid to the town of Keene. The first seven miles include gentle, but sustained stairstep climbs to the Cascade Lakes. Then, the road turns downward for a screaming seven mile descent to Keene. As I reached the Cascade Lakes, and I started seeing signs on the side of the road warning trucks to use low gears for the coming descent, I thought I heard cheering. At that point, Highway 73 was a two lane road with guardrails blocking the steep drop into the lake on the right, and high cliffs on the left. Yet I was sure that I heard people cheering! I was utterly confused until I looked up to the rock face on the left, and I saw a dozen climbers, dangling by ropes more than 100 feet up, cheering for the triathletes.

I descended to Keene, tucked deeply with my chest as close to my aerobars as possible. During the first half mile of the descent, even in my highest gear, I could not have applied any force to the pedals. I centered my weight over the bike and let gravity take over.

At the bottom of the descent, in Keene, volunteers and signs directed the athletes to take the sharp left onto Route 9N. The second 14-mile section of the course would take us from Keene to Upper Jay to Jay on the flattest part of the course. In Jay, we would take a left turn onto Highway 86, which we would follow over a series of short, rolling hills to the town of Wilmington.

As soon as I took the left turn in Keene onto 9N, starting that second 14 mile section of the course, I realized that I was starting to fall behind on my nutrition plan. The first 14 miles of the ride had required so much focus that I had forgotten that I needed to eat. Between Keene and Jay, I didn't have to worry about any tough climbs or tricky descents, so I used the opportunity to eat a bit.

In Jay, as I took the left turn onto Highway 86—a two lane road, like most of the highways in the area—I could see cyclists out of their saddles, grinding up the hill for almost a quarter mile. It is certainly not the longest hill on the course, but if there's any hill on the course that is steep enough to get you out of the saddle, it's the climb out of Jay.

I passed several cyclists on the way up, but many of them passed me back as we descended down the back side of the hill. Then I passed most of them on the next hill and they passed me yet again on the back side. For several miles, I was stuck leap-frogging with a group of a dozen riders, all of whom had the same average speed as me. In our group, the climbers would lead the way to the summits, and the descenders would blast past us on the way down again.

The third 14 mile section of the course started with the turn onto Haselton Road. Haselton Road is another two-lane road. The course winds seven miles along the road to the turn-around, then seven miles back to Highway 86. The road rolls with only a couple of noticeable hills. Otherwise, the out-and-back on Haselton Road is a nice opportunity to see who is ahead of you, and who is behind. During the first loop of the bike course, I rode along Haselton Road feeling strong, surprised at how easily the miles were passing. But I was less than 40 miles into the ride at that point. The bike course consists of two 56 mile loops, and during the second loop, it was during the out-and-back when the wheels started to come off, metaphorically speaking. More than 90 miles into the ride, as I was returning to Highway 86, I realized that I was slowing down.

I finished Haselton Road for the second time and only had 14 more miles to ride — from Wilmington to Lake Placid. After riding 98 miles, I realized that to ride well in this race, you have to be able to ride those last 14 miles well. Or more to the point, you have to be able to ride the last 11 miles well. The first three miles out of Wilmington are gentle, then the road turns up. It's not a steep climb; it's not the kind of climb you can power your way up. It is 11 miles of gradual, sustained climbs, punctuated by occasional plateaus. During those last 11 miles, I started calculating and recalculating what my final bike time would be. I had ridden an evenly paced 100 miles, and I thought I could extrapolate a final time from what I had ridden so far. But as I completed each remaining mile, inch by inch, I found myself adding minutes to my expected finish time. When I would reach one of the short plateaus where I might have been able to push back against the forces that pulled my average speed ever lower, I found that I only had the energy to stretch my neck a bit and coast while I prepared mentally for the next incline.

I reached the top, and I was exhausted. After a few short turns, I was back at Mirror Lake, then riding through the town of Lake Placid. Spectators lined the roads and cheered. I wouldn't have thought I had the energy to smile, yet somehow, a smile crept across my face, and stayed there for that final mile through town. I felt the fatigue of 112 miles on the bike and 2.4 miles in the water. But the reception I got as I rode through town made me forget it for a short while. It made me forget that fatigue for at least long enough to get through my second transition. As during T1, volunteers sheparded me through T2, and before I could remember how tired I was, I was starting the marathon.

The run starts with a long, steep, quad-busting downhill, and then continues out of town along the same route that the bike course followed. The spectators grew sparser and sparser as I ran on Highway 73 farther and farther from town. Three miles out of town, I was immediately below the Olympic ski jumps. A volunteer directed me to take a left turn onto Riverside Road. The course is easy enough to follow, even for exhausted triathletes. Head out of town to Riverside Road, turn left, and run on Riverside Road for a few miles. After a few miles, turn around and retrace your steps back to town. Add a short out-and-back that takes you part way around Mirror Lake, and then do it all over again.

As I started running on Riverside Road during my first loop, I was beginning to really understand what an ultra distance triathlon was all about. Swimming 2.4 miles: That's no mean feat. Following the swim with 112 miles of bike riding: That takes an impressive amount of endurance and tenacity. But somewhere in the early miles of the marathon, it becomes something different. It's not just a matter of doing more, or going farther. Less than five miles into the marathon—with more than 20 miles ahead of me—the excitement of doing this event was almost completely replaced by deep fatigue that made me want to do nothing but stop, sit, be done with the task at hand. It was during those difficult miles early in the marathon, when the finish was still so far away, that my motivation changed. I swam and I rode my bike because during the swim, I wanted to finish the race, and during the bike ride, I wanted to finish the race. As I started running on Riverside Road, I no longer cared about finishing the race. Somehow, the finish line seemed arbitrary and irrelevant to my life. Yet I continued to race. I continued to race only because I knew that the "me" who trained for so many months to get to Riverside Road, and the "me" who would have to live with decisions I made on Riverside Road both desperately wanted me to finish. Even if the "me" who was running on Riverside Road didn't care so much about finishing an ultra triathlon, I was no longer running for that me. I was running for the other mes because I felt I owed it to them.

So I started focusing only on the intermediate goals. First, I had to reach the turn-around. Riverside Road is mostly flat, with a few very small hills. After the first mile through open fields, the road wound into the woods. I had ridden my bike on the run course earlier in the week, so as the road began to twist and turn, I started to think that I was almost at the turn around. After each turn in the road, I expected to see the turn-around. I had almost given up all hope, and resigned my self to running out Riverside Road for the rest of eternity, when I finally got to the end of the course. As I ran back toward Highway 73, I wanted to tell people on the other side of the road—people who were still looking for that turnaround—not to abandon hope. Unfortunately, I was too tired for compassion.

Somewhere on my way back, I looked up, and I could see the Olympic ski jumps towering on a mountain just ahead of me. Ah ha! I could just focus on those ski jumps, they would indicate how far I had to run to get to the turn onto Highway 73! Little did I know that on that particular segment of road, conventional laws of optics and geometry did not apply. I ran for five minutes, and the ski jumps did not appear any closer. After another five minutes of running, I could have sworn that they appeared to be farther away than when I first saw them. It did not take long for my feelings about the phenomenon to change from curiosity to resentment. By the time I reached the turn, the ski jumps and I were not on good terms with one another.

I started walking as soon as I reached the first of two big climbs on the way back into town on Highway 73. Other racers who were trying to run up the hill were moving no faster than I was. Seeing the spectators on my way back into town made me realize how lonely Riverside Road had been. Climbing the second big hill on the run course — the "quad-busting" descent that started the run — was fun only because of the spectators who filled every inch of sidewalk space on both sides of the road, encouraging the athletes to "Keep it up" because we were "Lookin' good" and "Doin' great!"

I ran past the transition area and finish line. At about that time, the first man was finishing the race. I could hear the announcer and the cheers for the winner as I was starting my first out-and-back around Mirror Lake. I reached the turn around, and a short while later, I crossed the timing mat that marked the half-marathon point. I had finished half the run. I wasn't sure how to feel as I crossed that timing mat. My initial feeling was that I still had a very long distance to cover. I felt like the turnaround at the far end of Riverside Road was a world away. Then again, for the first time, I felt like I was going to finish the race. Before then, the idea of finishing the race was very abstract. "Theoretically, based on the training I have done and the shape I am in, I should be able to finish the race." Halfway through the marathon, I finally felt, in a very concrete way, that I would finish.

The sign in front of me said, "Second Lap LEFT, Finish RIGHT." I went left. During the second lap, everything was familiar. The spectators on the way out of town, the left turn onto Riverside Road, looking for the turn around, the ski jumps that never got any closer, the hills on the way back into town... Everything was familiar, but the mile markers were just a bit farther apart. There was something else, too. I had aged during that first lap. I looked at all the sights of the second lap with the eyes of experience, as if I was visiting a childhood home, or returning to school years after graduation. That second lap was much more difficult than the first lap, but having been there once, there was less doubt in my mind about what needed to be done: I just had to keep moving.

My emotions caught up with me when I could finally take the right fork in the road. "Second Lap LEFT, Finish RIGHT." At that moment, everything I had experienced in the months of preparation for this race rushed through my head. The sacrifices I had made, the work I had done, the people who helped me: they all came to me in a moment. I'm not one to get caught up in flights of fancy, but if ever there was a moment when I could swear I was literally floating, it was at that moment. I don't recall any fatigue or pain. I don't even recall my feet touching the ground. I floated through the crowds, I floated onto the Olympic speed skating oval that surrounded the transition area, I floated past the jumbo-tron, past the bleachers of cheering spectators, past the grandstand, and I floated across the finish line. And everything I did, it was all for a simple six word proclamation...AARON SCHWARTZBARD, YOU ARE AN IRONMAN!

About the Author

Aaron Schwartzbard has been racing triathlons since 1999. He has finished events at every distance from the short course to the double ultra distance. As a stronger runner than cyclist or swimmer, he currently focuses primarily on marathons and ultramarathons. However, over the years, he has put far too much money into bike gear and wetsuits to give up triathlons entirely.

When not swimming, biking, or running, Aaron does some kind of something with computers. His other interests include cellophane, shiny objects, and Persian tambourine music of the early Qajar dynasty.

Full Vineman Triathlon

santa rosa, california

Race Distance: Ultra
2.4 Mile Swim, 112 Mile Bike, 26.2 Mile Run
Month: August
Race Web Site: www.vineman.com

Author: David B. Glover
Racing Category: Professional

The t-shirt reads "Since 1990," so 2009 will be the 20th anniversary of the Full Vineman Triathlon—a classic race that is the oldest ultra distance triathlon in the United States after the Hawaii Ironman®. The appropriately named Vineman takes place around Santa Rosa, CA in the heart of California's wine country. Sonoma County, the Alexander Valley, and Russian River Valley, make the race a destination race and an "easy sell" to friends and family as in, "I'll do the race on Saturday then we can tour wineries on Sunday."

I did the Full Vineman for the first time in 1998. The experience of a beautiful yet challenging course, superb volunteer support, and overall excellent race experience, cemented into my mind of how incredible a race Vineman was and why it would remain one of my all-time favorites. I subsequently returned in 2001, 2004, 2006, and 2007 for the Full Vineman and plan to race there again in the future.

There are several other races held concurrently with the Full Vineman. There are relays, an Aquabike (swim and bike only), and a special woman's only long course triathlon called Barb's Race (which is also featured in this book).

Relay athletes can race in either the long or ultra distance formats. The Aquabike, also available in both the long and ultra swim and bike distances, is a nice option for someone who does not relish the idea of or is unable to run a half marathon or marathon after swimming and biking. I attempted the Aquabike in 2005 because of nagging run injuries, but a broken crank arm bolt 100 miles into the race prevented me from finishing.

A few months before the 2007 race, I received a call from Russ Pugh, the Vineman Race Director. Russ asked me, "Are you planning to come back to Vineman this year?"

"Absolutely," I said.

"Great, we'd like to induct you into the Vineman Hall of Fame," he replied.

My jaw dropped. As the Hall of Fame inductee, my image would be engraved on the back of all the finishers' medals. I still shake my head at one of my friends who subsequently changed his entry at the last minute from the Aquabike to the Full Vineman just so he could get a medal with my face on the back of it.

There are no qualifications for entry into the race other than to register, although I would strongly recommend not tackling an ultra distance event without experiencing a long course race first. Registration can be completed either online or by mailing in an application form. The race has not sold out in the past, although with the rise in popularity of ultra distance triathlons it will likely sell out in the future. There is, however, an incentive to register early, as there is a discount on entry fees prior to February 1. After February 1, the price goes up a small amount every two months.

With three large airports—San Francisco, Oakland, and Sacramento—within a few hours of driving from Santa Rosa, finding a flight is easy. Even though it is the furthest drive of the three, my preference is to fly into Sacramento because of the simplicity and ease of passing through a mid-sized airport with a bike case. Be forewarned that the traffic on Highway 101, which passes through Santa Rosa, can be stop and go at most any time of day.

There are plenty of hotels in and around Santa Rosa. The Vineman website advises staying in Windsor, Northern Santa Rosa, Healdsburg, or Guerneville, since the race actually takes place to the north and to the west of Santa Rosa. A friend of mine rented a riverfront house in Guerneville for her family, which made for a lovely vacation, but be aware that August is a peak travel time for vacationing in the area so make your reservations early.

Packet pickup and the race expo take place at Windsor High School on Friday afternoon before the Saturday race. The high school also serves as the bike to run transition area and the finish line. There is usually no wait time when picking up your race packet and t-shirt.

The race director holds a pre-race meeting on Friday with a slideshow that discusses the course, logistics and any course changes. The meeting is worth attending, especially for first-time Vineman athletes. At the expo, there are a good variety of vendors available and the last time I raced there I was able to easily pick up a set of lace locks for my running shoes and CO_2 cartridges in case of a flat tire. Friday is also the best time to drop off run gear so that you don't have to deal with it in the morning when it's dark and there are other things to worry about like the race start.

I highly recommend viewing the course a day or two before the race. My preference is to drive my bike to Johnson's Beach for an easy swim followed by an easy bike ride along the first five miles of the bike course. About five miles into the bike course, there is a right turn from River Road onto Sunset Road that is a little tricky so it helps to see the turn from the perspective of being on a bike. Afterwards I drive the bike course. There are a plethora of wineries along the way plus a few places to grab a sandwich so this can be done with friends and family without too many complaints.

The swim is staged at Johnson's Beach in Guerneville, approximately a 20-minute drive from Santa Rosa. After the race, there is a shuttle bus that runs from the high school back to the river for athletes who leave their vehicles parked near the swim start. There is designated parking a short walk from the swim start.

The out-and-back swim takes place in the Russian River. Full Vineman athletes swim two out-and-back loops while the long course distance racers do a single loop. "A river?" you may wonder. "What about current?"

The Russian River is dammed during the summer dry season so there is very little flow—I have never noticed it in any of the years that I raced. The course is well marked with large bright orange buoys and purple buoys at the turnaround making course sighting while swimming a breeze. There are wave starts so crowding is never an issue. Finally, the river itself is probably no more than 80 feet wide at its widest point with an average depth between four and seven feet making it an ideal race for athletes who are uncomfortable in open water.

Early in the morning, air temperatures generally range from the low- to mid-50s with water temperatures typically in the low to mid 70s. The swim has been wetsuit legal every year that I have participated. I typically swim with a sleeveless long john wetsuit and feel comfortable with the water temperature. Sometimes the mornings are foggy, making sighting of far buoys somewhat challenging but this is not a real issue given that the course is narrow and it is impossible to stray off course.

In 2007, I came out of the water in a little under 60 minutes, which is a typical finishing time for me at this distance. I was about five minutes back from the leaders.

The 112-mile point-to-point bike portion of the Full Vineman starts from the transition area at Johnson's Beach and heads straight out for approximately ten miles to the main course loop, then loops twice to finish at Windsor High School (site of Friday's packet pickup approximately 15 miles away). It passes by miles and miles of vineyards. Effectively, the course is a lollipop shape with the end of the stem at the swim start.

Bike aid stations are located approximately every ten miles along the course and have bottled water, Gatorade® Endurance Formula, gels, and bars available.

The race Website states: "The gently rolling hills are challenging, but not overwhelming." I agree with this assessment. The course has a nice variety of terrain that is challenging and interesting.

At the halfway point on the bike in 2007, as I passed by Windsor High School, the race director who was riding on a scooter held up a small white board with my elapsed time after the leader. I was in second place overall and 7.5 minutes back having lost 2.5 minutes since the start of the bike—I stayed "in the zone" and kept pushing my big gear.

Although a cool morning, temperatures were expected to be somewhere in the 80s on race day so I decided to start consuming electrolyte capsules early on the bike to mitigate cramping. I popped a capsule each time I passed an aid station on the bike then every mile or two on the run. Consuming the electrolyte tablets paid off later in the race as I avoided cramping.

As I rode, my mind drifted back to when I first heard about Vineman on a message board in 1995 when I first began competing in triathlons. At the time, Vineman was one of only a handful of ultra distance races in North America. As I read through the positive comments about Vineman on the discussion threads, the race stuck in my mind as a "must do" race.

During the bike segment, the course passes approximately 20 wineries and dozens of vineyards – I hope to get a more accurate count one day, but whenever I start counting, I lose track at some point during the race. The infamous Chalk Hill— a long climb around mile 46 and mile 102—has its own prestigious Chalk Hill winery.

With two miles to go, I saw the lead police vehicle and the lead rider. I dropped the hammer and flew by him in the last mile. I came into the Bike to Run Transition

Area to an empty bike rack in just under five hours and in the lead. I quickly transitioned from my bike helmet and bike shoes into my running visor and running shoes.

Starting from the Windsor High School, the 26.2 mile Full Vineman run course is a three loop out-and-back course that I consider flat to rolling. Athletes competing in the half-relay and Barb's race do 1.5 loops. Aid stations are staged approximately every mile and serve sports drink, water, gel, cola, assorted fruit, cookies and salty pretzels. Athletes return to the high school at the end of each loop to run around the transition area, where they are given "glow-in-the-dark" green and purple Vineman bracelets to track laps, before heading out again.

The transition area at Windsor High School is the best place for spectators to watch the bike and run portions of the race since the bike leg passes by the high school for the second loop and the runners always return to the transition area. There are also food vendors on hand and two race announcers to provide non-stop commentary that is both funny and informational. Downtown Windsor, which has restaurants and shops, is also only a short walk away from the high school.

I told the race director in 2007 that my goal was to do a sub three-hour marathon, but I quickly realized that this goal was not in the cards that day. I ran instead to build then maintain a lead over the trailing runners. I felt comfortable and in control, "I should be able to maintain this pace," I told myself. I did maintain my pace for the most part although I experienced periods of lows, which are common to athletes racing at this distance.

The three out-and-backs make for a very spectator friendly and athlete friendly course. As I passed friends going in the opposite direction, we exchanged slaps and words of encouragement. I also knew exactly where I stood relative to the athletes chasing behind me by measuring the time gap after each turnaround.

As I approached the finish line, I slapped the outstretched hands of the crowd and waved my arms overhead for victory. I crossed the finish line in 9:17 in first place, with a big smile on my face and a new course PR for me.

The awards ceremony for the Full Vineman Triathlon takes place on Sunday and includes an outstanding slideshow that is set to music and covers the entire event in pictures from pre-race to finish.

Vineman offers unique awards — logo engraved wooden boxed bottles of wine from La Crema, a local winery and longtime sponsor of the event. On Sunday during the awards ceremony, I collected a super magnum-sized bottle of 2005 La Crema Pinot Noir — which is a very nice wine by the way — for my win.

A special thanks to all the folks at the Vineman World Headquarters plus the other staff and hundreds of volunteers that make this event so special!

I look forward to racing Vineman again.

About the Author

David B. Glover has competed in almost 100 triathlons since 1995 including 25 ultra distance events with an 8:51 PR at that distance. The 2007 Full Vineman race was his 23rd ultra distance event and fifth time doing this race where he has finished first twice, second twice and fifth overall. In 2007, David also had the honor of being inducted into the Vineman Hall of Fame. To find out more about David, please visit www.davidglover.net.

Ironman Louisville Triathlon®

louisville, kentucky

Race Distance: Ultra
2.4 Mile Swim, 112 Mile Bike, 26.2 Mile Run
Month: August
Race Web Site: www.ironmanlouisville.com

Author: Jean Colsant
Racing Category: Age Group 35-39

As the old adage goes, you have to walk before you can run. I started doing triathlons in the summer of 2004. A girlfriend of mine had completed a few triathlons and asked if I wanted to do a short course race with her. I said, "Sure, why not, it'll put something on the calendar and it'll get me exercising again." If someone would've told me then that in a few years I'd be doing Ironman Louisville I would've died in a violent fit of laughter.

Having one short course triathlon under my belt I thought an ultra distance race would be complete insanity; it's a race for the mentally unstable, the super human, the genetically gifted, and the freaky athletes of the world.

Over the next couple of seasons I did more short course races and a few intermediate distance triathlons. I even made the leap and signed up for a long course race. I thought that distance was going to break me, and I'd never be whole again. When I crossed the line feeling relatively strong, I started thinking about what a marathon might do to my body. It's incredible how these thoughts in your head start to snowball.

With the encouragement from a friend, we decided to sign up together for the inaugural Ironman Louisville. Good thing we didn't drag our feet because the race filled within a week. Participants do not need to qualify to race at Louisville, you just need to pay the entry fee, prepare mentally and physically, and bring your suitcase of courage.

To prepare for this daunting race, I signed up for a marathon in March to see what 26.2 miles would do to my body. While training for the marathon, I tweaked the IT band in my right leg. I managed to run the marathon without any significant IT band evils, but it got me thinking that maybe I needed a coach to guide me though the rigorous training demands for an ultra distance race.

I attended a swimming clinic and one of the instructors was a coach and professional triathlete currently accepting new clients. After learning he had completed over 20 ultra distance triathlons, even winning two of them, I thought this guy obviously knows what he's doing. Where do I sign?

Working with an experienced coach and accomplished triathlete was one of my smartest decisions. In addition to the training plan, he also helped me visualize and mentally prepare for the big day. Of course you need to be physically ready to race this distance, but I learned that mental fitness is equally as important.

In a moment of serendipity, my coach decided at the last minute to race at Louisville too. I was beyond thrilled. It was a huge mental boost to know my coach was going to be there suffering with me.

Training for the race flew by. Before I knew it August was upon us and the race was only a few days away. My beau and I, along with my coach and friend I signed up with, made the 10-hour drive from Arlington, Virginia to Louisville, Kentucky. My family was coming from all corners of the country to rendezvous in Louisville and cheer me on. I was so excited to have them all there, plus my mom even made everyone a special, bright red t-shirt with "GO JEAN, the IRON BEAN!" on the front. When we arrived in Louisville the weather was very similar to the conditions in Arlington, Virginia—hot, sticky and humid. Several days before the race I was drinking water and sport drink to stay well hydrated and keep the tank topped off. The forecasts were all predicting a hot race day and it didn't disappoint.

Several months prior to the big day, the race organizers did a great job of emailing important race information to the participants. The first wave came early and it gave us information about lodging deals with local hotels. As race day neared, we received an athlete information guide. The guide included information about athlete check-in, bike check-in, the transition area on the Great Lawn, course maps, course descriptions, spectator parking, all the race rules, a schedule of events, medical information, aid stations, etc. Having never done an ultra distance race before, I was a newbie and had lots of questions. I printed it off and referred to it frequently.

Knowing I had a sizable crowd coming to Louisville, we took advantage of the hotel discounts and booked rooms at the Galt House several months in advance. Also, the location of the Galt House was situated a stone's throw from the race start. The last thing you want the morning of your race is to be stuck in a traffic jam. When we arrived, the 1,200-room hotel was teaming with racers and their support crews. I've never seen so many extraordinarily fit people in one place in my entire life. What a spectacle!

We arrived a few days before the race to take care of registration, go for a practice swim in the Ohio River, check our bikes in, attend a race briefing, and walk through the sports expo. Triathletes often recommend to never do the inaugural race because the organizers haven't worked out the kinks with the first one. But after going through all these pre-race activities, I was confident the Ironman Louisville folks knew what they were doing; the level of organization was like a well-oiled machine.

The sports expo was entertaining for racers as well as the support crews. There were plenty of triathlon sponsors selling their gear and demonstrating their products. In case you needed something adjusted or fixed on your bike, there were several mechanic stations available. One of the sponsors set up tables with poster boards and markers so that supporters could create signs for their racers. I saw one sign that said "Daddy race faster, mommy wants a trip to Hawaii!" My family must have spent considerable time at these tables. As I crept out of my room at 5:00 a.m. to head to the race, the entire hallway was decorated with these carefully-crafted, hand-made signs. What a boost to get right before the race!

During the race briefing we were told that because of the recent heavy rainfall, the race director decided to go to "Plan B" for the swim. They altered the course slightly and changed the format from the traditional mass start to a time trial start. I must admit, I was not looking forward to the pandemonium of jumping into the river at the same time with 2,000 other racers, so I was ecstatic about the more orderly time trial start, leaping off the end of a pier, three at a time. Because the water temps were in the 80s, wet suits were prohibited. The speed of the current, however, made up for missing the buoyancy of my wet suit. The current was fast and it shot us down the river in record time.

I cannot say enough great things about the legion of volunteers the City of Louisville provided for this race. I heard there were 4,000 volunteers dedicated to help 2,000 racers. Hands down, those are excellent numbers if you're a racer. The volunteers were quick, efficient and always ready with a free hand to help you in whatever way.

With the help of a kind volunteer in the women's transition tent, I was off for a long bike ride through beautiful Kentucky horse country. I remember hitting mile 90 and thinking, bummer, it's almost over. The course had just enough changes in elevation to make it interesting, without completely frying my legs. The course included a two loop section that passed through the town of LaGrange. This was a brilliant idea and a great location for family and friends to gather and cheer on their racers. As I approached the town I could hear the cheers and it instantly boosted my adrenaline and spirits. I scanned the throngs for my exceptional support crew sporting their specially made, bright red t-shirts. They were easy to spot!

For the most part, the roads that comprised the course were in good condition. It even seemed like some of the roads had been recently paved. There were a couple of areas in the road where racers hit a bump and the area directly after the bump was littered with water bottles and spare tubes. As for course support, there were eight well-stocked, well spaced and abundantly-staffed aid stations.

In the past I've never been much for running. My strategy has always been to enjoy the swim, rock the bike, and hang on for the run. Since I raced a marathon earlier in the year I knew I could run the distance. There was something mind blowing though about running 26 miles after all that swimming and biking, and to do it in 90 degree heat with 90 percent humidity at 3:00 in the afternoon. This is where your mental training comes into play. I tried not to think of it in terms of 26 long miles, but more like a 10K with a 20 mile warm up. Thankfully for me, the course was relatively flat. The run took you on a tour of Louisville. We went past the University of Louisville campus, Churchill Downs, the waterfront, and historic neighborhoods. There were fully stocked and well staffed aid stations at almost every mile. The only cruel design of the two loop, out-and-back course was how close you came to the finish line after you completed the first loop. You could see and hear the crowd going crazy at 4th Street Live, an urban center filled with retailers and restaurants, cheering for whoever was just about to cross the finish line. But no, I'm not finished yet; I've got another loop to go! I managed to dig deep and push on, finishing strong with a huge smile on my face.

Lucky for me, I had my beau with me who without protest accepted the role of Tri Sherpa. After I headed out for the marathon, he picked up my bike at the transition area, along with my bags of disgusting gear and brought it all back to our room in the Galt House. By the time I finished, all my gear had already been taken care of.

Considering this was my first ultra distance race, I didn't have others to compare it to. However compared to other triathlons I've done, I felt Ironman Louisville was well organized and well executed.

About the Author

Jean Colsant is an age group athlete from Arlington, Virginia. She is the IT Director for a committee in the U.S. House of Representatives. At the time she authored this chapter, she had completed four short course triathlons, five intermediate distance triathlons, three long course races, and one ultra distance triathlon.

Ironman Wisconsin®

madison, wisconsin

Race Distance: Ultra
2.4 Mile Swim, 112 Mile Bike, 26.2 Mile Run
Month: September
Race Web Site: www.ironmanwisconsin.com

Author: Brad Culp
Racing Category: Age Group 20-24

When I was a sophomore in college, I transferred to Miami University, in Oxford, Ohio. I spent my freshman year swimming out East and had a less than satisfactory season, to say the least. I had planned on transferring and swimming for the next three years, but after a month of try-outs, I was cut from Miami's team.

The coach told me that my strokes weren't efficient enough and it would be hard for me to develop the kind of endurance needed for further progression in the sport. I kindly thanked him for his time and told him that I would do an ultra distance triathlon the following year.

He thought that sounded like a great idea and the last thing he said was "Keep smiling." Up until that point I wasn't the least bit upset. I knew it would be hard for a transfer to make the team, and I understood his reasons for letting me go. However, when he said those two words it made my blood boil. It sounded so patronizing, like he had broken me and my life would be somewhat less satisfying without swimming. I know this wasn't his intention, but I was a little emotionally charged at the moment and I couldn't help getting upset. I smiled and walked out of his office.

I jogged from the pool back to my dorm room. It was the first time I had run in years, but I had to start training at some point. A half mile later, I was at my computer and filling out the registration form for Ironman Wisconsin.

My roommate was very confused.

"I thought you were on the swim team," he said.

"It's a long story," I replied. "I'm going running."

I laced up my basketball shoes (I didn't own running shoes) and logged about eight miles on the local trails. Those eight miles would prove to be harder than finishing my first ultra distance triathlon.

I slept like a baby that night and dreamt about Mike Reily exclaiming "Brad Culp, you are an Ironman!"

I could hardly walk the next morning, so I decided that an early jog was out of the question, but I wasn't about to take a day off. I had 11 months to make 140.6 miles doable. At that point, I weighed 195 pounds and could bench press almost twice that. I knew neither of these attributes would help me make it to that finish line. Needless to say, I had work to do, but time was on my side. I'm pretty sure I skipped a few classes that day to get in a long bike ride and shed some of that triathlon un-specific muscle.

That Christmas, there was an indoor trainer under the tree, which helped me get into triathlon shape that winter. I completed my first long course triathlon that April and damn-near killed myself en route to a respectable 5:15 finish.

I also started a triathlon club that spring and managed to get a small group of athletes to travel to Arizona to compete in the Collegiate National Championship. It was nice to feel like I was part of a team again. Unfortunately, none of my new teammates were planning on doing an ultra distance race so most of my training was done solo.

I spent the summer leading up to Ironman Wisconsin working as a swim coach, which left most of my afternoons open for training.

I made the long drive from Ohio to Madison on the Thursday before the race. I wanted to get up there early and have a few days to unwind. I had considered flying, but Madison and Milwaukee tend to be expensive places to fly into. I booked a hotel well in advance of the race, but I still couldn't find anything near downtown. Instead, I stayed on the east side of town, which ended up working out, since it was easier to get around that area. I ended up staying in East Towne again the following year.

I thoroughly enjoyed the pre-race festivities and made sure to soak up the whole Ironman® experience. I was even called up on stage at the carb-load dinner. I had no idea beforehand, but it turned out I was the youngest athlete at the race (I had turned 20 a few days beforehand). They threw the microphone in my face and wanted to know why the heck a college student would do something like an Ironman. I talked about my experience being cut from the swim team and walked off the stage to the cheers of 2,000 other athletes. That was the first time during the weekend that I really got pumped up for the race. Before I was nervous, now I couldn't wait until race day.

I sprung out of bed on race morning without an alarm, which is extremely rare for me. After a brief walk-through of the transition area I headed down to the beach at Lake Monona to get ready for the swim. The transition area is actually a giant building called the Monona Terrace, which is perfect for staging a race of this size. Bikes go on top of the parking garage and spectators are treated to a panoramic view of the swim.

Before I got in the lake for a quick warm up, I made sure to ask a volunteer for a marker. In big, bold letters I wrote "KEEP" on my left arm and "SMILING" on my right. I knew that when the race began to get the best of me all I needed was one glance at those words to get my blood boiling like it had in my coach's office one year ago.

By the time we started the swim, the mercury was already over 70 degrees. There was no doubt that it was going to be a tough day to make it through 140.6 miles. Wisconsin has wildly unpredictable weather in September. The following year, the temperature barely reached 50 degrees. This made for a frigid bike ride, but one of the best marathons of my life. Don't expect the temperature to be anything less than extreme on race day.

The swim in Madison is typically tame, although there can be a little chop, especially on a windy day (note: it's almost always windy in Central Wisconsin). Even though the weather can be hot, the swim is always wetsuit legal.

During my first time at Ironman Wisconsin, the lake was absolute glass, and I made my way through the swim in a tick over 50 minutes, which was even faster than I was expecting. I was lucky and I got away from the pack at the start and avoided any elbows or knees to the face.

I never rush through transition, especially at long events. To my surprise, a friend of mine was volunteering in the transition area. He helped me get all my bike gear ready to go and after a very brief chat, I was on my way out to Verona to complete two very hilly bike loops.

The bike course heads 16 miles west of Madison and remains relatively flat for this stretch. I say relatively flat because the rest of the course is an absolute beast — unless non-stop hills are your kind of thing. I think I consumed three salt tabs during the first 20 miles. It was only 9:00 a.m., but the temperature was already north of 80 degrees and showed no signs of cooling off.

The goal was to complete each of the 40-mile loops in as close to two hours as possible. However, once the wind picked up and the heat hit its midday high of 94 degrees, I had given up all hope of hitting my goal time. After my first loop, I was already in survival mode—something I hadn't planned on reaching until halfway through the marathon. At this point, my mind switched from focusing on my goal of finishing in around 11 hours to just finishing, period. At times, especially when the wind was gusting hot air at my face, a 17-hour finish sounded just fine to me.

Thankfully for myself and the 2,400 other competitors, there were huge crowds along every steep climb, helping to get us to the top. At the Old Sauk Pass—by far the worst climb of the day—there was a guy dressed in a devil costume cooking bacon on the side of the road. I almost stopped for a strip or two.

Another relief was that the wind was howling at our backs as we made our way back to Mad-town. This gave me about a 1/2 hour to loosen up my legs before I attempted the first marathon of my life.

I'll never forget the feeling I had when I attempted to dismount my bike. I literally collapsed into the arms of the guy who was there to catch my bike. After about 20 seconds on the pavement, I was hobbling through T2.

It's probably a good thing that I was so delirious from the heat, because the fact that I was about to run 26.2 miles under that sun never really hit me. My family was there as I made my way out of the Monona Terrace, which gave me a much needed boost.

The race fell on September 11, which, among other things, was my Mom's birthday. I was so out of it at the start of the marathon that I forgot to wish her a happy birthday. However, I promised myself I wouldn't forget at the finish line.

The run course in Madison is spectacular and relatively easy, compared to the bike. The two loop run remains in the heart of Mad-town the whole way and the streets are packed with fans, spectators and University of Wisconsin students enjoying a few afternoon drinks. They all do wonders to take your mind of the fact that this is a really hard race.

Much to my surprise, my legs felt strong for the first 18 miles of the run. I definitely wasn't moving fast, and I felt like a snail as the eventual winner lapped me en route to a nine-hour finish.

"Someday," I said to myself, as I watched him charge toward the finish, "But definitely not today."

With about six miles left, my body shifted from survival mode to desperation mode. My legs were cramping, my stomach was in revolt, and I couldn't get any electrolytes to stay in my system. The sun was finally sinking, which offered a bit of a reprieve, but it certainly wasn't cool, by any stretch of the imagination.

I took a glance at the words written on my arms to give me that final push. It was a much needed reminder of why I was doing this. It was something that so many people, including myself thought to be impossible for so long. Now, I was only a few miles away from a finish I would never forget and the best tasting beer of my life.

Miles 18 to 25 were a blur, which was probably a good thing. I walked through the aid stations and sucked down chicken broth as if it actually tasted good. All the pain subsided about a 1/2 mile from the finish. At that point in the race, you reach the heart of downtown and all you need to do is make the steep climb back to the Wisconsin state capitol building and one of the most scenic finishes in the sport.

My parents were waiting in the chute and after wishing my mom a "Happy Birthday," I tuned in to hear the words which I had been waiting on for 12 hours. I still remember every word.

"Coming to the finish is Brad Culp, our youngest athlete here today. Brad was cut from his swim team because he didn't have enough endurance. I think he proved that wrong today. Brad, you are an Ironman!"

I broke the tape and collapsed from a combination of tears and exhaustion. It was the most fulfilling moment of my life, and I just wanted to slow it down and remember every second.

When I stood up, my brother was waiting there with two Sam Adams® in hand. My stomach was a wreck, but I wasn't about to turn that down.

"Why the hell do you have 'Keep Smiling' written on your arms?" he asked.

"It's a long story," I replied. "Just give me that beer."

At the awards ceremony the next morning, we learned that almost 20 percent of the athletes didn't make it to the finish — the most ever for the event. That number was almost as high the following year, when temperatures failed to reach above 55 degrees.

With Madison, you never know what you're going to get. Rain, heat, wind, or cold — it makes you work for the finish and that's what makes it the most rewarding race I've ever done.

About the Author

Brad Culp, 23, currently resides in La Jolla, California. He is the editor of *Triathlete* magazine, where he has worked for three years. He's been competing in triathlons for eight years and has raced in over 50 competitions, including six ultra distance races. Feel free to contact him at bculp@competitorgroup.com.

Ford Ironman World Championship®

kona, hawaii

Race Distance: Ultra
2.4 Mile Swim, 112 Mile Bike, 26.2 Mile Run
Month: October
Race Web Site: www.ironman.com/worldchampionship

Author: Hope Hall
Racing Category: Age Group 40-44

Aqua-Rock (ah-kwuh•rok) - noun: Derogatory term used at the U.S. Naval Academy for one who swims poorly.

I was an aqua-rock. Just my luck that I selected a college with a mandatory yearly swim test. Of course, it stands to reason that if young officers will be serving this country while sailing across the seven seas, the ability to swim might be a valuable skill. I approached each yearly swim test with gut-wrenching apprehension and passed each one by the skin of my teeth. Every year, I ingested gallons of chlorinated water, fighting the urge to simply give up and sink to the bottom of the pool. I sputtered, gasped and cursed my way through each test. My only comfort, my saving grace was the knowledge that with each passing grade, I was one year closer to NEVER, EVER having to swim again. I swore I would keep myself firmly planted on solid ground. I would run marathons. I would ride my bike. I would remain happily dry for the rest of my natural days! So, wait. Doesn't the first leg of each triathlon begin with a swim? What happened, you ask? How did a land-loving, water-hating midshipman become a four-time finisher of the Hawaii Ironman World Championship®?

My friend Doug and I were stationed together at the Joint Intelligence Center Pacific, located in Pearl Harbor, Hawaii. Now, Doug was a smart fella, but not much of a betting man. Ask me what the wager was over and I won't be able to tell you, but what I do know with certainty is that Doug lost a huge bet to me. His penance? He had to teach me how to swim. That would prove to be a monumental task, but it would also be the catalyst for my love affair with the sport of triathlon.

While stationed in Hawaii, I caught the triathlon bug, diagnosed as "triathalitis." Truth be told, triathalitis is like a tropical disease. Symptoms include: 1) inability to sleep beyond 5:00 a.m., even on the weekends and holidays; 2) insatiable appetite for such marvelous taste sensations as sport gel; 3) rapidly dwindling savings account as "better" equipment is procured each season; 4) hairlessness; and 5) an inexplicable drive to qualify as a competitor at the Ironman World Championship. Possible side effects may include: Dry mouth, blackened toenails, overactive bowels, sore muscles, sunburn, windburn, saddleburn, and death. Okay, I'm just kiddin' about the death part.

As soon as I arrived on the island, I noticed groups of people swimming in the ocean as the Hawaiian sun rose over Ala Moana Beach Park. This same group would then scurry out of the water and hop on fancy tricked out bicycles for a quick pedal around the island, followed immediately by a running tour of Diamond Head. Who were these people and how could I infiltrate their exclusive tribe? As I studied this unusual species of athlete, I became intrigued, obsessed even (another symptom of early onset triathalitis). I knew my days of staying out of the water were coming to a close.

Back to Doug. Each afternoon, he dutifully took me to the pool. I can only now imagine the horror he must have felt when he witnessed my first pathetic lap. Doug had been a swimmer at the Academy. I'm sure he must have thought, "Hope's a pretty good runner. How is it possible that she is so horrible in the water? I should probably update my CPR license." True to his word, Doug upheld his end of the bargain and patiently taught me the basic elements of swimming. As time passed, I gained confidence and enough skill to make me think I might be able to join the ranks of those crazy triathletes.

In Hawaii, triathlon was already a mainstream sport in the early 90s. The U.S. mainland was lagging behind the islands and triathlon was still an obscure "fringe" sport in most parts of the country, save California. Sure, many sports enthusiasts knew of the famed Julie Moss crawl to the finish line of the Hawaii Ironman. Remember that image splashed on television screens worldwide, forever marking the sport as suitable for only a few lunatics with way too much time and energy on their hands? Triathlon fever was rampant, contagious and encouraged in Hawaii. Triathletes swarmed the local beaches, rode through the pineapple fields of the North Shore, all the while swapping stories about watching first hand the epic battles in the lava fields between Dave Scott and Mark Allen, or watching Paula Newby Fraser and Erin Bakker duke it out on the Queen K highway. The legends of this sport were revered and athletically without parallel in the minds of Hawaiian triathletes.

From a historical perspective, Navy Commander John Collins is credited with the concept of combining the Waikiki Rough Water swim (2.4 miles), the Around Oahu Bike Race (112 miles) and the Honolulu Marathon (26.2 miles) into a single endurance event. Folk lore tells us that a friendly argument erupted over who is the best endurance athlete — a swimmer, a runner, or a cyclist. Whoever finished the combined three Hawaiian endurance events first would be crowned the "Ironman."

I braved the waters of the Pacific for my very first Ironman World Championship in October of 1995. I had been participating in triathlons for three years, always with the idea of trying to qualify for "the big show." I have always believed (and still do) that qualifying for this race is a special mixture of skill, luck and selecting the right qualifying race. In the mid-1990s, before many of today's qualifiers existed, there were a handful of North American races of the long course distance or shorter that would allow an athlete to punch a ticket to the Big Island. In 1995, I qualified at the Fairmount Park race in Philadelphia. I would qualify at this same race in 1996. When this event was moved to Allentown, Pennsylvania, I qualified again in 1998. Three exciting and memorable trips to the World Championship resulted, but it was only when I qualified more recently at Ironman USA® in Lake Placid, New York that the impact of the championship race finally hit me. Perhaps it was because I was older. Perhaps it was because I had taken a bit of a hiatus from the sport to focus on other life events. Perhaps it was because my close friends and family had agreed to join me for the adventure. Whatever the reason, my most recent trip to the Big Island of Hawaii carved a special niche in my soul.

I called a few close friends and family members on my drive back home to Virginia after accepting my Hawaii slot at Ironman USA in Lake Placid. I was on cloud nine! Little did I know that most of my friends already knew the outcome as they had watched the race unfold courtesy of online race updates. When I returned to work a couple of days after the race, I found my co-workers dressed in Hawaiian shirts and my cube completely converted into a Hawaiian tiki hut. My friends had taken me by surprise and I was moved to tears by their actions. They understood how important qualifying for Hawaii was to me and they celebrated with me. I was thrilled at their response, but moreover, I was determined to be at my best when I arrived on the Big Island. I didn't want to disappoint myself or my incredibly supportive friends.

I poured my soul into my training. I had work commitments that couldn't slip, but I managed, with the help of tireless and dedicated training partners, to train upward of 20 hours a week. My friend Bill Beyer dragged me up and down the hills of rural Virginia on epic bike rides. He taught me the healing power of humor as he entertained me with endless stories that had me laughing too hard to continue pedaling. Another friend, Gary Grilliot, ran the local trails with me for upwards of three hours and his wife, Lindsey, allowed me to draft off her for countless laps in the YMCA pool. Holding down a full time job, keeping family commitments and basically performing those tasks required to keep your life in balance while training for such a race can be an interesting and challenging juggling act. But, believe me when I say that it can be done.

In October, I boarded a Continental Airline flight ultimately bound for Kona, Hawaii. Both of my sisters, my mom, and five close friends formed my "entourage." Having these eight important people accompany me meant more than I could begin to express. We arrived on the island completely jet lagged on the Tuesday afternoon preceding the race. I stepped off the plane onto the sizzling Hawaiian tarmac. After being trapped inside an air conditioned capsule for the better part of a day, the heat of Kona smacked me in the face like an angry hand. There was a six hour time difference between Virginia and Hawaii, and I felt completely out of sorts. You know that feeling when your brain and body are just a quarter beat out of sync? Well, that's how I felt. To add to my discomfort, my bike had been shipped via UPS two weeks prior to my departure. I tried not to panic as I realized it had not yet made it to the island. Fortunately, the bike made an appearance on Wednesday and was quickly assembled so I could get in a couple of short rides before the required bike turn-in on Friday afternoon.

I rented a sprawling Hawaiian house situated on a hilltop overlooking Kona Bay. The house had been decorated in the mid-70s and by the looks of it, had not been updated since. I liked the retro feel of the place and took no exception to the invasion and residency of the abundant tropical bugs. Geckos peered down at me each morning as I brewed Kona coffee and the centipedes simply rolled up in a ball the minute I scooped them up to fling them outside. Sunset from the lanai of this house was worth the price of the ticket alone.

My first foray into the hustle and bustle of the downtown Kona area was early Wednesday morning. Like most other athletes, I headed to Dig Me Beach, the official swim start area, to squeeze in a last minute swim. Okay, time for total honesty here. Dig Me Beach is one intimidating venue for an easy morning swim! I was surrounded by the best long distance triathletes in the world and it looked like each one of them had been recently chiseled from a piece of flesh tone marble. These folks were race ready! My friend, Lindsey, and I eased into the warm Pacific Ocean and within a couple of strokes, we were in deep water looking down at coral reefs and darting schools of tropical fish. The Hawaiian waters were crystal clear and thanks to the high salinity, even without a wetsuit, I was buoyant. I briefly wondered if I would be able to distract myself on race day by looking down at the fish while swimming the course. Probably not a good idea, given the fact that I would be thrashing through a sea of bodies, trying not to get clocked by a competitor's wild swim stroke!

My next step in the Ironman journey was packet pick-up, held at the official race hotel, the King Kamahamaha. The Kona race officials and volunteers had athlete check-in and packet pickup down to a science. I was guided through the process by a slew of friendly, smiling, tireless volunteers. (Note to self: Volunteer at a race. It's the best way to give something back to the sport.) Even though my nerves were already on edge, the kindness of the volunteer who patiently explained the contents of my race packet had a way of putting me at ease. I emerged from the packet pick-up process with a numbered band affixed to my right wrist. Now, I was marked for all to see as an Ironman competitor. There was no hiding anymore.

While an athlete may be tempted to keep to themselves and focus on the task at hand, it was impossible to avoid getting caught up in the excitement of the race. The entire town of Kona participated in the race preparations the week before race day. There were banners welcoming the athletes. All of the shops and restaurants catered to the shopping and dining desires of a triathlete. The Ironman "M-dot" logo was literally EVERYWHERE.

People watching was a favorite pasttime of mine. I sat on the sea wall and watched the groups of excited athletes and their family members walk past. I caught snippets of conversations, some of which went something like this: "Oh, that's not deodorant I put on my butt. That's Body Glide." "I sat beside Natashia Badmann last night at dinner. I'm pretty sure she remembered me from last year." "I hate tapering." "I've never seen 'Grey's Anatomy.' If it's on past 9:00 p.m., I'm already asleep."

With the bike and gear bags turned in, I worried that I would not be able to sleep the night before the race. I was right. Despite the fact that my family cooked a huge pasta dinner at our retro house, I tossed and turned for hours before sleep finally found me. My alarm was set for 4:00 a.m., and I bounced out of bed the minute I heard it. It was race day. My friends drove me to the athlete drop off for body marking, entertaining me with an a cappella version of Mariah Carey's "We Belong Together." That song would remain with me the entire race. Gee, thanks guys!

To say the athletes were on edge would be an understatement. Many carried that 1,000 yard stare. Many wore headphones. Some chatted nervously. Some actually warmed up. Every single one of us pondered the same unanswerable question: What would the day bring? Would we get seasick in the rolling ocean? Would the notorious winds blow the bikes sideways? Would the "fry an egg on the lava" heat bring us to our knees? I waded into the warm water and took one last look at the crowds gathered on the sea wall before swimming out to await the cannon.

Breathe. Wait. Settle. Breathe. Wait. BOOM! And with that, 1,800 athletes began a life altering journey.

I emerged from the water a little disoriented, my lips swollen from the salt water and my eyes puffy from the goggles. I raced into the changing tent to put on a jersey and slather myself with sunscreen. I began the bike, telling myself to keep my heart rate in check. The bike course is deceptively hilly. At the risk of alienating some hardcore lava enthusiasts, the course is not exactly scenic. Ocean on one side, lava on the other. That's it. That's all you get to see for 112 miles. I would have been somewhat lonely if Mariah Carey wasn't having a concert in my head!

I reached the halfway point of the bike course in the town of Hawi after having ridden for close to three hours. I remembered from racing here in the past that I should prepare myself for the famed winds on the return trip, but much to my joy, the winds remained suspiciously calm. I waited nervously to get blown sideways, but the gods smiled on the athletes and the wind never materialized. I rolled into the second transition, posting a sub-six hour ride. Now, for my favorite part of the whole day…the marathon!

I loved, loved, loved the third and final leg of the race. Even in the heat of the Hawaiian lava fields, I felt at home with my feet planted on the earth. I appreciated the rhythm of the marathon. I told myself to run with the measured stride of a demanding metronome. During the marathon, I could talk, even if only briefly, to other athletes. We all got a little lonely out there, so a kind word or encouraging nod never went unnoticed.

The marathon course was fairly spectator friendly for the first 10 miles. However, once I ran up Pick and Save Hill and turned onto the Queen K Highway, I quickly learned the definition of the lonesome marathon. The road shimmered with rising heat and I could barely make out the outline of the next aid station. I ticked off the miles by telling myself that I would run between each aid station and then just walk a bit at the station, downing a combination of Coke®, Gatorade®, and bananas. The sun was setting as I neared the town of Kona. I could feel the blisters on my feet swelling to maximum capacity. I wanted to finish this race more than words can describe. The crowds grew louder as I neared the turn onto Alii Drive. This was my moment. To my absolute delight, I heard the sweetest phrase in the sport of triathlon: "Hope Hall from Reston, Virginia, you are an Ironman!"

10 hours, 58 minutes, and 10 seconds after hearing the cannon fire, I had completed my journey. In retrospect, I wonder if crossing the finish line of the Ironman World Championship was the end of a journey or merely the beginning. Ask 100 athletes what the most difficult part of the race is and you will likely get 100 different answers. Here are a few of the hurdles a triathlete must clear:

1) The training time required. You forego trips to wineries with your friends in order to spend all day Saturday with your butt firmly planted on a bicycle seat.
2) The elements encountered on race day. Kona is windy and hot. Not exactly optimal conditions for peak athletic performance.
3) The cost. An Ironman race is expensive, so is the travel to the race, and so is the equipment required to do the race.
4) Work gets in the way. Your manager is in town and wants to have a team outing the same night as Masters Swim practice.
5) The juggling act with family priorities. Your daughter's team has qualified for the state championship soccer match the same day as your last 100 mile training ride.
6) Personal relationships. The alarm is set for a 5:30 a.m. trail run and your partner is feeling frisky at midnight.
7) Pure statistics. If there are 80 slots available for Hawaii at a particular qualifier and there are 2,500 participants, calculate your odds of winning a slot.

So, why in the world would anyone want to even attempt to race on the Big Island? I'll tell you my opinion. It's that last 200 meters of the race, when either side of Alii Drive is packed with cheering supporters and you can see the finishing banner directly ahead of you. That moment is worth every hardship, every hurdle. In that moment, you realize you have achieved what very few other humans have. You have covered 140.6 miles along side the best athletes in the world. No other obstacle will seem quite as insurmountable. Oh, and by the way, the finishers' t-shirt is sweet! When the stars align just so and you are the recipient of a slot to the Ford Ironman World Championship, take it and, let your journey begin.

About the Author

Hope Hall resides in sunny Southern California where she works as a Project Manager for Tishman Construction. She has been competing in triathlons for about 15 years and is currently preparing for her 12th ultra distance race, this time in Nice, France. She has been lucky enough to have made five trips to the Hawaii Ironman World Championship. While she loves the competitive aspect of the sport, Hope contends that the very best part of being a triathlete is the people you meet along the way. Oh, and the fact that you can continue to eat anything you want even as you age!

Great Floridian Triathlon

clermont, florida

Race Distance: Ultra
2.4 Mile Swim, 112 Mile Bike, 26.2 Mile Run
Month: October
Race Web Site: www.greatfloridian.com

Author: Rob Weitzel
Racing Category: Age Group 40-44

The Great Floridian Triathlon, or GFT as it is better known, has been in existence since 1990. It is an ultra distance triathlon that occurs toward the end of October in the quaint town of Clermont, Florida (about 20 miles outside of Orlando). The GFT is run by Sommer Sports. Sommer Sports hosts a number of triathlon events in the region which end each season with the GFT.

Why would anyone want to endure a race of this distance and at this particular venue? That same thought occurred to me in 1998.

I began my triathlon career of sorts back in the fall of 1997. I entered my first triathlon, a local hometown intermediate distance event when I was 30 years old. Toward the end of the 1998 season I learned that a couple of the guys that I trained with had signed up for a race called the Great Floridian. I inquired about the race and learned that it was an ultra distance race. At that time I never thought it was something I could do because I just could not conceive that ordinary people could enter an event of such magnitude. I found the web page for the GFT and read all about it.

I ended up following the results of that 1998 race, and spoke to my friends about their experiences there. Slowly, I began to feel that maybe it was something I could achieve after all. I realized that there were all kinds of people of differing backgrounds, ages, and speeds that had competed and finished the race that year and that the sport was not closed to mere mortals like me. In fact, all you had to do was pay the entry fee.

I pulled the proverbial trigger when the 1999 registration for the Great Floridian opened. There I was with a full season of racing under my belt and a full season to train and get ready for the biggest sporting event in my very short triathlon career. I thought about all of the things that I needed to do, and I very quickly came to the realization that if I wanted to make it across the finish line in one piece that I would need some kind of help. I also realized that the equipment that I had been using was not quite sufficient for a race at the ultra distance. I acquired a new state of the art triathlon bike. That made a huge difference in comfort. I also acquired a personal coach. It was worth every penny.

My training build up started in the spring of 1999. I religiously tried to follow the training plan that my coach had designed for me. I asked a ton of questions, and tried various nutritional products during my workouts. Some products seemed to work while others did not. It was all one big moving lab experiment while I was out on my bike. I logged on to the GFT forum page. I found that there were a lot of people in the same boat as me and it was a great place to share and learn from others that had already been down the road I was heading.

The heat where I live in Virginia was oppressive that summer. I suffered tremendously on some of my long training rides. What did I get myself into? Would I be able to swim 2.4 miles without drowning? What would happen if I had a mechanical problem on the bike? How in the heck will I ever be able to run a marathon after suffering 112 miles on the bike? My coach told me that the training would get me through most of the race, but there would be variables that could throw a monkey wrench into the works. The pure physical aspects of training can only take you so far. There is also the mental edge and fortitude that one has to forge to train and compete in a race of this distance. You also have to have a very understanding family.

Given the close proximity to Disney World®, I decided to make a full blown vacation out of this trip for me and my family. We stayed about 15 miles outside of Clermont, and about 10 minutes from downtown Disney at one of the many local hotels.

I picked up my race packet the Wednesday afternoon before the race; it was very quick and expeditious. The race packet had all of the essentials in it including a swim cap, race number for the bike, helmet, and race number for the run. It also had a bag for each of the transitions including a swim-to-bike bag, a bike-to-run bag, a special needs bag for the bike course, and a special needs bag for the run course plus a warm up clothes bag for after the race. The packet also contained information about the course as well as a timing chip. There was also some other race schwag including a t-shirt, water bottle and other assorted goodies. There is a race expo where the various gear can be bought. If you forgot something you can typically find it at the expo.

I took my first look at the swim venue. It was a nice clean lake called Lake Minneola. The water was the color of tea from the local trees. The water is safe, but the water clarity makes it hard to spot people. When I saw the lake for the first time I thought it was huge. The swim is a two-lap triangular affair. After you finish the first loop you have to run onto shore and through a timing area before you begin the second and final lap. I did not bother to drive the bike course that year. The course was a single 112-mile loop. Most people do not equate hills with Florida. I can personally tell you that there are hills in Florida and that every one of them sits within the confines of the GFT bike course. The run course that year consisted of a five mile out section that included several very tough hills that snaked through one of the local neighborhoods before it headed back down the local trail and around Lake Minneola for 3-laps for a total of 26.2 tough miles.

I spent Wednesday night and all day Thursday hitting the Disney theme parks. It was a great time, but a lot of walking and I was getting tired out. This was probably not a good thing considering I should have been conserving every ounce of energy I had for race day. It actually turned out to be very stressful because I wanted my family to have fun, but I also needed my time to prepare and that caused some conflict. The Friday before the race I took my bike down to the transition area. They had a bike mechanic onsite that I asked to run my bike through its gears just to make sure everything was working properly before I racked it up for the night. Bikes have to be racked the Friday night before the race and cannot be removed after they are racked. You do have access to your bike when the transition area opens on race day morning to pump up your tires, and to put your race day nutrition and water bottles onboard.

I had a very fitful night of sleep and awoke at 4:00 a.m. The race started at 7:00 a.m. sharp. I wanted to get up early enough to begin fueling my body for the long day ahead and to make sure that I had everything that I needed as well as enough time to drive the 20 or so minutes to the race venue.

I threw up on the drive to the race site. Not a good start to the day. I got body marked with my race numbers on both arms, both thighs and my age on my calf. I donned a large "V" on my other calf which designated me as an ultra-distance virgin. I checked my bike out and placed my bags that I had been given at registration in their proper places. I decided to put a couple of Snickers bars in my bike special needs bag. I would be able to retrieve that bag at a designated spot at approximately 60 miles into the bike ride. I also placed a long sleeve shirt into my run special needs bag. Typically you place anything in either of those special needs bags that you think you might need during the event and to which you can forego getting back afterwards because they typically dispose of them and they can not be retrieved after the race is over.

I put on my sleeveless wetsuit. Most of the time, the GFT is wetsuit legal. Orlando typically gets a major cool off during October that lowers the water temperatures just enough to make it wet suit legal by USAT standards. I temporarily lost my timing chip, and found it before I reached a state of panic. There was nothing more I could do at this point except go racing.

The swim began from the beach and was a mass start. There were close to 900 people ready to go toe to toe with this beast. The gun went off promptly at 7:00 a.m. The start is always confusing and hectic. The swim start is usually like a giant washing machine, and it takes close to half of the first leg to thin out. There was not as much thrashing and bumping and pulling as I had actually felt in some of the smaller races I had done leading up to this event and this was okay by me. The first loop went well and by the second loop I began to fade a bit as expected as I am not a very strong swimmer. I hit T1 in a little over 1:20. That was fine by me as I had not drowned and I was on to the next leg. I entered the changing tent. Stripping off my wetsuit and stuffing it into my swim-to-bike bag. I got everything out of my bag that I needed for the bike ride and proceeded to my racked bike.

I realized later that I had entirely too much stuff on my bike, but I did not want to leave any rock unturned. I proceeded with my nutritional plan but at mile 40 I became violently sick. Race day temps were in the 80s, and it was humid and there were spots on the course that were windy. I struggled through the course with intermittent vomiting. I was unable to hold anything down except water and an occasional cookie that I picked up from one of the bike aid stations. Bike aid is located at about every 10-15 miles and typically offers some sort of electrolyte sports drink, water, and bananas. These stations are manned by volunteers who give up their days to stand out in the heat to assist in making your day go better. These races could not function without the aide of volunteers.

The course has many hills and most begin after a sharp turn which causes a deceleration and lack of speed to begin the climbs. The course was smooth in some parts and rough on other parts. Some parts had sand and gravel that made for potentially treacherous riding if you were not careful. The course in and of itself is not very scenic but I rate it as the toughest bike course I have ever ridden. I suffered tremendously for close to seven hours before I finally made it back to T2.

I handed my bike off to the "bike valet." Yes, they have people who take your bike and rack it for you. I headed into the changing tent and changed into a new top to run in. Inside the changing tents they have volunteers that help apply sun screen, get your food and drink and they also take your bags. I tried to assess my condition and realized that I had lost a lot of fluid through vomiting, and was unable to take in enough calories to give me any strength to survive the run. I left T2 feeling a rush but that soon diminished as I moved away from the crowd surrounding the exit to T2.

Out on the run course I realized I was still pretty sick. I could barely move forward. The first five miles of the run course were hilly and hot. The run course aid stations are placed at about every mile so there was some solace there, but there were times when I just could not make it to the next station without being sick. The aid stations are very well stocked with everything from sports drink, cola, cookies, salt, pretzels and sometimes chicken broth. They typically have a contest to determine who has the most unique aid station. These folks offer lots of encouragement.

The sun finally went down and the atmosphere became somewhat surreal. There was a full moon over the lake and there was not a single cloud in the sky. It was one lap down, two laps down, and on the third lap I could see the lights of the finish line lighting up the night sky. I felt at peace. I felt no pain, no sickness nor weakness. I knew that I was going to finish no matter what and it provided me with a huge adrenalin rush that led me to the finish line.

It took me 13:48 to get to the end of my journey, but I felt a huge sense of satisfaction. I collected my medal and a bottle of water. My mom was the only one waiting for me at the finish line as my girlfriend, sister, and kids were enjoying the theme parks. My mom drove me back to the hotel where she ordered a pizza at 10:00 p.m. while I sat in a hot shower drinking Gatorade®.

I never went to the awards ceremony as I was off again to Disney World for another day with the family. It was a great adventure that I swore I would never do again. Since 1999, however, I have competed in nine ultra distance triathlons including GFT in 2000, 2001, and 2007. The swim course remains the same and the bike course has gone back and forth from a single loop to a double loop and in 2007 back to a single loop. In 2007 the run course saw a much easier five mile out-and-back without the hills of the past before heading out on the three laps around Lake Minneola. I lost my ultra distance virginity at GFT in 1999 and set my second fasted time in 2000 in a time of 11:24.

I highly recommend the Great Floridian to any first timer. It is a very low key race but it can also be one of the hardest and most unforgiving races because of the hills, heat and wind. It is a very well run race and typically offers a Wednesday afternoon reception, a Thursday evening pasta dinner, a Friday morning breakfast, and an awards brunch on Sunday morning. All of this is included in your entry fee and extra tickets can usually be purchase for your friends and family.

GFT has some of the best and most enthusiastic volunteers I have ever seen. I have made many new friends through GFT that I will never forget. I consider GFT one of the greatest and most rewarding experiences in my life.

About the Author

Rob Weitzel began competing in triathlons in 1997. His background was not in any particular sport. He was a lifeguard throughout college, but never competed in any swimming events and the swim training did not require any real distance workouts nor did it offer any experience in open water swimming. Rob biked a lot for both sport and pleasure but never competed. A lot of his commuting in college was done by bike. His running experiences were limited to some short two plus mile runs which eventually lead to some 5K and 10K road races. Rob joined a local running club and found that the running club had members who were not only great runners, but also triathletes that ranked up there with the best in the mid-Atlantic region. In Rob's own words, "I began to train with this group and glean and sponge as much information as I could about the sport of triathlon including what type of training to do, how to pace, information on nutrition, and advice on which equipment I needed to compete in this sport effectively."

Ford Ironman Florida®

panama city beach, florida

Race Distance: Ultra
2.4 Mile Swim, 112 Mile Bike, 26.2 Mile Run
Month: November
Race Web Site: www.ironmanflorida.com

Author: Teresa Byrnes
Racing Category: Age Group 40-44

It is minutes away from 7:00 a.m. on November 3, 2007, and I am standing on the shore of the Gulf of Mexico in Panama City Beach, Florida. With the music blaring and my heart pounding, I glance at my heart rate monitor; it reads 123 beats per minute. Did I mention I am just standing? This will be my first ultra distance triathlon. Let me explain how I got here.

I began triathlon in 2001 with an intermediate distance race, but the ultra distance was my ultimate goal from the start. Deciding to have a second child sidelined me for a while, but I returned to the sport in 2004. Prior to competing in Ironman Florida, I completed one short, three intermediate, and one long course triathlon for a total of five triathlons.

I decided on Ironman Florida after talking to other athletes as well as a former professional who all told me it was a great race for a first ultra event. I was warned, however, not to get lulled into thinking the course was easy because it was flat, as I would be using the same muscles all day. I also chose the race for ease of travel since I live on the East Coast. Another factor was that I like warm weather and at Ironman Florida the highs are usually around 70 degrees and it's often sunny.

One of the most nerve racking parts of the Ironman Florida experience was gaining entry into the race. Entry for the next year's race opens up online the day after completion of the current year's race. I sat at my computer minutes before the online entry opened. At 12:00 p.m. I typed like crazy. The race sold out in less than an hour, but I did get in. Were there that many crazy people out there willing to pay $425 to go 140.6 miles in less than 17 hours? I guess its popularity speaks for itself!

If you don't get in online there is another way to gain entry. You can purchase a Community Fund slot for $1,000. Half of the entry fee goes to charity and the other half to your race entry.

The first Friday in November (two days before the race), I flew to Panama City. I checked in at the Boardwalk Condos which, in my opinion, is the best place to stay. It is located at the heart of everything including check-in, transition area, race start/finish. The condos also have kitchens so you do not have to eat all of your meals out.

The Boardwalk Condos sit right on the beach and have a pool and kiddie splash area. This gives family members something to do during the race so they aren't bored to tears waiting all day to catch a glimpse of you. Perhaps the best part of staying right at the race staging area is not having to stand in line for the port-a-potties. You can prepare at leisure, then don your wet suit and walk right down to the swim start.

There are numerous other hotels and condos available in close proximity as well. A good resource for finding lodging information on the area is www.getawaytothegulf.com. It is best to secure your lodging as soon as you obtain your entry, as the closer establishments fill up quickly.

My next stop was Tri-bike Transport to pick up my bike and gear bag. I highly recommend this service. For about $100, they transport your bike by van, fully assembled, to the race site. For an additional fee you can also send a duffle bag, which I found very handy. I packed all of my race gear in this bag including CO_2 cartridges, which you can't take on an airplane. Not having to worry about lost race gear on the way to the race alleviated a great deal of stress. The pick up and drop off location (for after the race) was also right at the Boardwalk Condos.

After securing my bike I was off to registration. I was pleasantly surprised at how smooth a process this turned out to be. They really have this down to a science.

Saturday was bike and gear drop-off day. I placed my gear in specially marked bags specific to the bike and the run, which they provided at registration. I dropped each bag in the designated spot at the transition area, and then racked my bike. This was an excellent opportunity to check out the bike start/finish and run start so I had an idea of where to head on race day (although I knew there would be plenty of great volunteers on race day to provide directions).

Normally, the night before a race for me does not involve a great deal of sleep. However, the night before Ironman Florida I had surprisingly little trouble falling asleep. When I awoke I thought, "Hey I actually slept!" Until I looked at the clock and realized only a half hour had passed! I was in for a long night.

At 4:00 a.m. my alarm went off. I had set it just in case I wasn't already awake at this time. I choked down "breakfast," the only real food I would have for a while. I then read a very inspiring note written to me by a very dear friend and placed it in my run "special needs" bag just in case I was in bad shape at that point and needed a little pick me up. I then headed off to the transition area to place my nutrition for the day on my bike and to pump up my tires. The race does provide bike pumps in the transition area, but my suggestion is to bring your own to avoid the long lines. Your neighbors in transition will appreciate this as well. Good race karma? I like to think so!

My next stop was the drop off point for the bike and run "special needs" bags. You can fill these with pretty much anything you want, extra nutrition, tubes, CO_2 cartridges, anything. I never used mine, but it felt good knowing the stuff was there just in case.

At the special needs drop off, I met up with a good friend who gave me some much needed words of encouragement and then it was back to the condo so I could go to the bathroom about 10 more times before putting on my wetsuit and getting down to the swim start.

Now back to my pounding heart. As I looked out on the Gulf, it was incredibly beautiful and calm. Thank you triathlon gods! Although the water has been choppy in past years, the Gulf does not typically have the surf one would associate with an ocean swim. This usually makes for a relatively smooth open water swim.

As the cannon sounded to start the day, chaos ensued. The mass start of an Ironman® race is truly something to see, so I watched and entered the water at my leisure so as not to become a part of the human washing machine. The water was beautiful and clear. It was wonderful to be able to see while swimming.

The 2.4 mile swim is a two loop course with a short beach run between loops. About halfway through the first loop, you face the rising sun so I was glad I had worn my mirrored goggles. The two loop set up was psychologically great for me. I was able to check my time and had a better idea of what I needed to do on the second half of the swim. I had previously done a 2.4 mile point to point swim and breaking it up into two loops just seemed easier than constantly seeing just how far I had to go.

Exiting the water, I was met by the loud cheers of spectators, including my family. The announcer told everyone that I was a stay-at-home mom, but today I would be an Ironman. People were yelling "Go Iron Mom!" as the wetsuit strippers went to work. (Clarification: not strippers in wetsuits, but volunteers helping me strip off my wetsuit.)

After a short run up the beach to the transition area, a volunteer handed me my bike gear bag, and I entered the changing tent. There were more volunteers to help in any way possible. As I exited the tent, there were even volunteers waiting to slather me with sunscreen.

There is a nice hill next to the transition area that is lined with spectators. My family waited on that hill to cheer me on before I left on the 112 mile bike course. I knew I wouldn't see them for a while, I just didn't realize at the time just how long a while that would end up being.

The bike course is a single loop course. It is very flat; the highest point on the course is only 161 feet. The winds are usually low, thus this course is said to be a very fast one. I guess "fast" is a relative term because I was out there for 7 1/2 hours.

Once I was on my bike, it was time to come up with a new time goal. My original goal was no longer attainable since my swim took me almost two hours. Don't get me wrong, I was very thankful to have made the 2 hour 20 minute cutoff for the swim, and I was happy to be on my bike. This would change from time to time during the 112 miles. About halfway through the bike ride I set a finish time goal of 15 hours. At this point, I was very happy I had trained extensively in my aero bars. This flat course has you in them most of the way.

I felt good on my bike with the exception of the time I lost my ability to do math. As I passed the 80 mile marker, for some reason I had it in my head that I had only 20 more miles to go. Imagine my mood when I realized this mistake.

I was determined not to get off of my bike. I was worried if I stopped, I would not want to get back on, so I sat in that saddle for 7 1/2 hours. I even learned to pee while on the bike. My mom would be so proud.

The end of the bike course runs along the shoreline. While it was true that the winds were light most of the day, as time passed they picked up. A few times I felt as though I might be blown across the road. I came out of the aero bars and held tight to the handlebars and made it without incident.

As I finished my ride a volunteer took my bike from me, and I was more than happy to see it go. Another volunteer handed me my run gear bag, and I was once again off to the changing tent. I changed into clean running gear (remember my newly acquired talent on the bike?) and I was off once again to the cheers from my family as well as the other spectators.

The run is a flat two loop course. The highpoint on the run is only 17 feet. I was off my bike before the cutoff, which is 10 1/2 hours into the race. I had now been racing for 9 1/2 hours. I knew that even if I had to end up walking the marathon, I would indeed make it in time and I would be an Ironman today. I had a big smile on my face as I started running.

The run course starts off along the shoreline and is packed with spectators. Some are cheering, some have music blaring, and some have some interesting costumes on. It was very entertaining and a welcome distraction from the little aches and pains that were beginning to emerge.

As in the swim, the two loop course was a great set up for me mentally. I thought of it as just that, two loops, not as 26.2 miles. I tried not to pay attention to the mile markers and this strategy worked pretty well. I had done two other stand alone marathons prior to this and my marathon at Ironman Florida was by far the best marathon I have experienced. The two loops made me feel like I was never alone and it gave me a chance to see some familiar faces, some of which I had just met in the days before the race.

The Janus inspiration station is around mile eight. In the days before the race, there is a computer at Ironman Village where family and friends can enter messages for their athletes. These messages appear on a computerized board as each athlete passes. Because it is a two loop course, you see this sign twice. The second time through for me, it was dark and seeing the message was very inspiring as it came at a much needed time. No one would own up to entering my messages, but whomever it was, if you are reading this, I really appreciated it!

It was dark as I finished my first loop but it was still warm enough that I didn't need the long sleeved shirt I left in my special needs bag. I saw my family once again, told them I felt great, which to my surprise at this point in the race, was actually not a lie! I also heard the party going on at the finish line and told myself "One more lap and you will be there!"

By my second loop, I could no longer stomach the drink that I had brought. I instead began to alternate between flat cola and warm chicken broth that was available at each aid station. Who knew chicken broth could taste so good? I allowed myself to walk through the aid stations, but not to stop at any other time. I was afraid to stop for fear the pain would seem even worse and prevent me from starting to run again.

Somewhere about halfway through the second loop, I lost my senses for a minute or two. My surroundings looked strange and I felt as though I had taken a wrong turn somewhere. I started to panic that I would be disqualified. This temporary insanity passed quickly, however, and I was able to get back to the task at hand. I looked down at my watch, and as much as it hurt, I was going to have to pick up my pace in order to cross the finish line in under 15 hours! At this point, I could faintly hear the announcer welcoming people into the Ironman club as they crossed the finish line. I could also hear the blaring music. I was almost there!

As I approached the finishers chute I was overcome with emotion. As my eyes welled with tears, I suddenly heard my mom call me. She had found a folding chair and in her lap was my four-year-old daughter, Jordan, sound asleep. My eight-year-old daughter, Jamie, ran to me and grabbed my hand. This was the moment I had been dreaming of since I had started this journey, and my husband, Joe, was at the finish line catching it all on film! Jamie and I ran down the finishers chute together. Everyone was shouting my name, as it was printed on my number, and extending their hands in congratulations. At 14:58:52 I heard those words "Teresa Byrnes you are an Ironman!" as my daughter and I crossed the finish line together, arms lifted in triumph.

This was one of the greatest moments of my life.

About the Author

Teresa Byrnes lives in Damascus, Maryland with her husband Joe and two children, Jamie and Jordan. She is currently a stay-at-home mom, working toward a certification as a Personal Trainer. Teresa also hopes to soon take a USA Triathlon coaches course.

Teresa started competing in triathlon in 2001 at the Columbia Triathlon in Columbia, Maryland. Her background was in running, so in her own words, she's still learning about swimming and biking. Teresa has a passion for triathlon and doesn't see ever giving it up. She hopes to do another ultra distance triathlon in the next couple of years. Her ultimate goal is to someday compete in the World Championship in Kona, Hawaii.

American Triple-T Ohio

Race Distance: Non-traditional
Three-day, Four event, ultra+ distance
Month: May
Race Web Site: www.americantriple-t.com

Author: Daniel J. Brienza
Racing Category: Age Group 25-29

On October 10, 2005, eight days after my first long course triathlon, I was introduced to the American Triple-T (Triple-T) and my life has never been the same since. It all started rather innocently, when in between sets of 200s, a swim buddy and I were talking about the previous race season. When he began to describe Triple-T, only one thing kept going through my mind, "You have to be crazy to do something like that." He went on to explain how it is a great training weekend, how wonderful the racing and accommodations are, how it is the best bang-for-your-buck in triathlon, and what a great sense of community and camaraderie you feel throughout the weekend's event. Needless to say, before that practice was over, I had already signed up to be his partner in that year's race.

Before I proceed, here are ten things you should know:

1. Triple-T is both my most difficult and most favorite race
2. Triple-T is the best value you will find in triathlon racing (in my opinion)
3. Triple-T is the perfect race in preparation for a mid-late July ultra distance race
4. Bring your climbing gears for the bike
5. All races are a time trial start
6. Complimentary massages are available after each race
7. The field of competitors at Triple-T is very talented but there is not a cut-throat sense of competition. Instead, there is a sense of community that develops out of respect for each others' participation in the race
8. HFP racing is organized, friendly and puts on a world-class event

9. Accommodations at Triple-T are perfect—there are two bedroom cabins with a master bedroom and the second bedroom has two sets of bunk beds which sleep five. The cabins are onsite and less than one mile from the race start

10. Triple-T is limited to roughly 500 competitors

So, what exactly is the American Triple-T?

It is a three day, four event, ultra plus distance tour located at Shawnee State Park in the "Little Smokey's Region" of southern Ohio (beginning in 2009, a second event is scheduled in California). The events are broken down as such:

- Race 1: Prologue
    - Friday, 5:00 p.m.
    - 250m Swim - 5 mi Bike - 1 mi Run
- Race 2: Individual Time Trial
    - Saturday, 7:30 a.m.
    - 1500m Swim - 24.8 mi Bike - 6.55 mi Run
- Race 3: Team Time Trial
    - Saturday, 3:00 p.m.
    - 24.8 mi Bike - 1500mi Swim - 6.55 mi Run
- Race 4: Team Time Trial
    - Sunday, 7:00 a.m.
    - 1.2 mi Swim - 55.5 mi Bike - 13.1 mi Run

The swim portion of the race is in Turkey Creek which is fairly warm, clean, and pleasant. The bike courses are all on lightly traveled fairly hilly, challenging, and scenic terrain. The run course, also fairly hilly and challenging, takes place on fire roads within Shawnee State Park.

Participants either compete as individuals or in two person teams. Placing for the event is based on your cumulative time for all four races with time bonuses awarded to stage winners. In the first two races, the team's time is the sum of the team members' individual times. For the two team time trials, drafting is legal within teams and the team's time is the time of the last team member who crosses the finish line. All of the races are time trial start and the third race of the tour is unique in the fact that the order of disciplines is bike, swim, run.

The only true way to understand exactly what is so special about Triple-T is to compete in it; nevertheless, hopefully the details below regarding my experience will help get you to the starting line a little more prepared.

Race #1: Prologue, Friday, 5:00 p.m.—Swim 250 meters, Bike 5 miles, Run 1 mile

On Friday around 2:00 p.m., all of the triathletes began to swarm the cabin grounds and there was a buzz in the air. As early as 3:30 p.m., you were able to see people starting their pre-race rituals and warm-ups. By no later then 4:00 p.m., all participants could be seen warming up in one way or another. About 20 minutes before start time, most people made their way down to the water, were warming up and started to line up for the time trial start. For the prologue, some individuals chose to wear wetsuits but given the distance of the swim; most people decided to simply wear their Triple-T provided tri top. As the race started and the top team members went into the water one-by-one in five second intervals, I could feel the adrenaline pumping through my body.

As my turn approached to hit the water, it was a quick sprint and then dolphin dives for about the first 75 meters. Personally, I prefer to dolphin dive for as long as possible and the water is shallow enough well past the first buoy to continue to do so. The swim was over before it started and I was off on my bike chasing my teammate down. (Your teammate either starts five seconds in front of or behind you.) The bike course is an out-and-back that stays within the park. On the way out, there is a fairly long and steep hill; about 600 yards, then another shorter ascent up to the cabins where everyone stays. The long descent on the way back is appreciated as your heart rate is typically in the red the whole way out due to the steep ascent and the competition to go faster as the course is fairly bunched up due to the short distance. The run is a flat, out-and-back that is mostly on grass.

The best part of the day is heading to the complimentary massage tents which are available throughout the weekend. A word to the wise; you better get there to sign up as soon as possible as the slots fill up quickly.

Each night, HFP provides dinner for the athletes right at the lake where the race start/finish and transition area is located. This is a great time to meet all of the fellow competitors, trade stories and re-fuel before the next day's races.

Race #2: Individual Time Trial, Saturday, 7:30 a.m. — Swim 1500 meters, Bike 40 kilometers, Run 6.5 miles

Similar to the first race; participants began warming up about 45 minutes to an hour before the race and everyone seemed to be buzzing. This race is also a time trial start with swimmers entering the water every five seconds. I really enjoyed these races simply because of the starts. It becomes really exciting to watch each person take off into the water. What makes it even better is that this format spaces the swimmer out so there is not much bumping or jostling for position.

On the bike course, we finally hit the roads outside of Shawnee State Park and were met with many steep inclines and a lot of climbing. After about 15 minutes of climbing and then a brief downhill; there is a 120 degree turn onto the infamous Thompson Hill.

Thompson Hill is about a 500 yard climb in about one mile. The course is fairly technical and you are never able to fully let loose on the down hills. There is one downhill on Tick Road that captures a victim every year and it is not a pretty picture. This year, the participant who fell hard still ended up finishing the entire race. Completing this event is difficult enough, let alone without being scabbed, bruised and bandaged all over your body. I guess we should not be surprised though knowing the type of person an event like this attracts.

The run is an out-and-back. This single loop is utilized for all of the remaining races and is fairly shaded to give some protection from the sun. Despite this; this run course is unforgiving. For the greater portion of the way out, it is a steady climb with a few fairly steep inclines. Just as you are beginning to wish for a downhill; there is a quad burning half mile descent to the turn around. After turning around and climbing that hill you just almost lost your legs going down; it is a gradual downhill the same way you came up. As a word of caution, the way back is much faster then going out but I caution participants not to let completely loose at this point as there is still another race to finish in less than six hours.

Upon completing the race it is extremely important to get your massage, eat, drink, and get off of your feet as quickly as possible. Personally, to minimize preparation time in between races; I organize all of my race gear, equipment and nutrition before the Friday race. By 11:30 a.m. the park is silent as every good triathlete is fast asleep dreaming of their next race in 3.5 hours.

Race #3, Team Time Trial, Saturday, 3:00 p.m.—Swim 1500 meters, Bike 40 kilometers, Run 6.5 miles.

After a much needed nap; my cabin mates and I rolled out of bed, into our triathlon gear and down to the race start by 2:30 p.m. for the 3:00 p.m. race. Unlike previous races where most participants were feverishly warming up; most have now congregated underneath the tents for some much needed shade while trying to get a few last minutes of rest. With about five minutes until the race start; there was a cluster of nearly all of the participants about 10 yards from the start line all trying to hide with their bikes underneath the shade of a tiny tree. I have never seen so many triathletes so close together; not even during a swim start.

This race starts on the bike with teams taking off, time trial start, in 30 second intervals. During this race, you are allowed to draft off of your teammate and are supposed to stay with him/her throughout the duration of the event. Having your teammate with you really makes these next two races bearable as you have someone to pull you when you are tired and because it adds additional elements of strategy to the event which takes your mind off of the fact that your legs are about to explode. The bike course is an out-and-back. The first eight miles of the course is moderate climbing, followed by a long downhill and then four miles of flat out and four miles of flat back where you climb the same hills just in reverse. The eight mile flat stretch is the perfect time to get a look at all of the other triathletes and to try to size up where you are stacking up. In addition, this eight mile stretch is the first truly flat section of the course which is nice; but beware, the winds can get very strong.

After pulling in off the bike, the last thing you want to do is put on your wetsuit. Fight the urge to forego it as you will regret it later. Wearing your wetsuit will make the swim easier because of the buoyancy factor but more importantly; it will help keep your muscles warm and less likely to cramp. This portion of the race is the hardest all weekend as there are many cramping victims in the water and even more so when participants are getting out of the water in between laps or at the end of the swim. I personally was feeling great during the swim but the minute I stood up, I fell to the ground with cramps in my hamstrings, calves and feet. It was not a pretty sight as my partner ran to drag me out of the water and stretch me out. Beyond the pain of cramping and my muscles locking up, his helpfulness was accompanied by a few choice words that I let him remember later in the weekend as I was dragging him on the bike and run. In this event, it is critical to realize that you could bonk at any minute and you should be drinking fluids non-stop throughout the event.

The run portion of this race is that moment where everything starts to click and you realize that you are going to finish or the walking shoes come out. For the teams; it is crucial that both teammates are able to motivate and push each other through the events. For my team, my partner was able to help me with my cramps getting out of the water and I helped pull him through the run. At this stage of the race; you will see teams where one team member holds onto the other's race belt going up the hills for that little extra help. I have even seen some teams use a leash; it reminded me of seeing joggers and their dogs in the park.

Nonetheless, I equate the dynamics of the team during this time to that of a man and woman during child birth. The suffering person hates the person that is feeling fine and trying to help them out. The suffering person just wants the other person to shut up and leave them alone. The person who is feeling great feels bad for the other person and does not know what to do; so he/she continues to encourage. The one difference is that during this race; one minute you could be feeling great while your partner suffers and the next minute, it could be you who is suffering.

Despite the run course seeming much longer then the identical course that morning, you finish and hurry over to the massage table hoping that there are still open slots. It is critical to drink as much as possible for the remaining hours that you are awake. It is also critical to eat a substantial meal even though you might not feel very hungry. To help you out with this, HFP puts on another great dinner just outside of transition area. The food is great and the camaraderie is excellent.

It is refreshing and simply fun to be around people of like minds and passions as they trade war stories. Nonetheless, most people still head back to the cabins fairly early as there is still a long course race to do the next morning.

Race #4: Team Time Trial, Sunday 7:00 a.m. — Swim 2100 yards, Bike 56 miles, Run 13.1 miles.

As my partner and I drove down the road and parked the car near the transition; there was a flurry of activity. It resembled the scene on Friday with hundreds of people biking, running, and stretching. There was a buzz in the air but it was not from fellow Triple-T competitors but from the Little Smokey's race that is held in conjunction with the final race. Fellow Triple-T competitors are typically huddled underneath a tent waiting for the first lap of the swim to warm up. Watching the fearless competitors slowly shuffle out of the tents and barely put a toe in the water before the race started juxtaposed with my memories of the Friday start is something you will never forget. Contrary to what you might believe, I woke up on Sunday feeling fresh and ready to race. Properly hydrating leading up to and throughout the race was critical to keeping my energy levels up and my legs feeling fresh.

The swim start is a time trial start like the previous races except now the first five teams are ranked according to their time differentials in the previous races. This adds to the race as the team to cross the finish line first; is the overall winner. The rest of the teams line up just like they did in previous races. After the Triple-T race starts, the Little Smokey's race begins as well. In the water, you can definitely feel more bodies around you and it helps if you can find a good draft.

The bike course is a two loop course that is the most challenging of the three with about 10 climbs and some very treacherous descents. Either way, it is a lot of fun to be out on the course with your partner, pulling each other, talking strategy, picking off teams one-by-one or just trying to survive. We went out conservatively for the first lap and it paid off. On our second lap, while many teams were losing gas, we were picking up steam, riding confidently and ended up passing a lot of teams. It is much more enjoyable to pass people instead of being passed. With that said, one word of advice is to put your pride aside and let competitors, especially the Little Smokey's racers, go by you and do not try to hang on. We saw a few teams not want to get passed and pushed really hard, only to later bonk badly.

The run course is the same out-and-back you have done all weekend so by now you should know it very well. I recommend taking it easy on the first lap and then leaving whatever you have left out there on the second lap. The final lap is a truly special experience as your doubts begin to fade away and you realize you are on your way to conquering the race. Furthermore, by now, you have become very friendly with your fellow competitors and are able to feed off of each other's energy. There is even a greater sense of camaraderie and encouragement among the Triple-T competitors now that there are other racers on the course. Every time you see someone with that blue and white Triple-T top; you know that you both have endured and are proud of each other.

As my racing partner and I crossed the finish line together for the last time we were both relieved the race was over but sad we would have to wait until next year to do it all over again. With a long race season and many important races ahead, Triple-T, my "training weekend," had become my favorite race. It had helped prepare me for a very successful season and left me with memories and the confidence to last a lifetime. On Sunday afternoon before leaving the cabin, we already booked our cabin for the next year and began to speak about what we could have done differently. Triple-T was a great race, but more then just being a race it is an experience…an experience that has changed me forever.

About the Author

Daniel Brienza stumbled upon the triathlon world because of a bet with his roommates one day after they returned from their weekly bike ride. Two weeks later, in his first race, Daniel broke the course record and was immediately hooked on the sport. He now aspires to race at the elite level and currently manages the sponsorship of triathlon event marketing for Toyota. Daniel's athletic background includes playing professional soccer for Lask-Linz FC in Austria, Sao Paolo Futbol Club in Brazil and various stints with the U.S. Olympic Development program. Daniel first raced TTT in 2006 on a recommendation from a friend and it is now a mainstay on his race calendar. See you at the finish line.

Escape from Alcatraz™ Triathlon

san francisco, california

Race Distance: Non-Traditional
1.5 Mile Swim, 18 Mile Bike, 8 Mile Run
Month: June
Race Web Site: www.escapefromalcatraztriathlon.com

Author: Martin P. Desmery
Racing Category: Age Group 45-49

Escape from Alcatraz embodies everything we love about the sport of triathlon. The race is unique, challenging, and extreme. Strength and technique are essential, but physical skills are not enough. You need to be "mental" about this event, both in training and on race day. If you know what to expect, and if you're prepared for the unexpected, you will have one of the most amazing experiences of your triathlon career.

You can't just sign up for Escape from Alcatraz. This popular race is reserved for 2,000 fast or lucky triathletes from around the world. There are half a dozen qualifying races in the Escape "To" Alcatraz series. These events are held in different geographical regions of the United States, as well as the U.K. and Europe. The top age group finishers in the qualifying races, plus the division champions from the previous year's race, receive automatic invitations. The rest of the field is comprised mainly of lottery winners, relay teams, and athletes who participate in certain training camps.

I placed my name in the lottery for the June race before the deadline in mid-November of the previous year. At that time I had been into triathlon for less than two years. A training buddy convinced me to fill out the online registration form. I must confess that I wasn't keen on the idea because I disliked swimming in cold water. Back then, if I stuck my toe in a chilly pool it would take me three minutes to gather the nerve to jump in. I just couldn't picture myself crawling through the frigid waters of San Francisco Bay. Still, I knew I had only a remote chance of winning a lottery slot, so against my better judgment I entered my name.

When the lottery results were announced in December, my friend had been picked but I had not. Perfect! "Congratulations, man! Gee, what a shame I can't do that swim with you." Instead, I entered the race as part of a two-man relay team, with another good friend who agreed to be the swimmer. (By the way, you don't need to qualify or enter the lottery to race this way. Relay teams are accepted through online registration on a first-come, first-served basis.) The three of us made plans to travel from Boston to San Francisco the following June. Just the guys. No wives, no kids, and no chilly swim for me. I was happy.

In February, the race organizers announced the second wave of lottery picks. "Second wave? What second wave?" I'll never forget the feeling in my stomach when I checked the website and saw my name listed as one of the "lucky" winners. I was trapped. I couldn't back out. I already had my plane ticket. To make matters worse, the friend I signed up with as a relay team contacted the race organizers, explained how he had suddenly become a one-person relay team, and somehow managed to convince them to give him an individual race entry. I had no choice. The time had come for me to suck it up and conquer my fear of cold water swimming.

I have several recommendations for anyone racing Escape from Alcatraz for the first time, especially if you're nervous about the swim. Obviously, you need a well-fitting, quality wetsuit. You also need a "squid lid," which is a neoprene hood that fits over your swim cap and protects your head from the cold. Silicone ear plugs are helpful too, as they help prevent the heat from seeping out of your skull. And, most importantly, you need to practice swimming under race conditions. The temperature of San Francisco Bay in June can range from 52 to 56 degrees. The only way to acclimate your body and mind to the numbing cold is to practice, practice, and practice. Start by swimming in the coldest water you can find for five minutes, then 10, then 15, 20, and so on. In a few weeks, you'll realize that you've stopped thinking about the temperature and moved on to related challenges, like how to take off your wetsuit when you can barely feel your fingers. Anyway, the body is a highly-adaptive machine. With the right gear and enough practice, swimming in cold water is not a problem.

I also recommend buying two items. The first is a short book entitled, *Alcatraz Swimmers Manual*, compiled by a Bay area resident who has crawled to and from Alcatraz Island dozens of times—all without a wetsuit. The book has many open water training tips. It also sets the record straight on certain facts about the swim, such as the number of people who have been attacked by sharks in the past 130 years (zero) and how good a swimmer you really need to be (average). My second suggestion is that you purchase a copy of the DVD of the race from the prior year. Escape from Alcatraz is a nationally-televised event. Every year, the producers put out a slick DVD that describes the logistics of the race and the layout of the course.

It's an invaluable tool for a first-time racer, especially if you're not from northern California.

My buddies and I flew to San Francisco on the Thursday before the race, which gave us two full days to see the sights and prepare for the drama on Sunday. We stayed at an inexpensive motel near Fisherman's Wharf. This is a popular tourist area with many restaurants and hotels; and it's just a short bike ride to the expo/transition area. Over the next 48 hours, we embarked on a full recon patrol. We took the ferry to Alcatraz Island (intimidating); we swam in the Bay (cold); we biked most of the course (hilly); we walked all over San Francisco (dumb); and we took early morning runs up and down the streets of the city (dumber). I'm sure our pre-race activities were not ideal for three slightly nervous, middle-aged, jet-lagged triathletes, but we were having too much fun to simply kick back and relax.

We hit the race expo on Saturday. The booths were plentiful and well-stocked with the usual assortment of tri-products and race merchandise. The official t-shirt was absolutely the best ever. (Even today, I imagine other bikers and runners whispering in awe as I fly by in my dark blue shirt with the bright red "Escape" logo emblazoned on the back.) We enjoyed the race briefings presented by several legends of the sport. Over and over, we were told to be mindful of the currents in San Francisco Bay. In order to hit the swim exit 1.5 miles southwest of the start at Alcatraz Island, we were instructed to aim due south toward the city and allow the current to pull us west. Any athlete who failed to heed this warning would overshoot the swim exit and, in theory at least, be swept under the Golden Gate Bridge and out into the Pacific Ocean. Of course, numerous boats and kayaks are on hand to keep athletes from becoming castaways, but we understood that misjudging the current meant the end of our race.

In addition to the usual T1 & T2, Escape from Alcatraz has a third transition called "T1/2." The swim exit is about one mile from the bike racks. Many of the pros run barefoot to T1 with their wetsuit pulled down to their waist. Most athletes, however, put a second pair of sneakers in a bag supplied by the race organizers. The bags are transported to the swim exit on race morning and arranged by bib number. As you exit the water, you find your bag, throw your wetsuit inside, put on your sneakers, and run to your bike. This has the advantage of literally warming you up after the frigid swim, so that by the time you hit T1 you're ready to jump on the bike and fly.

On race day, we woke up before dawn and biked over to the transition area, which was spread out over a large grassy field near the waterfront. After racking our bikes and setting up our gear, we boarded one of the many buses to the ferry terminal. One large boat transports all of the athletes to the start of the race off

Alcatraz Island. The boat is very comfortable, with numerous bathrooms and just enough floor space for each athlete to stretch out and contemplate the day ahead. Consider the pre-swim anxiety of your typical wave start, with 100 or so athletes standing for a few minutes on the beach or in the water before the race begins. Then imagine the nervous energy generated by almost 2,000 people, who are forced to wait in close quarters for an hour as they chug out towards the middle of San Francisco Bay. I was very grateful to be with my good friends. Instead of our usual pre-race trash talking, we traded silent nods and wide eyed grins. "Oh man! Can you believe we're really doing this?"

It turned out to be a gorgeous day, without a cloud in the sky and temperatures in the mid- to upper-60s. As the boat approached Alcatraz Island, we lined up by age group and quickly snaked our way through the ship until we reached the timing mats on the outside deck. I felt like a paratrooper or maybe a lemming, as I jumped off the edge and hit the water five or six feet below. Suddenly, it seemed like I was all alone. With the moving boat and the rolling waves, the parachute analogy holds true because the athletes enter the Bay over a wide area and spread out. I put on my goggles and did my best to get into the rhythm of swimming without any warm-up.

After a few minutes I rolled over and caught the silhouette of the prison against the clear blue sky. "That's pretty cool," I thought. About five minutes later I looked again and saw the exact same thing. "That is definitely not cool." I had been swimming for almost 10 minutes and my position relative to Alcatraz had not changed. I fought back a brief surge of panic, picked out a tall building for my sight line, put my head down in the water and focused on executing long, smooth strokes. I kept telling myself, "Mind the current and head south." I swam strong through long rollers, washing machine waves and endless swells. I wondered if anybody else had noticed that even the waters off San Francisco seemed hilly.

Although the swim distance is 1.5 miles, you're supposed to be assisted by the current so the swim leg should last a little longer than your one-mile time. I expected to be in the water for no more than 35-40 minutes. After almost half an hour, however, I could see that I wasn't even close to the swim exit. Also, it didn't look like I had moved very far to the west so I assumed that the current must be closer to shore. I had almost reached land, well to the east of the swim exit, when I finally realized that the water seemed to be moving in the wrong direction. I spent almost an hour in the Bay, with the last 10 minutes stumbling over submerged boulders while trudging through thigh-high water at the shoreline as part of a long line of cold and tired athletes. We learned later that over 200 people had to be pulled from the water because the unusual cross current had dramatically lengthened the swim.

I finally emerged from the swim exit and found my bag at T1/2. Somehow I managed to peel off my wetsuit and put on my sneakers. As I started out on the one-mile run I heard someone call my name. It was another triathlon friend from home who just happened to be in San Francisco on business. Small world. The unexpected support from 3,000 miles away gave me a huge boost. I ran a relatively quick mile to the bike transition, switched shoes and donned my favorite Grateful Dead bike jersey. It took a few minutes to navigate out of T1; and then I headed off on the 18-mile trek up and down the famed streets of San Francisco.

The bike course opens with a one-mile stretch of flat road, followed by a series of climbs. Like a pilot, I scanned my instruments—speed, cadence, heart rate— trying to stay focused on the physics of my ascent. I passed within two feet of a very enthusiastic spectator who looked exactly like Robin Williams. "Whoa! That really was Robin Williams!" My fear of not having a gear low enough to climb the hills gave way to concerns about lacking the technical skills necessary to handle the descents. These are well-traveled city streets with the usual assortment of hazards that you don't want to encounter at 40 miles per hour. It can be difficult to concentrate, however, when almost every mile presents a stunning view of San Francisco Bay, the Golden Gate Bridge, the Pacific Ocean, the Presidio, or Golden Gate Park.

For most triathletes, 18 miles is barely a training ride, and I completed the bike leg almost wishing I could do it again. By the time I exited T2 my mind had already blocked out the swim and I found myself thinking, "This race isn't nearly as hard as I expected." Then the fun started. The eight-mile run begins and ends with two flat miles along a paved footpath. In between, you run on dirt, gravel, asphalt, grass, wood, and rocks, as well as hard- and soft-packed sand. There are long stretches of wooden stairs and steep hills where the course is only wide enough for a single lane in each direction. You definitely want to keep an eye on your heart rate or perceived effort. If you allow yourself to redline too early or often, you'll fall off a cardio cliff and climb back up.

After you pass under the Golden Gate Bridge you head down to the turnaround at Baker Beach. The half-mile beach run ends with a 400-foot climb, known as the infamous Sand Ladder. You don't want to encounter this obstacle for the first time on race day. Watch the DVD. Visit Baker Beach. Talk to people. Read race reports. You should have a clear plan before the race about how to approach this unusual part of the course. It consists of wooden railroad ties spaced about two or three feet apart up a vertical hill of sand, with thick cables on both sides to use as handrails. Whether walking or running, you want to try to land your feet on the railroad ties and not on the sand in between, although this gets harder as the race progresses and hundreds of athletes kick sand in all directions. Put your head down, shorten your stride, and either pump your arms like a maniac or use the handrails to pull yourself up to the top. With the Sand Ladder behind you, it's almost literally all down hill from there. You've got about one more mile of tricky descents, and then you're back on the flats heading for home.

My friends and I ended our day feeling like we had accomplished more than just a mid-pack finish in a famous race. It was an extreme test of endurance, strength, speed, technique, and mental toughness. We passed. We were now ready to move on to century rides, marathons, and long course triathlons. In a sport where "Iron" is the definitive word, and "Kona" is the ultimate destination, "Alcatraz" is in a class by itself.

About the Author

Martin Desmery is the father of three wonderful kids—Emily, Virginia, and Alexander. He lives in Duxbury, Massachusetts, and practices law in Boston. His training buddies include K'Boom, Shack, Condor, Goose, Dr. P, Double D, and the members of Team Pegasus. He is coached by Beth Kenney of Pegasus Elite Athlete Management. The love and support of his wife, Diane, makes everything possible. Although her patience can wear thin at times, it never seems to run out. Almost never, anyway. Thanks Dee!

Escape from the Rock Triathlon

san francisco, california

Race Distance: Non-Traditional
1.5 Mile Swim, 2.5 Mile Run, 13 Mile Bike, 10K Run
Month: Varies (June – September)
Race Web Site: www.envirosports.com/events/

Author: Stephanie Falkenstein
Racing Category: Age Group 30-34

By accident I ended up signing up for one of my favorite races to date, Escape from the Rock. When I was a newbie triathlete, with only three intermediate distance races completed, I heard of an almost mythical event that involved swimming from Alcatraz called Escape from Alcatraz. Completely smitten by this new sport and up for a challenge, I couldn't wait to sign up. The only catch was that there was a short time frame in which to enter. You had to sign up the day registration opened which was unfortunately a day that I would be traveling. I wasn't about to be deterred so I convinced a friend to sign up as well and asked my father to register for me in my absence.

When I returned from vacation I had a few surprises. First, my father had signed me up as a professional triathlete which I could be if I were allowed to subtract nearly an hour off my intermediate distance race times to date. My lack of professional status meant I had no choice but to relinquish my coveted spot for Escape from Alcatraz. Meanwhile, my friend was convinced that she had gotten into the closed-out race. It turns out that my friend signed up for Escape from the Rock not Escape from Alcatraz. Since I was the one who talked her into an Alcatraz race, I had no choice but to sign up. Ironically, this same friend ended up dropping out about a month before the race but that's another story entirely.

At this point, you can be relatively leisurely in signing up for Escape for the Rock. This could change, however, as more and more people discover how great a race this is. Entry is capped at 700 participants.

While I had only a vague idea of the hilly run and bike courses gathered from the online maps, I was aware that many people are physically repositioned on the swim after the current pushes them far off course. In preparation, I practiced swimming two miles continuously in the pool to ensure I'd be set for the 1.5 mile swim plus currents. When I arrived in San Francisco from my home in New York City, I went for a practice swim in Aquatic Park. I was glad I did. I had never swum in water that cold in my life. While swimming around the buoys, I familiarized myself with the key landmarks I would see on the swim from the perspective of the water including the MUNI pier (the cement-colored oval structure surrounding Aquatic Park), the Fontana Towers (a key landmark of the twin apartment buildings facing the park) and the historic ships. For those with extra time in San Francisco, Water World Swim coaches frequent swims at the Aquatic Park where you can learn more about the shifting currents and acclimate to the chilly waters.

Normally race check-in is the mindless part of the race but for me it was a stressful experience. You need to set up your bike transition the day before the race inside one of the former army buildings. There is no logic to the set up; there are no numbered racks and several bikes were leaned against the walls. Basically, the earlier you get to check in the more choice spot you can snag. Not knowing this, I arrived less than an hour before closing, set up in a less than ideal location, and then discovered that I no longer had bar end plugs. Being a low-key race there were none available. Yikes! Not wanting to risk a disqualification, I scoured the unfamiliar city of San Francisco for bar plugs and arrived back to transition just minutes before closing. For forgetful types or those who always need that one extra gel, you can take advantage of the Sports Basement Presidio which is located less than a mile away from transition.

I think the first time you complete any race it is the most vivid and memorable experience. The first time I did Escape from the Rock this was no exception.

I arrived at Aquatic Park early to set up my swim to run transition and was struck by the low key atmosphere. There weren't masses of people setting up under the glare of rented lights. Instead, just prior to the race all the participants gathered like a family or team in a huddle and recognized personal milestones such as who was doing their first triathlon, celebrating a birthday or getting married. After this pep rally of sorts, we began the wetsuit procession from Aquatic Park to Pier 39 where our boat would depart. My parents, who live about an hour from San Francisco, were able to join me on this walk.

Just before the boat departed for Alcatraz, the race director announced that he had several spaces open on the boat for spectators. Amazingly my father turned down this photo opportunity because he and my mother wanted to make sure I got out of the water. That really did a lot for my confidence.

On the boat people exchanged tips for what landmarks to site of off and the best angle to the shore. Of course this depends not only on the currents for the day but how fast you swim. All I knew is that I was starting to get very nervous.

Once we jumped off the boat I had my first surprise of the day — the water seemed warm. Okay, maybe warm is an exaggeration but it was definitely warmer than Aquatic Park. I took this as a good omen for the day. Gradually everyone started lining up in the water between two kayaks. This race has a water start which allows you to have some time to appreciate the stunning site of San Francisco from the waters of the bay. I glanced back at Alcatraz and then took in the amazing feat that I was about to undertake; swimming to the city before me.

When the race started I kept my eyes on the Transamerica Pyramid per a friend's recommendation. Because there are so few people in the race relative to the size of the bay, there were precious few people at my pace taking the same route. This is when I started to question my initial race plan. The pyramid seemed so far left from the finish area. Surely my friend just mentioned that building because you can see if from anywhere. So blessed by relatively calm waters and a view unobstructed by thick fog, I began to personally sabotage my race. Before I knew it, the Fontana Towers were looming before me. This is when I knew I screwed up. The current tends to be quite strong just before you enter Aquatic Park. It is much better to aim too far left (east) and have the current assist than do as I was doing and end up swimming against the current. I couldn't actually see the finish but I knew it was there because I was stuck on the other side of the dreadful MUNI pier for what seemed like an eternity. You can't see over or around the pier. It's simply a looming obstruction. I saw the many others who misjudged the current and the hordes of kayakers ready to rescue tired swimmers or relocate those who were extremely off course for their own safety. I really didn't want to be one of those people. I wanted to swim the distance of my own accord. That was really my only goal for this race. Do the swim. I kept telling myself to keep strong. Somehow I finally swam inside the opening to Aquatic Park where there was STILL a current. But I had made it. I knew that I could swim the last bit.

I slowly warmed up as I ran through Fort Mason and conquered the one and only hill of this section. My feet remained frozen but I figured that running would warm them up eventually. Mostly, I was ecstatic for having completed the swim from Alcatraz. I was so happy that I think I was a bit delirious. Then it happened. I fell. There was no real reason to fall. It was completely flat. Not only did I fall but my reaction time was non existent. I didn't really bother to break my fall. As a result, my chin was bruised, my knuckles were raw, and my left arm from wrist to elbow was thoroughly scraped. I told fellow racers that I was fine and I decided that I would deal with it later. Luckily, I am one of those people with a thoroughly stocked transition area. I knew that band-aids and Neosporin would be waiting for me.

After administering to my wounds and jamming on my bike gloves, I set off on the bike. While the bike course is short it should not be underestimated. Throughout the three-loop course you are either climbing or descending. These are not rollers either. They are sustained climbs. Luckily I love to climb. I'm normally overly cautious on the descents but this time I wasn't as fearful. I already had my fall and the views were stunning. I was either biking through the tree-filled Presidio or staring out at the deep blue ocean water and admiring the contrast of the white homes lining Sea Cliff. My parents were at the top of one of the climbs cheering me on with each loop. The only downside was pulling off my gloves as the blood had started to dry and stick to them. Also, there are no aid stations on the bike so carry what you need.

The second run started with a flat warm-up along Chrissy Field before making a sudden turn to a long series of stairs. I knew about the hills but I had no clue that these stairs were coming. I ran up the stairs and then continued up the short switch backs of the hill. I started to feel that I was on more of an obstacle course than an actual run. In addition to the paved areas, there were sections with dirt, wood chips, a sandy beach and a tunnel where even I at five feet needed to duck my head. The most famous part of the race though is the sand ladder. In reality it's not a ladder at all. It's more a combination of wood lodged into a hill with a rope "railing" on the side. The distances between the wood are a bit off and sometimes the wood is completely under the sand. I couldn't seem to run the lower section and instead focused on powering up the ladder in a bit of a speed walk instead of grabbing onto the rope and acting like I was a mountain climber. Several others had chosen the mountaineer technique and they seemed to be moving at a glacial pace. At some point the wood disappears and then there is just sand and a more gradual incline. As I was contemplating what to do at this section, I heard people cheering my name. Apparently not only had my father religiously studied the pre-race info and decided the infamous sand ladder was the place to be but he had brought along binoculars so that he could actually see me from the top of the hill. I had no choice but to start running. Once you reach the top of the sand ladder you turn left and continue to climb on more stable ground. However, that's that last hill. On a challenging run course where you seem to be either running up a never-ending hill or running across a beach, knowing that the last section is entirely downhill or flat is phenomenal.

Since the distances and course terrain are unusual, I had no previous race times to compare against and could simply enjoy my accomplishment of completing the race. At first the post race food provided by Bubba Gump seemed more revolting than appealing. Shrimp post race? However, after going to the first aid station and attending to my wounds, I was ravenous. I enjoyed one of the best post race meals I have ever had while lounging on the grass.

Enviro-Sports races are always an adventure. In addition to Escape from the Rock's challenging race course and stunning scenery, I think this is one aspect of the race that makes it so fun. While there are definitely enough kayakers and boats for the swim and the race date is chosen based on a careful study of the currents, the aid stations tend to be sporadic and the run and bike volunteers minimal. If you are fussy about race food be sure to bring your own favorite drinks and gels. Otherwise, you may end up with some less traditional race fare like red licorice with your water.

Although the Escape from the Rock is nearly 30 years old, the feel of the race is more grass roots than slick. There are no big corporate sponsors and there is no flashy race expo. There is also no $300 plus race fee. Instead you feel like you're a part of an extended Enviro-Sports family.

While the looped bike course and out-and-back run are extremely spectator friendly, the race does not draw the local crowds of spectators that other races do. This race is not an official USAT race and does not draw the volunteer support of the local tri clubs that it should. However, it offers a chance to swim from Alcatraz and embrace the geographic challenges of San Francisco without dealing with the hoopla of a lottery.

If you love a challenge with bragging rights, take advantage of Escape from the Rock while you can. It is typically held between June and August each year. On some years there has been drizzly rain and fog at the start and in other years the post-swim skies have been a clear blue. Since the race takes place in San Francisco, it is rare that the temperature is above 75 degrees. More likely, it will be in the 50s at the start.

About the Author

Stephanie Falkenstein currently resides in San Francisco less than a mile from the race start. Stephanie started competing in triathlons with the New York City Triathlon in 2002. Since then she has completed about a dozen intermediate distance triathlons, seven long course races, and Ironman Canada® twice. She currently races age group in the female 30-34 division. While Stephanie started endurance events as a marathon runner, she quickly grew to love cycling. Her proudest accomplishment to date is biking 7,000 miles across Africa, from Cairo, Egypt to Cape Town, South Africa. She hopes to bike from Istanbul to Beijing some day soon. When she isn't training, traveling, or eating like a foodie, Stephanie works in marketing and serves on the International Board of Directors for the non-profit, Amigos de las Americas.

Santa Barbara Triathlon

santa barbara, california

Race Distance: Non-traditional
1 Mile Swim, 34 Mile Bike, 10 Mile Run
Month: August
Race Web Site: www.santabarbaratriathlon.com

Author: Marie Claire Lamb
Racing Category: Age Group 20-24

A row of evenly spaced palm trees lines the bike path bordering the brilliant blue ocean. Tourists pedal by on rented bikes and roller bladers glide along in their cut-offs and bikini tops. I can't help but wonder, "What year is this?"

I was doing the Santa Barbara Triathlon Long Course for my first time. This is a unique triathlon, as you may already be able to tell. It not only takes place on the beach, but the distances are unlike any race most triathletes have ever done. The swim is a one mile ocean swim, the bike course is a 34-mile loop in the Santa Barbara foothills (sometimes longer depending on detours in Montecito), and the run is 10 miles. This was the longest race I had signed up for to date, but have since done it again, as it became my all time favorite triathlon.

I had heard about the Santa Barbara Triathlon for a long time, as I am a local Santa Barbarian. My dad actually did this race a couple of weeks before I was born, but back then it was a standard long course race, and up hill the whole way in the snow... It wasn't until college that I became a triathlete myself, and then not until the summer before my senior year that I entered this race, actually by chance. One of my junior lifeguard's moms gave me the entry because of an injury. This race quickly became my favorite, not only because of the home court advantage and the camaraderie, but because it is one of the most well organized races I have ever done.

The Santa Barbara Triathlon consists of two races. The long course is on Saturday and a short course race takes place on Sunday. This grand event always takes place in late August, at the end of the summer when

all of us should be fully rested and trained but also enjoying margaritas! As many people have heard, Santa Barbara is famous for Fiesta, which celebrates the Old Spanish Days of Santa Barbara in early August. As a result of this heritage, there are delicious Mexican restaurants all over town. I would recommend forgetting about a pre-race meal of pasta, and trying something new for a change, say a burrito mojado from Los Arroyos on Figueroa and State Streets. For those who refuse to break their pre-race habits, or in some case compulsions, "Santa Barbara offers the most restaurants per capita of any city in the U.S.," as some tourist guide once said. So a hungry triathlete will have no problem finding something good and healthy on State Street or nearby.

Lodging accommodations are not a problem for the race since Santa Barbara offers a range of options less than a half-mile from transition. There is the luxurious Double Tree Resort with an average room price ranging in the hundreds per night, or Motel 6 (which is literally across the street from transition) for less than $100 per night. Other options include the cozy Old Yacht Club Inn (265 steps away, as counted by two cute little residents), the Radisson, the Mar Monte, and a variety of other hotels. Just reserve a room early as they fill up fast.

The expo takes place on Friday and lasts all day. It consists of about 10 tents full of samples and merchandise right on the sand in front of the Bath House. Last time I raced, exhibitors at the expo included Trader Joe's, local gyms, De Soto, triathlon clubs, FRS, and even a lettuce company. On race day there is a tent with excellent masseuses for exorbitant prices, but hey, it's Santa Barbara.

Packet pick-up is hassle-free and straightforward, and you even know what transition rack to put your bike on the next day. A local bike shop also comes out and offers all the gear you need and free mini tune-ups. There is a transition clinic as well for those who are new to the sport. This race has everything right there.

Race morning has always felt stress-free. I don't know if it's the bike mechanics at your disposal, the witty (and sometimes garrulous) emcee, or just the fact that you're in Santa Barbara with the general vibe of a laid back beach town. Plus there are ample porta-potties and even some flush toilets. Parking has never been a problem either. There are various public lots around, and many curb spaces lining soccer fields and the zoo.

The race starts at 7:00 a.m. which is late enough for the sun to warm the sand just a tad, and make the water shimmer and appear warmer, but early enough that the final stretch of the run isn't unbearably hot.

The racers start lined up on the sand and run into the refreshing waters of East Beach. Most opt to wear wetsuits for the speed and colder water. I didn't wear one this past year, and wished I had, but warming up on the bike doesn't take long at all, as the first half is a net uphill gain. You swim with the sun at your back on the way out towards the pier, and the sun blaring in your eyes on the way back. Luckily, there are big orange buoys and lifeguards on paddleboards to guide you, not to mention the neon caps of your opponents, although I no longer trust the open water skills of the average swimmer after following a few out to sea.

The transition to the bike is up the sandy beach and into the parking lot. It can get a little hectic, but as long as you know where to go, and don't forget your helmet (no, I am not talking about myself!), you'll be fine. Once on the bike, you'll find the roads are in good condition and the course is well marked. The only downside is that it can be crowded at the beginning. Although most people are polite, some curse and yell to get their spot in the pack. The course takes you through neighborhoods in Montecito, over the rolling hills of Summerland, and behind Carpentaria. You make a quick loop on Gobenator, which goes through an avocado orchard and has a nice little cardiac hill. Then there is some long straight aero time, until you hit Toro Canyon. People have been known to scream going up this grueling beast of a hill, but going down never felt so sweet. The rest of the way back is rolling downhills back the way you came and by this time, the volleyball courts are full of people playing beach volleyball. You may get a fleeting desire to go join them instead of embarking on a 10-mile run, but triathletes don't quit.

The final leg of this triathlon is no walk in the park. It is flat for the first few miles and turns into a gentle up hill, with the ocean constantly in view to distract you from your plight. After some weaving turns through the Mesa neighborhoods and an aid station with little kid volunteers cheering you on, the course sends you down, down, down Cliff Drive and no sooner do you hit the turn around and go up, up, up the same hill. If this isn't hard enough, you hit the six mile marker a few minutes later and this is the point where most triathletes are ready to cross that finish line, but no, four more miles to go! However, the course starts to slant down, the ocean comes back into view, and you start to feel, well, good.

There is nothing like the final couple of miles of this race. To your right is the harbor with hundreds of boats bobbing in their slips. On a clear day (which they always have been when I've done this race), you can see the Channel Islands, and all the way down to Ventura. The ocean is glistening, people are cheering, and you can see the finish line waaaaay down at the Bath House. You want to go faster, but every triathlete knows that this isn't always an option, so you sit back, and enjoy the view as you cruise into the finish line.

The announcer shouts your name as you go through the shoot and trod into the sand. You are given fluids and invited to a food tent with a grand buffet just a few steps away. But the most attractive thing of all is the big, blue, salty, ice bath waiting for you to float in just beyond the tents. After recovering you realize what a great race this has been. The energy is high, people are all around, and the location couldn't be better. The award ceremony is punctual, before noon that is, and quite generous. USAT age groupers four deep get a tile that says their place and has a cool Santa Barbara triathlon graphic. There is also a nice little grill for celebrating with rounds of beers.

All in all, this race offers a great experience for triathletes ranging from professional to beginner. For the real newbies, and triathletes who prefer the short course distance, the race the following day is a better option. I have never done the short course, but many of my friends have, and some infamous Santa Barbara triathletes are known to do both the long and short course in the same weekend. This becomes a challenge in which more partake every summer. The course for the short race is in the same direction as the long course, just different distances. The swim is 500 yards, the bike is six miles, and the run is two miles. These mini distances make for an excellent first triathlon. There is even a women's only race at the same time as the short course race. After the races are over, most opt to enjoy the beach, because if you haven't caught on by now, Santa Barbara is a nice town!

About the Author

Marie Claire Lamb has been a triathlete for a little over five years. She has competed in roughly 30 triathlons, mostly at the short and intermediate distances and two Santa Barbara long course races. Marie Claire was a member of the Cal triathlon team and trained seriously for four years at Cal. In her own words, "I initially joined to meet cool people and to not gain the freshmen 15 (lbs). Then I did my first triathlon and was hooked."

Marie Claire had her best season during her final year at Cal. She was the top female in the West Coast Collegiate Triathlon Conference, which consists of the collegiate teams in California. She also placed 9th at Collegiate Nationals in Tuscaloosa Alabama. Since then she has been training for fun with friends and with the Santa Barbara triathlon club and hopes to soon do a long course triathlon and eventually an ultra distance triathlon. According to Marie Claire, "I don't know if I am made for that distance, but I have to remember that it is only to finish!"

"SOS" – Survival of the Shawangunks

new paltz, new york

Race Distance: Non-traditional
30 Mile Bike, 4.5 Mile Run, 1.1 Mile Swim, 5.5 Mile Run, .5 Mile Swim, 8 Mile Run, .5 Mile Swim, 750 Yard Stair Climb
Month: September
Race Web Site: www.ulster.net/~sosnyta

Authors: Mary and Allen DeLaney
Racing Category: Age Group 55-59 and 60-64 (respectively)

Think you've done it all in triathlon? Ultra distance, long course, intermediate, short course, "escape-froms," off-roads... with nicely organized transitions areas, a buffet of energy foods at your fingertips, bottle hand-offs, convenient port-a-potties? Well, you haven't done it all until you can call yourself a "Survivor."

Part adventure race and part triathlon, Survival of the Shawangunks (SOS) was the brain child of Don Davis, a two-time ultra distance competitor. He started this race for himself and a few masters' swimmer friends in 1983. SOS is classified by the New York State Triathlon Association as a triathlon, but that is where any similarity to the average plain 'ole American Apple Pie triathlon ends. This may just be the hardest triathlon t-shirt to get in the country!

We discovered this amazing race while having a pre-race dinner with other triathletes at the Crab Shack in Delaware City, Delaware. Discussing what other races we would like to do someday, while carbo loading on crab cakes and beer, we noticed a guy sitting in the corner with an old, obviously much-loved t-shirt. On the back it said, "SOS" Survival of the what? "Shawangunks?" We asked the guy about the race and how you pronounce it ("shawn-gum") and so began our trek toward the crenellated Smiley Memorial Sky Tower at the finish line of the SOS triathlon outside New Paltz, New York.

First of all, we had to qualify to enter the race. Traditionally, only 150 participants are allowed to participate (although recently the number was increased to 170). After certifying that within the past 18 months

289

you finished a long course race in less than seven hours or an ultra distance triathlon in less than 15 hours, you must also certify that you swam 1.5 miles in under 50 minutes, biked 56 miles in under four hours, and ran 13.1 miles in sub 2:10.

Just finishing this race requires more than swimming, biking, and running. It also requires more planning and organization than the average race. Distance-wise it compares to a long course race but it is a point-to-point race.

To understand the high standard for application requires that you examine the overall race logistics. This is definitely not a beginner's race.

Leg 1: Bike 30 miles (1000' climb) into the Shawangunk mountains with a final one mile climb up a 12+% grade
Leg 2: Run 4.5 miles uphill on a trail to Lake Awasting
Leg 3: Swim 1.1 miles in Lake Awasting (temperature ±58 degrees)
Leg 4: Run 5.5 miles along a rolling trail to Lake Minnewaska
Leg 5: Swim .5 miles across Lake Minnewaska
Leg 6: Run 8 miles on trails through the forest and under Trapps cliffs to Mohonk Lake
Leg 7: Swim .5 miles across Mohonk Lake with a six foot rock climb exit
Leg 8: Run a 750-yard stair climb and switchback trail to finish at Sky Top Tower (elevation 1542 feet)

That is a total of 30 miles biking, 2.1 miles swimming, and 18.7 miles running. There are several thousand feet of elevation gains and losses throughout the race.

Once notified that we were in the race, along with Chas and Dave, two friends from our TriCATs Triathlon Club in Virginia, we had to enlist the services of bike handlers or "tri-sherpas," which are a race requirement. Our friends and endurance athletes Randy and Susie willingly enlisted for tri-sherpa duty. Without a support team, your bike would be left in a gravel lot in the woods about 10 miles from the finish line and 25 miles from the start. It would take the rest of the day to sort out and locate gear and vehicles.

Training was challenging. Traditional triathlon training wasn't sufficient. We devised brick workouts that included swim, run, swim, run, swim, while all the time carrying everything we needed. In this way we could practice the transitions as well as train. We learned to swim with our back packs. We had to learn to run with wet feet. Some competitors race in just a swim suit and then either swim in their running shoes or stuff them in their swim suits. Some devise a bag that they tow behind them holding their shoes.

The night before the race there was a pasta dinner at SUNY New Paltz and the race briefing. The walls of the gym were covered with memorabilia from the race. There were old race results, photos, press coverage, and shirts from past races. The organizers also gave awards to volunteers who had been involved in the race for many years. Like the entire race, this was well-organized. There was no expo.

We don't usually take part in pre-race dinners, but prefer to have a quiet dinner without all the race-talk. As the town is rather small, reservations should be made ahead of time if you want to have your choice of restaurants. We ate with our friends at a small Italian place, outside of the town of New Paltz, but not far from our hotel.

Race morning was foggy with temperatures in the 50s as racers and tri-sherpas gathered at the starting line. From the start line at the Ulster County Fair Grounds in New Paltz, and from several other points along the race course, you can see the tower on the mountain top at the finish line, way far away… Did I mention, WAY far away?

As the fog burned off, we stared at the finish line tower in the far distance and wondered exactly what we had gotten ourselves into. We got body marked and went through an informal bike and helmet inspection. The race crew is very experienced, and there is little mass hysteria as the field of competitors is small. Last minute instructions were given to racers and their helpers. The multi-waved bike start went off at 7:00 a.m. Most folks were in their 30s and 40s. Not many young or beginners and only a few in the 50+ range. Overhearing conversations, we could tell that many racers had done the race multiple times and knew each other. They appeared totally relaxed.

Although we have 50+ triathlons under our race belts, six years of relay adventure races, and 20+ years of running races before that, we were still nervous at the start line. This was unlike any previous race, so the unknown left us uncertain as to how the day would unfold.

Wetsuits are legal and since the mountain lakes are 58-60 degrees, we opted for wetsuits. Chas and Dave did not. To make the multiple transitions between run and swim more efficient, we cut off the legs of our old sleeveless wetsuits. It was still frigid. Many competitors without wetsuits were clearly hypothermic.

The bike course is incredibly scenic. Riders are rewarded with views of the Catskills and the Hudson River Valley. We saw no course marshals, but there was minimal drafting. It was every athlete for themselves although racers cooperated and encouraged each other along the way. The ride terrain is generally uphill with some rolling climbs and was topped off with a gut-wrenching 12+ percent one mile climb to T1, where Randy, Susie and sherpa-dog Lucy were waiting with bikes and run gear laid out. You are required to have someone there to take your bike since the finish line is over 20 miles away. We were thankful to have our good friends there with hugs and smiles and encouragement! Thanks guys!

Leaving the bike-to-run transition you start to climb on the trail toward Lake Awasting. It is uphill the entire way, but since we had previewed the course the day before, we knew what to expect. There are many trail sections where footing is an issue, so street racing flats aren't the best choice for foot gear. Our hydration packs contained our energy drink, as well as wetsuits, caps, goggles, and gels. Compared to other racers who carried nothing except their caps and goggles, we felt heavy and slow. But our goal was to finish, and we knew we would need everything we had.

We swam the 1.1 mile swim and slowly started out on the 5.5 mile run toward Lake Minnewaska, trying to thaw out our legs. Here, we were running together encouraging each other, reflecting on how beautiful this country was when we rounded a corner at Castle Rock and we came upon the first aid station at the edge of an unbelievable white quartz cliff several hundred feet high.

We took time to gaze out at the countryside below us where they say we could see half of New York state. Now our legs warmed up and we picked up the pace, passing some other athletes.

Running downhill to Lake Minnewaska, we could see a line of buoys had been set out. Each leg of the race has its own director and this director added buoys to make navigation easier. We appreciated that touch and the encouragement of the volunteers at lakeside. The right side of this lake is a beautiful rock wall. The water seemed just a bit warmer.

At the other end, Randy and Susie greeted us again with loud cheers and "Go Get-ums!" Here the volunteers gave us hot tea and pretzels, nice salty pretzels! If only I could get my legs to work. There are about a dozen steps to get out to the road and they were brutal. I was running like a tin man without knees. At this rate, the eight mile run would be very long.

Meanwhile the first finishers were enjoying hot soup and warm towels and the elusive "SOS Survivor" t-shirt at the tower. Times for this race are similar to the long course distance. The fastest male course record was 4:10:43 in 1993. The fastest female finisher was in 2000 at 4:44:49.

This race is not without perils and pitfalls. Hypothermia looms large. Trail runs can trip the fatigued runner, especially the last eight mile run, as it parallels a stream and has long stretches of uneven rocky terrain. As Allen ran past the Trapps, the rock climbing cliffs that were covered with climbers and their dangling ropes, he took his eyes off the rocky path and fell hard, knocking himself out. When he came to, people were standing over him offering assistance, which he declined. He just sat on a rock, letting the fog clear. When he got his wits about him, he took off, looking forward to the cold water of the last swim to clean off the blood and dirt and clear his head.

We met up at the last run-swim transition, since Allen sat out the race for about 10 minutes after hitting his head, and by this time we were ready to get the race over with. We had given it our all and it was taking a toll on us. But, we were thrilled to realize that the finish line was a mere .5 mile swim and a little jog up the hill away. For this swim we left our shoes on. Greeting the swimmers at the end of the lake at Mohonk Lodge was a six foot rock wall. Glad to have the shoes on. Many swimmers who were cramping, too fatigued, or too cold, climbed part way up, only to fall back into the water. We climbed out, left the wetsuits on and hustled up the stairs and trail to the tower.

Although this is definitely not a spectator friendly race, there were lots of cheering, and folks at the Mohonk Resort grounds as we started up to the tower and on the way back to the post-race feast.

The tower, the finish line… Although many of the athletes had already finished, it was a SWEET finish! The warm towels, hugs, hot soup, and cold soda were fabulous! The cheers of friends and volunteers were even warmer. And, "The Shirt…" We now understood why that guy's SOS shirt had been so worn, back at the Crab Shack.

Now, the walk back down the 750 feet we just climbed—it was slow going, but we were elated! It was getting chilly and windy, so we changed into SOS Survivors shirts and headed to the Mohonk Resort post-race feast. This was the best post-race meal ever! There was a huge barbeque with every kind of meat, chicken, hotdog, hamburger you could want. The salad and side dish table was huge, and the bread and pasta table was loaded. There was a make-your-own sundae bar and massive dessert table. There was beer, soda, and plenty of thirst-quenching beverages. There were enough picnic tables, so no trying to balance all the food while standing.

The awards ceremony followed and was mercifully brief. There were many well-deserved kudos for the volunteers. Eventually, they got to Female 50-54 and Mary won her age group. With a finish time of 7:19 we wouldn't have imagined taking home hardware, but you just never know.

Since we had sherpa-dog Lucy with us, our choice of hotels was limited and we ended up staying at a "Best-Forgotten" motel not far from the New York Turnpike exit. We would absolutely never stay there again, as the management was surly and the place was disgusting. There are apparently several nicer places to stay, but they wouldn't take pets. If we do it again, we will most likely rent a house for a week or stay at a B&B. The race ends at the fabulous Mohonk Resort, which is well worth staying at if you don't mind the $300+ per night rates.

This race is essentially the road bike leg of an intermediate distance triathlon, followed by three off-road runs interspersed with three frigid swims and a straight uphill dash to the finish. You are essentially self-supported during the race. You aren't competing against other athletes. You are racing to be an SOS Survivor!

About the Authors

Allen and Mary DeLaney are USAT certified coaches and experienced healthcare professionals with years of experience dealing with injured athletes. They have over 80 triathlon podium placings between them. Members of Team USA, they represented the U.S. at the Long Course World Championship in the Netherlands in 2008. Their consulting business, Rehab To Racing, (www.rehabtoracing.com) provides coaching and training services for healthy athletes and assists the injured athlete's return to the field of play. They have a particular interest in older athletes.

Virginia Double IRON Triathlon/Virginia Triple IRON Triathlon

spotsylvania county, virginia

Race Distance: Non-Traditional
4.8 Mile Swim, 224 Mile Bike, 52.4 Mile Run (double ultra)
7.2 Miles Swim, 336 Mile Bike, 78.6 Mile Run (triple ultra)
Month: October
Race Web Site: www.usaultratri.com

Author: Christine Couldrey
Racing Category: Age Group 30-34

Why only race for one day, when you can race for two or even three? A silly question you might say and to be honest, a few years ago I thought exactly that. The distances seemed insane, why would you ever want to do that? But little by little, after six years of competing in triathlons of all distances as an age group athlete I began looking for a challenge beyond the ultra distance race. The Virginia double and triple ultra distance triathlons (previously called Odyssey double and triple) have been taking place since 1998, and I have been involved in these races for five years as an athlete, a support crew, and part of the race management.

The current location, Lake Anna State Park in Virginia in early October is by far the best of the three locations in which the races have been held, and it looks set to be the race site for the foreseeable future. Lake Anna State Park, is a beautiful 2,328 acre pine forest covered park containing a 13,000 acre lake (but don't worry, only a very small portion of the lake is used for the race) located 60 miles northwest of Richmond, Virginia.

With only a handful of athletes competing in each of these races (usually around 20 between the two races), the race briefing is a very different affair than any of the other triathlons that I have done. The race briefing occurs at the race site after a casual barbeque the night before each race begins. This meeting is usually the first place that competitors from around the world greet old friends and meet new ones. The race briefing is first given in English and then often translated by competitors and support crews into French, German, and Italian to ensure that everyone knows where to be and when. A description of the race course is given for the first timers along with how laps will be counted and how much help is allowed from the support crews.

Athletes and their support crews have a variety of options for the night before the race. Some athletes choose to camp at the race site, but for a comfy bed, you only need to travel a few miles away to one of the few motels, inns, or B&Bs a few miles from race central. More recently, self contained cabins have been built inside the park.

The swim takes place just off the swimming beach within the park. The 4.8 or 7.2 mile swim consists of multiple laps around a 176 yard lane rope. Or for those competitors that prefer not to swim, a 16 or 24 mile kayak option (on a much longer course) is available.

This swim format has a large number of benefits. First, you get the benefit of a lane rope to swim around so there is no spotting a small speck of buoy in the distance with the sun in your eyes, you simply have to watch the white and blue lane rope and stay an appropriate distance away. Second, unlike swimming in a short pool, you don't have to turn every few seconds. You do, however, need to be careful not to swim into the poles that are holding up the lane rope, sounds silly, but after swimming for between two and five hours it can happen! Third, this swim format allows support crews to feed their competitors (competitor supply much of their own food throughout the race). One end of the swim loop is shallow enough for support crews to wade out and bring water/food to their competitors and this makes for good spectating from the beach.

In October, the water is fairly cool, so supports crews will do well to bring wetsuits for themselves. Swim laps are counted and race time at the completion of each lap is recorded by a member of the race staff/volunteers.

Transition one at these races is the most relaxed that I have ever seen. Before the swim, competitors place their bike somewhere along a fence near the lake. When you are done with the swim you are welcome to take a shower and get changed or simply get on your bike. Once you are ready to ride, it's just a matter of riding up the hill and checking in with the closest person holding a clipboard. You then get to ride your bike for the foreseeable future while your support crew tends to your every need.

Unlike shorter triathlons, the sheer distance that each athlete must travel, often in the middle of the night in a sleep deprived state, means that a one or two loop bike course is pretty much out of the question. Staffing such a course would require a small army of people for this handful of athletes. As with ultra distance triathlons around the world, the bike portion of the Virginia double and triple IRON triathlons is a short loop. More precisely, an out-and-back loop 200 feet short of five miles, yes, that is a lot of laps to complete the 224 or 336 mile ride all without leaving Lake Anna State Park.

Most people not familiar with ultra distance triathlons will, by now, have thought, "How awful," but it really isn't so bad. Riding the same stretches of road actually makes the race easier for the competitors as they become tired, easily disorientated, and lacking in concentration. Of course, this format also makes the race manageable and increases the safety for everyone and means that medical attention (from doctors and paramedics that have vast experience with ultra distance athletes) is never more than two and half miles away. The fact that the loop is completely within the park also minimizes problems with traffic, especially at night.

The terrain: well, if you weren't riding 224 or 336 miles before running two or three marathons, most people would probably describe the ride from the lake end of the course up to the park gate, as a false flat. However, if you ask anyone who has done either of these races, they would describe it (more accurately) as a "climb up to the gate and then a bit of a downhill back." The road itself has enough curves to keep it from being boring, but not enough to be technically challenging. The road surface is okay, there are a few small holes, but most people have those memorized after the first few laps. When you get tired, these holes can actually make notable landmarks to help tick off the miles and remind you that with every pedal stroke you are getting closer to the end of the bike!

Ultra distance triathlons are governed by the International Ultra Triathlon Association (IUTA) with its own rules and regulations based on the different demands that ultra distance triathlons place on the athletes and race staff. Competitors may be kept company during both the bike and the run legs of the race as long as they are not receiving any assistance in forward momentum i.e. drafting or being pushed/pulled. The Virginia double and triple IRON triathlons are also governed by USAT which endorses IUTA rules for ultra distance races. Although not compulsory, or necessarily vital, having a support crew that can come out and keep you company really helps breaks up the long ride. Some people have support crews that ride a few laps, but others don't. The short out-and-back format does mean that you see all the other cyclists each lap anyway, so you tend to have a fair amount of interaction with the other competitors.

The world changes when it gets dark, and whether you are doing the double or triple, you will still be on your bike when it gets dark! At this time my world became very small, just me, my bike and the road. A good lighting system definitely helped keep my speed up through those dark hours. During the double, most athletes will be off their bikes before it gets light, for me that was around 2:00 a.m. and it gave me something to focus on. In contrast, all triple competitors are still on their bikes at first light, I was third off the bike at 11:00 a.m. the next day! The difference in mental attitude required between knowing that you will still be on your bike in the morning and knowing that the faster you ride the less darkness you will have to ride in is huge! Both rides are hard, but the triple ride is something truly unique.

Transition two is again a very casual affair. After being given the all clear that you have completed all your cycle laps, you are free to change at your chosen transition area. Once your feet are released from those hard cycling shoes and find themselves in some cozy (at least for the time) clean sox and running shoes, it's time to check back in with the race staff and complete the last (and for me the most difficult) part of the journey.

By the time you get onto the run course, you have seen either half or all of it, depending on which of the park roads were used for the bike loop. You head uphill for approx 0.6 miles of the bike course and make a right hand turn. The remaining 0.4 miles is flatter and you make a U-turn around at an orange cone where one of the race staff sits day and night to record your number and the race time, then you head back to have your number and time recorded at the transition/race headquarters where the support crews are waiting patiently. This process is repeated time and time again.

This format allows for great spectating of the race (the most amazing sights are usually in the wee hours of the morning) and makes planning a nutritional strategy an easy task. I always had one bottle of water/sports drink at each end of the mile, most times I would finish a lap, my super support crew would provide me with a tasty (or not so tasty since after many hours most forms of calories don't have much appeal) snack.

The final lap has the feel of a victory lap. All the competitors and support crew (by this stage, many support crews are cheering for everyone) know that you are nearly done. There are congratulations to be had, it's also a time to reflect on all of the feelings that you have had over the race, and think about the awesome accomplishment you are about to complete, and of course, the thought of sitting down or sleeping. The final lap of my double ultra triathlon was definitely one of the most emotional times I have experienced in my life, and they were all wonderful emotions. The hard times seemed to disappear from my mind and were replaced by the good ones. Those last 200 yards are incredible, and if you choose to, you can carry your national flag and finish to the music of your choice blasted on the stereo. What a way to finish! It's these touches by the race organizer that puts the icing on the cake of these two incredible races.

Many athletes stay at the race course to watch the remainder of the race. After spending one or two nights awake with this small group of people, there is very much a feeling of family. Tough times have been shared, and strong bonds have formed during the highs and lows of the race.

The weary support crews set about packing up the competitors' worldly possessions (preferably sealing any clothing that was worn into plastic bags) as things begin to wind down and the competitors finish one by one. It's hard work for the support crew, and repayments will need to be made, but in my experience as a support crew, it was also nice to sit and watch the race from the other side of the fence and live the race vicariously through the athlete I was supporting.

Once the official time is up, the last few things are packed into vans and there is a mass exodus to the prize-giving dinner, often held at a local winery a few miles away. A meal is enjoyed and awards are given. In each of the years that I have been involved in these events, every finisher has received a plaque showing their accomplishment. Each competitor is encouraged to get up and say a few words. Most of these impromptu speeches are very emotional thank you's to the race management, support crews, competitors, to the familiar faces from around the world that gather together each year.

Those who don't speak fluent English often find willing volunteers to translate. In my opinion, you don't get anything this wonderful at a shorter triathlon. Everyone is exhausted but happy and no one seems to have a bad word to say. It's a fitting ending to an incredible weekend. The five years that I was privileged to be a part of this family have given me some incredible memories that will stay with me forever and the only reason I won't be at the next event is that I now live on the other side of the world in New Zealand.

So, why would you want to only race for a day when you could race for two or three?

About the Author

Christine Couldrey has competed in a wide variety of world class endurance events over the past decade. In addition to her second place finish at the Virginia Triple (which earned her a world 8th place ranking), some of her major accomplishments include her 1st place win in the 2008 TransTaupo Kayak race in the mixed tandem division in New Zealand, 2nd place mixed tendem award in the GoldRush 3 day multisport race (New Zealand), a 4th place finish in the 2007 New Zealand National marathon kayaking championships, 1st place finish in the 2006 Lake Taupo maxienduro bike race (640km road bike race) in Taupo, New Zealand, and the 2005 OC1 (1 person outrigger) winner of the East Coast USA point series: novice division.

Chris also has experience in adventure racing/triathlon race management through Odyssey adventure racing, has a basic wilderness medical certification and was an adventure racing instructor for EX2 in 2004. Chris currently lives in New Zealand and her major goals include:

1.   DecaIron distance triathlon (40 km swim, 1180 km bike, 420 km run)
2.   Compete in Race Across America cycling race solo
3.   Continue expedition length adventure races
4.   New Zealand 24 hour swimming record

Ultraman World Championships

big island of hawaii, hawaii

Race Distance: Non-traditional
6.2 Mile Swim, 90 Mile Bike, 171.4 Mile Bike, 52.4 Mile Run
Month: November
Race Web Site: www.ultramanlive.com

Author: Peter Nickles
Racing Category: Age Group 65-69

The Ultraman World Championships Triathlon is the big one, the ultimate race on the Big Island of Hawaii! It encompasses three days of racing and it is spectacular! Day One starts with a 10K swim in the ocean from Kailua pier to Keauhou Bay and that's not all. Once you are out of the water — and generally you come out battered by the waves, currents, and bent over from seasickness — you grab your bike and continue the race with a 90-mile bike ride ending with a 4,000-foot climb to the rain forest at Volcanoes National Park. If you complete the swim and the bike in 12 hours, you have earned the privilege of moving to day two as a "competitor."

Day Two is imposing — a 171.4-mile bike ride around the Big Island of Hawaii with several 4,000-foot climbs. If you complete the ride from Volcanoes to Hawaii in 12 hours, you move on to Day Three — a double marathon through the lava fields of the Big Island and along the popular Ironman® bike course from Hawi to Kailua Kona.

The records in each of the stages will shock you. They are amazing human achievements. In the 10K swim the top three times are around 2 1/4 hours. In the first day 90-mile bike to the Volcanoes, the three-fastest times are in the range of four and half hours. On the second day 171.4 mile bike, the three fastest times are in the range of 7 1/2 hours. And on the third day double marathon, the fastest time is an incredible 5 hours 33 minutes through the lava fields in 90+ degree heat.

The overall three-day record for men is 21 hours, 41 minutes, 22 seconds. The women's record is 25 hours, 45 minutes, 51 seconds. Truly amazing!

Those are the facts! Now let's talk about the very special, what I would call almost spiritual quality of the race and my participation and that of my sons and son-in-law in the race.

From its humble beginnings in the late 1970s to its Olympic debut in 2000, the sport of triathlon has grown up. The sport has become mature, stable, with maybe a hint of mid-life crisis. And although no race can remain totally immune from the changes in society, there is a race on the Big Island of Hawaii that comes pretty close and it's not the one most people think of!

Ultraman came on the scene in 1983, springing from the imagination of three guys who were looking to take on a new challenge after the Ironman World Championships in Hawaii. With a route that took them all the way around the island, through pristine ocean waters, past an active volcano, through rainforests, and through the sheer lava fields of the Kohala coast, it was, as one author put it, a "sacred circumnavigation" of the island.

It would be a couple more years before the Ironman World Championships would make its network television debut in 1985 and take its place as the Mecca of the triathlon world. And even though Ultraman attracted some of the world's top triathletes, the race was given a "fringe" label by folks in the mainstream. As Hall of Fame triathlete Scott Molina put it, "People didn't want to know about this odd and ludicrous race more than twice as long as Ironman. It was almost as if giving the race a bit of credibility damaged the image of triathlon. But my thinking at the time was that perhaps it was ahead of its time. "

Now, 20 years later, the Ultraman epitomizes everything that is right about the sport of triathlon. It is a sanctioned world championship with many of the top triathletes in the world duking it out. It takes place in one of the most exotic spots on earth. And it has retained the original spirit of the race by embracing the decidedly retro Hawaiian values of aloha (love), ohana (family), and kokua (help). With the field limited to 35 (by invitation only), and each racer having a support crew, these values are on display throughout the three-day race. "Cowman," one of the original Ultraman characters, has a business card that sums up this spirit. It says: "We meet as strangers. We compete as friends. We part as brothers and sisters." Corny perhaps, but true. Ultraman can have a profound effect on people.

Eric Seedhouse, winner of the 1998 Ultraman put it this way: "From my perspective, ultra endurance is all about going on a journey that at the same time offers the athlete the opportunity to fully realize their potential. Although some of the races that I have competed in have been demanding, none of them could be described as the ultimate, that is until I discovered Ultraman. In Hawaii, the journey has to be the most spectacular of anywhere on the planet, the demands of the event the most challenging and the course offering an athlete every opportunity to test themselves emotionally, mentally, and physically. It is the ultimate challenge in endurance sports today."

So Scott Molina was right. The Ultraman was ahead of its time. And now, with its feet firmly planted in both eras, the race has managed to both stay true to its roots, while at the same time offering competitors the opportunity to compete at the highest level in the world. As one competitor put it: "[At Ultraman] I could feel the ghosts of Ironman past, when it was an insane distance for a small group of dedicated racers. I remembered why I am a triathlete." It truly is the ultimate race.

My own personal involvement with Ultraman began with, what else? The Ironman World Championships. In 1989, we began what would become our annual trip to the Big Island to watch my son John compete in the legendary ultra distance race. Finally, in 1994, after five years of watching the race, I got the bug and moved from marathoning to triathlons and on to the ultra distance. That was it! I was captivated. I fell in love with the Big Island and my goal was to go back—not to the Ironman World Championships—I had done that race—but to something smaller and bigger. Smaller in terms of the intimacy of the race, but bigger in terms of the distances and the challenge. So I set my sights on the Ultraman. John had done it. He encouraged me and my other son Philip to do it with him in 1999—the year he won the race.

That year my race ended on day two when I landed in the hospital after crashing on the final descent into Hawi. It was a bitter pill to swallow, as I was less than three miles from the finish line.

Six years later I once again stood at the swim start of the Ultraman wondering what the next three days would hold for me. I went through my list of items—Vaseline, goggles, seasickness pills, power gels, bananas, water, and Gatorade which were all stowed on my escort's boat.

The sun was just beginning to rise over Kona with the pier lights glistening around us when the athletes and crew formed a circle. We held hands for a moment of silence, and we thanked the heavens for that moment. I embraced my family, and wished my son Philip and son-in-law Rob (who were also racing) good luck, gave the victory sign to my son John and my wife Maria who were going to spend a lot of time with me over the next three days as my support crew then said goodbye. I was alone with my thoughts.

In the past six years a great deal had happened. Most of it good: I had a healthy family, with six new grandchildren, four of whom were there to cheer me on. But some of it not so good: After 40 years of running my right knee finally gave out. Following surgery in 2001, my doctor told me that there was no cartilage left and that my running career was over. Obviously, I didn't listen to him, but I would be lying if I said the knee felt good.

Even so, the running was still two days away and it was the last thing on my mind. I was looking out at 6.2 miles of ocean swells, jellyfish, currents, and who knows what else. I focused on the task at hand.

The horn sounded and I entered the water with 35 men and women. The first few strokes felt smooth and powerful. After about five minutes the pack broke up. I linked up with my escort and found a rhythm. Two strokes, one breath. Two strokes, another breath. "I have done this before," I told myself, as I prepared for the long haul.

Even though I have years of swimming experience and am comfortable in the water, the sight of the canoe to my right calmed my nerves. Unlike the Ironman World Championships, where you are constantly surrounded by competitors and never get out more than a quarter mile from shore, the Ultraman swim is generally a solitary affair that can take you a mile or more from shore, where the ocean depth approaches 1,000 feet. At these depths you are essentially swimming in a vacuum, and your only point of reference is your escort. It is only by seeing him paddle that you know you are moving forward.

My escort took me on a route closer to shore, so through the crystal clear water I could see fish, and coral, it was like swimming through an aquarium. And even more important, the current was with me.

I hit the four mile mark in just under two hours and was feeling good. But then, like a bad dream, the currents moved against us and the wave action became fierce. Marker buoys that were once in plain site disappeared behind the giant swells. I was tossed around, swimming in place for minutes at a time. At four miles, I was scheduled to finish in three hours. At five miles, I was struggling with seasickness and exhaustion, and my projected finish time was an hour later. Instead of taking a break every 45 minutes—as I did during the first four miles—I took breaks for food and water every 30 minutes, then 25 and finally every 15 minutes.

In 1999 with calmer conditions, I finished in a little over three hours and enjoyed the company of fish, dolphins, and a baby whale. But this time it took me over four hours. I lost my goggles, had to massage out serious cramping in my legs and was overwhelmed with dizziness. When I reach the finish, my daughter helped me out of the water to the change area where I rested, refocused, showered and, finally, after loading up on bananas, cookies, peanuts, water, and Gatorade, took off on the 90-mile bike ride to the Volcanoes.

"Took off" is not quite accurate since the first miles are long, tough climbs out of Kona and Keauhou Bay, and I struggled just to gain my balance. After clearing the initial climb, I headed south from Keauhou through small towns and along the coast until I hit Pu'uoKa'au, the southernmost point in the U.S.

It is there that the route turns north and the long, slow climb begins. It was also there that I turned my attention to the clock. It was 20 miles to the finish at the Mamakaui Paio Campground, and I had less than two hours to get there. Under normal conditions this would not be a problem. But the wind was in my face and a cold rain was falling. It was also getting dark and my prescription glasses were cracked. Four miles from the finish, I reached one of those defining moments. Give in to the pain or push myself into the unknown?

I blocked out the rain and howling wind and focused on the yellow line on the road in front of me. Without this line I would have ended up in a ditch somewhere, or worse. I crossed the finish line—with less than five minutes to spare. I got a massage, something to eat and tried to sleep. It was an exhausting and emotional day, but there was no time to reflect. I thought, "Tomorrow, as the sun rises, I will take to the road again."

The first 25 miles of the bike on day two were a breeze—straight down from the Volcanoes, at speeds exceeding 35 miles an hour (the faster guys were hitting 40 mph). It was cold at the top, sometimes rainy and it was great to be off—at first all together in one great rush—and then the field spread out. I was riding alone with my support crew cheering me on. My goal was simple: cover 171.4 miles in less than 12 hours. The ride was amazing. Its most startling feature was the Red Road, a 15-mile single-lane, red-paved road that hugs the ocean. Absolutely unforgettable—like something in the movies—the flowers, the colors—reds, yellows and blues—and the ocean smashing its waves at your feet as you pump it up. I reached Hilo—the largest city on the Big Island and the "fun" started—along the east coast of Hawaii. I climbed and climbed—through Honomu, Hakalau, Honoka'a, all the way to Waimea where I hit the toughest climb. There I reached the Kohala Ridge—seven miles up and then 13 miles down to Hawi. I rode to the finish at break-neck speed—and on this day I finished with about a minute to spare.

Crouched over my bike at the finish line, I told people I felt fine. But the truth was, I could hardly move. I took a hot, hot shower to loosen me up enough to get a massage. After the massage, I could move again—slowly, but there was 12 hours before the double marathon on day 3 and who knew what miracles awaited me. To state the obvious — running two marathons back-to-back after two days of pushing to the max is not easy. The thought was to run six minutes, walk four minutes, and vary the run/walk routine depending on conditions. The first 15 miles or so are generally downhill from Hawi to Waikui along the Kawaihae Coast, then the course flattens out on the Queen K highway — through the lava fields, past the spectacular Resorts — Mauna Kea, Mauna Lani, Waikaloa — past the Airport to the Finish at the Old Kona Airport State Recreation Area.

I didn't make it. My son Philip did — for the second time; and my son-in-law Rob almost did. My legs cramped fiercely. I dug deep for everything I had but my body had reached its limit. By the time I reached the Queen K, it was over.

Was I disappointed? Of course. In 1999, after my crash I had banged up my body so badly that I could not move, at even glacial speed, beyond 13 miles of the run. This time I made it 18 miles to the Queen K, but could never have reached Kona in 12 hours. It was out of reach.

As I rode with my crew to the finish with my legs soaking in ice, I saw my fellow competitors pushing themselves to their limits through the lava fields. We stopped often to cheer and give them support. For three days, I had been part of something very special. I was caught up in the spirit of Hawaii and this great event. I had spent three days — very long days — competing with exceptional athletes from around the world who had trained for months to spend but a few moments together on the Big Island.

About the Author

Peter Nickles was 67 when he competed for the second time in the Ultraman World Championships. In his own words, "Ultradistance sports represent the ultimate athletic challenge. Having competed in the 1999 Ultraman, I can say that, quite simply, Ultraman is the greatest sporting event in the world. Ever since my crash in 1999, I have wanted to return to the Big Island to try again. Finishing the Ultraman would be my greatest athletic achievement." Peter is an attorney and resides in Great Falls, Virginia.